BECOMING AN EMPOWERED PROJECTOR

Thrive with Wisdom and Guidance from Human Design

EVELYN LEVENSON

Becoming An Empowered Projector
Thrive with Wisdom and Guidance from Human Design

Edited by Laurie Knight

An Imprint for GracePoint Publishing (www.GracePointPublishing.com)

GracePoint Matrix, LLC
624 S. Cascade Ave
Suite 201
Colorado Springs, CO 80903
www.GracePointMatrix.com
Email: Admin@GracePointMatrix.com

SAN # 991-6032

A Library of Congress Control Number has been requested and is pending.

ISBN: (Paperback) 978-1-951694-86-9
eISBN: 978-1-951694-85-2

Books may be purchased for educational, business, or sales promotional use.
For bulk order requests and price schedule contact:
Orders@GracePointPublishing.com

Contents

Foreword

I have been surrounded by Projectors my whole life.

My first husband was a Projector. My middle stepdaughter is a Projector. In the first ten years of building a Human Design coaching practice, nearly all of my clients who wanted readings were Projectors. I owe a lot to Projectors.

Evelyn Levenson was one of my very first professional students and I don't think I would be where I am today with my writing and my Human Design professional school if it wasn't for her gentle but persistent Projector guidance during those first few years of learning how to be a teacher and a trainer.

My first husband used to say that Projectors are like sheep dogs, but instead of herding sheep, they're here to herd humans. If you ask any Projector, they'll likely sigh and say that herding sheep might be easier than herding humans and that being a Projector is more akin to herding cats.

Although I've been surrounded by Projectors, it wasn't until I gave birth to and had the privilege of raising one that I truly understood the power of the Projector. My youngest child is a 5/1 Projector with all centers defined except her Sacral. She's a powerhouse of a human being. She catalyzes magic wherever she goes.

I've watched my Projector daughter naturally grow into her Projector nature. When she was a small child, we lived in an apartment with a balcony that overlooked the street. The railings were high and closely spaced so I felt comfortable letting her stand outside, with my supervision, so that she could watch the people on the street.

By the time she could speak in full sentences, she was yelling corrections at the people walking by on the sidewalk. "Hey," she'd yell from the balcony, "Don't you know that smoking is bad for you?" or, "Why aren't you wearing a bicycle helmet? You're going to fall and hurt your head!"

She'd do the same while we drove around in the car. Every time we'd come to a stop light, she'd roll the back window down and try to manage the world from her car seat. I had to finally lock the back windows so we could keep out the cold -20-degree weather in the winter.

The degree to which my daughter innately understood the world from the moment she got here was beyond extraordinary. One afternoon, after my mother picked my daughter up from preschool, my mother came into the kitchen and sat down at the table looking quite stunned. When I asked her if she was okay, my mother replied, "I just had such a high-level conversation with a three-year-old that I had to do a double take and make sure there was an actual child riding in the back of my car."

Even now, at the age of twelve, instead of experiencing some of the natural drama that I expect from a tween in middle school, my daughter's interpretation of the school day includes deep psychological evaluations of the mental health of the teachers and her classmates. Her comprehension of the intricate workings of the human psyche and the stress of middle school teachers is beyond her years.

She prepares for the inadequacies of the human condition on a daily basis, bemoaning the fact that there aren't extra gloves and hats at school for the kids who forget them at home. Her backpack is full of extras, "just in case" someone needs them.

She is the class sage, the one that everyone calls when they need to share their troubles. She jokingly refers to herself an "emotional support human" and thinks she should have a red vest to go along with the job.

And yet, she tells me, that for all that she gives everyone else, she doesn't feel like anyone listens to her. She feels used and like she's giving everything to everyone, and no one recognizes her in return. Some days she is exhausted and bitter.

Having the knowledge of how she is configured and who she is born to be has helped me adjust my parenting to meet her unique needs. My daughter knows how to delineate the difference between being tired and being "Projector Tired" and nurtures herself accordingly.

She knows to proclaim at least one day every weekend to be her "pajama" day, a day when she stays in bed and rests so that she can go back out and guide the world for another week.

We work with her schedule carefully, protecting her from her own struggle to sometimes know "when enough is enough." We build into the day time for her to talk and process her daily experience.

I don't know how my Projector parenting journey is going to end up, but my prayer is that being armed with the information that Human Design teaches will help my daughter become the empowered Projector that she seems destined to become. I am so deeply grateful to all of the Projectors I've known, especially Evelyn, who have taught me how to raise an empowered Projector.

Projectors, as a Human Design Type, are fairly new on the planet. This powerful energy configuration is only a couple of hundred years old. The role of the Projector, to guide and direct the fulfillment of the potential of humanity, is a vital role that is essential to the evolution of the planet. We need empowered Projectors to help us do the work of finding the elegant solutions to the challenges facing humanity today.

The original teachings of Human Design about Projectors have given many Projectors a deep understanding of their unique role and why their life experience seems so different from the cultural norm. For many Projectors the understanding of why they are the way they are and why they can't do things in the same way as others is a relief. They begin to integrate the idea that they are not broken, stuck, or blocked.

Sadly, I haven't met many empowered Projectors. Most of the Projectors I have worked with arrive on the doorstep of learning about their Human Design already depleted, burned out, and bitter. Even though Human Design explains so much about their life and their overall experience in the world, just following the strategy of "waiting for an invitation" doesn't really give them what they need.

There is a gap between the information that traditional Human Design teaches about Projectors and the ability to live in the world as an Empowered Projector. Evelyn's book gives Projectors and those who love them a clear, easy-to-follow instruction manual that guides the Projector healing journey from burnout to empowerment.

Burned out Projectors need a concrete strategy to heal themselves, to unlearn all the ways that they've internalized the message that it's not okay to be who they are and how they are. The very first thing that they must unlearn is the old message that their value is tied to what they do and learn that they are inherently valuable because they exist.

In this book Evelyn gives Projectors a clear system to decondition the old cultural narratives about work, productivity, hustle, and self-worth. Evelyn's personal healing journey and the work that she's done with hundreds of Projectors to help them discover the true story of who they were born to be are beautifully woven into this manual designed to guide and enlighten Projectors everywhere.

We are standing on the cusp of a Creative Revolution that will be as transformative as the Scientific Revolution was hundreds of years ago. We are on the cusp of this Creative Revolution precisely when we are facing a creativity crisis.

We cannot get to where we need to be nor discover the solutions to the challenges facing humanity using the same ways of creating and producing that got us in this mess in the first place. The Projectors are here to guide and manage us out of this time of crisis.

If you are a Projector, you were born for this time.

I encourage you to read this book thoroughly and to follow each and every suggestion and recommendation that Evelyn has for you. She lays out a vital process that will help you (or a Projector you love) untangle yourself from the conditions of an outdated era and help you take your right place in the world as a leader in a cosmic revolution that will bring about the solutions to the challenges facing the world today.

But don't do this work for the world, do it for yourself first. You deserve to live a life that is the fulfillment of Who You Truly Are. Your own well-being adds to the well-being of the world and you being the person you were born to be IS the greatest contribution you can make.

Let yourself sink into the wisdom and the healing of Evelyn's work and then give yourself the gift of healing and aligning with a new narrative about who you are and the power and leadership you were born to give the world.

Thank you for being YOU!

Karen Curry Parker

January 2022

A Note to the Reader

It is incredibly powerful for Projectors to come together, share experiences, and feel seen and heard. It is in this spirit that I share my journey, to provide insight into the lived experience of a Projector and to offer a different approach than most Human Design texts.

When I first saw my Human Design chart in 2008, I did not like it. It looked angular, ugly, and weird. And was not helpful at all.

I had encountered Human Design a few weeks earlier. I attended a teleclass Karen Curry (now Karen Curry Parker) and Brad Yates offered on EFT (Emotional Freedom Techniques). I was particularly intrigued by Karen. She seemed to have a deep understanding and wisdom about how the world works and what is possible. There was something about the way she talked about people and life that spoke to me.

On Karen's website, I found an entire section about something called Human Design, which wasn't even mentioned during the teleclass. The more I read about it, the more interested I became. It sounded amazing, so I requested my free chart.

Life got busy, and it was several weeks before I read the email. I opened the attachment and saw my chart. *Eww. Weird.* I quickly scanned the free report that accompanied it. Nothing much there explained anything about my specific chart which was frustrating, and I was too busy to spend any more time on it.

A few months later, I finally had the chance to look at the chart again. I fully read the report this time. I saw that I was a Projector Type and learned what it said about us. A little lightbulb flickered then lit up in my mind. This information made sense to me. *How strange.*

How could this weird looking chart and generic description of my Type fit me so well? It explained so much about how my life had worked and had not worked.

I immediately thought back to my career and saw—to my great surprise—that the best jobs and career moves I had ever made were always from a personal invitation. I had never noticed that before.

Then I thought about the times I tried to force things to happen (which never worked) and the times I applied for jobs I wanted but never got (despite stellar credentials). The patterns were clear in retrospect.

I used to think (actually, worry) that there was something wrong with me. Why couldn't I land a job? Why was it so hard to make things happen in my life and career, while it seemed that others weren't having the tough time I was having? Was I somehow fundamentally flawed? Or was there some trick I just hadn't learned yet? What was I missing?

When I attended conferences and other large gatherings, I would feel overwhelmed and want to go to my hotel room early in the evening to be alone, rather than try to meet people and hang out with them. I wasn't an anti-social person; in fact, I was quite personable, and most people liked me. So, what was going on?

After returning home from these events, I would usually call in sick the next day so I could stay home and rest. I didn't want to go anywhere or get things done around the house or even watch TV or listen to music. I wanted to sit quietly, and maybe read or do a crossword puzzle. What the heck was wrong with me?

The more I read about Projectors (there wasn't much way back then), the more amazed I was. I had my partner's chart generated. It turned out that he is a Projector, too. *What?* That seemed impossible to me. We are so different in so many ways. But when he read the description of Projectors, it resonated with him. He said it explained so much about his experiences. *Wow.* Then I had a friend's chart created. She is also a Projector and the description totally resonated with her. I was amazed and started to think there was really something to all of this. I requested other charts (who were other Types, thank goodness), and their descriptions were a remarkable fit.

At this point I knew I had to learn more about Human Design, if only to help me understand myself and my quirks, and the people in my life and their quirks. Within two months of starting Karen's nine-month Specialist Training Course (it was one long continuous course at that time), I was hooked and knew in my bones and the depths of my soul that there was nothing on the planet I wanted to do more than learn this system and help others with it by doing readings and teaching.

Honestly, that shocked me. First, because it was such a departure from my background. I had two master's degrees, one in government and one in business, and had achieved reasonable success in both arenas. What was I doing diving into this woo-woo stuff?

The second shock was that I felt so certain. I had been notorious for having a hard time deciding things. I'm a Libra and always wanted to look at all sides and weigh the pros and cons to come to the best conclusion. This decision was totally different. I had learned from my Human Design studies that I have Splenic Authority for making decisions, which means that I get information in the moment about whether something is right or healthy for me. In this case, my splenic "YES" was unmistakable. Of course, my mind tried to second guess me and talk me out of it, but there was something about the deep certainty I felt that I trusted; that trust has grown daily ever since.

Another reason for the shock was that I would be working one-on-one with people. I had never done that. I didn't know if I would like it or be any good at it. My first few attempts at doing Human Design readings (freebies so I could practice) were a little rough, but I stuck with it and got better and more comfortable with it. It has turned out to be the most rewarding work I have ever done.

Since 2009 I've been doing Human Design readings professionally while taking dozens and dozens of courses to deepen my study and improve the quality of my readings. There is still nothing I would rather do on this planet.

As I learned more and more about being a Projector and worked with Projector clients, I slowly relaxed into and accepted my Type—despite my initial resistance and disappointment. Being unhappy about being a Projector is a fairly common reaction and completely understandable. How are we supposed to get anything done, let alone succeed and thrive, if we're "not here to work"? It sounded like the hardest and worst Type to be!

Gradually, I began to see some core truths about Projectors that were not being explained clearly anywhere. First, we *do* have energy, it's just different from the other Types. Second, we *can* take action, even without an invitation (although our results might not always be great, there is no rule to stop us). Third, we *can* manifest the things we want in our lives, our process just looks different. Fourth, we are *not* simply at the mercy of the world around us, powerless and overlooked. Fifth, we are critically *important* to the world.

As I learned to trust my process and pay attention to the flow of energy and the responses of people around me, I gradually began to step into my own power. This was huge for me. I had always been smart, but I never felt powerful. On top of that, classic descriptions of Projectors didn't include the concept that Projectors can be powerful, and those materials never described how Projectors could legitimately claim their power.

As I personally felt more empowered as a Projector, I saw how critical it is that many more of my fellow Projectors become empowered so they can fulfill their role of guiding others and be the full contribution of their unique selves. It's pretty obvious that the world could use some extra help right now!

I also became aware of the pivotal and vital role we are here to play in service to all of humanity. It is not acceptable to me that Projectors feel disempowered and struggle in this world. In that condition, we cannot serve as we are meant to serve—and everyone is worse off for that.

I now see my mission in life as "empowering people to know and love themselves." Human Design is the most amazing tool I've ever found to help do that. I further discovered that I have a vital specific mission within that to "help my fellow Projectors step into their crucial role in the evolution of humanity and joyfully live in their brilliance, power, and sweet success so they create a life they love."

This book is an expression of that specific mission. May you be empowered to live a joyful and confident life knowing that you are not broken, but that you are extraordinary, amazing, and more valuable than you can imagine. You are different from everyone else and thank goodness for that. The world awaits (and needs) the full expression of your brilliance.

The chapters of this book are organized in a progression leading to Projector empowerment, so I recommend that you read them in order for the fullest benefit. But if you are already familiar with Human Design and you have specific issues you are looking to resolve, feel free to jump to the chapters that call to you most.

Evelyn Levenson

Brief Introduction to Human Design

Thank you for your interest in discovering and aligning with your True Self—the authentic YOU. We are in a period of great consciousness awakening on planet earth, and each of us has an important role to play in the process and the outcome.

If you are already familiar with Human Design, you are welcome to skip this introduction and go directly to Part One.

It can be hard to put together the pieces of a puzzle when you don't have a good idea of what the completed puzzle should look like. So, before we dive into the details of becoming an Empowered Projector, let's look at the bigger picture of Human Design and what it tells us about ourselves and our world.

Human Design has been called the new science of awakening and the new astrology. It is a system of knowledge and wisdom that offers amazing insight into your personal energy blueprint. With this clarity, you are able to function with less stress and greater success, make decisions that align with your natural energy and your purpose, improve your relationships, and choose careers and jobs for which you are perfectly suited.

Human Design is *not* a belief system. It is a practical set of principles that describe with astonishing accuracy how life on this planet works. These principles are at work all around us, whether we know it or not, and whether we believe it or not. The founder of Human Design, Ra Uru Hu, encouraged everyone to experiment with the knowledge so we can each come to trust it for ourselves (or not). If you see its value and trust it, you integrate that trust at a full body, deep knowing level. It feels like Truth.

As you experiment with Human Design in general and your specific design in particular, it will take you to the core of Who You Are and awaken you to yourself. You will learn that only *you* know what is correct for you, no one else. You will also learn exactly how you can find your own inner truth, consistently and reliably.

Your Human Design chart holds the keys to unlocking your full potential and living the life of your dreams. It shows you the unique energetic blueprint you were born with and how you are designed to be successful in your life.

If you do not have your chart yet, see the Resources Page for the link to request one. Your chart comes with a free Decision Maker's Kit that includes introductory materials about understanding your chart.

As you read through this introductory chapter and your Decision Maker's Kit, you will be encountering new ways of viewing yourself, other people, and the world. You will need both time and practice to get used to applying this new perspective in your everyday life, but you will also receive insights you can use immediately to optimize your awareness, mindset, and behaviors.

What Human Design Shows Us

At its simplest, Human Design helps you to know yourself and love yourself. It also gives you the awareness of what is correct for you and the power to direct your life in ways that are aligned.

In remarkable detail, and with extraordinary accuracy, Human Design shows:

- How you are designed to function optimally in life.
- How to make decisions that align with your True Self and your purpose.
- Your overall life themes and life path.
- Your areas of vulnerability and how to minimize them.
- Your areas of strength and how to leverage them.
- Your potential for wisdom and how to develop and access it.
- The personality style you bring to all you do.
- How to enter relationships and interact with others in ways that are correct for you.
- Why you are drawn to the people you are drawn to.
- How to identify and break unhealthy behavior patterns.
- What you are designed to communicate and how.

- The challenges you are designed to grow from.
- The lessons you are designed to learn.
- Your greatest blessings and areas of expansion.
- What you soul needs to master to bring about healing.
- And SO much more!

When you understand your own configuration and know how to make decisions aligned with your True Self, you become activated, empowered, fully alive, and able to fulfill your innate potential. You are finally able to create the life you LOVE! You no longer feel like a victim of your circumstances, and you begin to have your hands on the steering wheel (instead of the rear-view mirror) of your life.

The most basic aspect of Human Design is the concept of Type and Strategy. There are five Types within humanity and every person belongs to one and only one of these Types. The Types are based on fundamental energy configurations that are shared within each Type. These configurations then determine the decision-making Strategy that is most advantageous (and most correct) for each Type. The beauty of the Strategies is that they naturally align us with our innate energetic structure and are therefore a reliable way for us to navigate through life with as much success, and as little stress, as possible. For excellent sources of information about the Types and Strategies, please visit the Resources Page.

Human Design can be quite complex and take years of study to learn fully. But it can also be sublimely simple: When you follow your particular Type's Strategy and your personal Authority (as shown on your chart), which refines exactly how *you* are designed to apply your Strategy, you minimize struggle and chaos and maximize the energetic correctness of your choices and actions.

So, the process for improving your life is simple: Live your Strategy and use your Authority for making decisions and taking actions. Doing this will allow you to unlock your full human potential and live the life of your dreams. You'll be more focused, more effective, more purposeful, make better decisions, take inspired action, and attract the right people, circumstances, and opportunities for the magnificent unfolding of your life path.

When each Type follows their Strategy and each person follows their Authority, they make better decisions and can better fulfill their role. When each Type fulfills their role, life functions more smoothly and correctly for everyone, and each person can feel successful in their own way. When we try to operate as a different Type than our birth Type, we struggle, and our struggle ripples out to others.

Basic Principles and Parts of the Chart

Every detail in your chart influences every other detail in your chart, so while the basic information about Human Design charts is fundamentally correct, it is always subject to the influence of other aspects of your chart—which is why a private Human Design reading is so valuable. But even before a reading, it is useful to understand the main principles underlying Human Design as well as the basic parts of the chart. Refer to your own chart as you learn about its parts and principles.

Gates

At the core of Human Design are the 64 **gate** energies which represent archetypes, or fundamental behavior patterns, of humans. A couple of examples include the Listener (Gate 13) and the Thinker (Gate 61). Similar in concept to astrology with its twelve signs and houses, the 64 gates are depicted as a wheel (a mandala) and the sun moves through all 64 over the course of a year. At the time of your birth, certain gates were "activated" and imprinted onto your energy configuration by the planetary bodies of our solar system, including our sun and moon as well as the earth itself and lunar nodes.

These activated gate energies are called **defined**, and they are listed in the columns of numbers on the chart plus they appear as colored bars on the triangular-shaped bodygraph. The black numbers and bars indicate the gates that were activated at the moment of your birth. These represent your Personality energies. They are considered your conscious aspects and relate to your soul. The red numbers and bars indicate the gates that were activated approximately three months prior to your birth. These represent your Design energies. They are considered your unconscious aspects and relate to your life and your physical body—your "vehicle."

The bars that remain white on your bodygraph are considered **undefined** or **open**. While your defined energies flow through you and broadcast out to the world constantly, your undefined areas are taking in the corresponding defined energies from others and amplifying them. Undefined areas allow you to experience those energies but indirectly, through others.

Thus, everyone experiences *all* of the chart. This is so important to remember. It is easy to use shorthand references like "having" a certain energy in your chart and "not having" others. But we are all made of the same stuff. We all have the same DNA although some genes are activated, and some are not. Similarly, some of our gate energies are activated and consistently experienced by us and some are not activated and are inconsistent for us, but we all have the identical basic configuration of energy potentials.

In addition to taking in other people's energies through our openness, we are affected by the gate energies activated through the movement of planetary bodies, known as **transits**. These effects are not as powerful as when we are born, or even as impactful as energy from people around us, but they still affect us every day, all day long.

Centers

You will notice nine geometric shapes on the bodygraph, called **Energy Centers**, which represent hubs of energy and govern many of our behaviors. For example, the Throat Center governs communication, and the Sacral Center governs lifeforce energy.

Similar to gates, when a center is colored in, we call it **defined**. A defined center gives you consistent access to that center's energy. When a center is white, we call it **open** or **undefined**. Look at your own chart to see which of your centers are defined and which are open. As described above, openness takes in and amplifies that energy from those who have it defined.

Our open centers can be areas of great confusion, distraction, and pain for us. They are our main source of **conditioning**, which is the energy and influence we take in from those around us and from the transits. The good news is that our openness is also where we develop wisdom as we experience life.

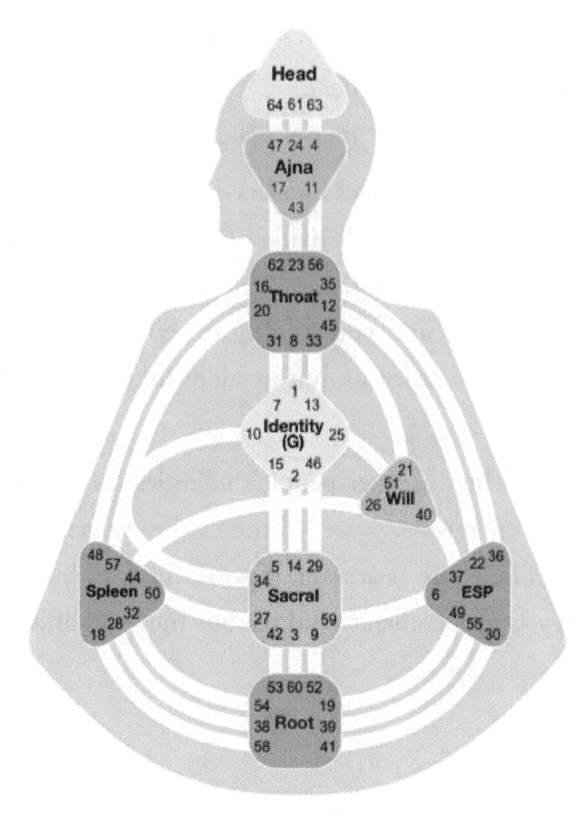

However, there are predictable negative behavior patterns and coping strategies associated with each open center. These are the "low" expressions of those centers. As you **decondition** your open centers, you will express the higher qualities and gain the wisdom of your open center energies while avoiding the potential pain and confusion associated with them. Deconditioning is the process of distinguishing the energy of others from your own and choosing to function from your own flow (which means from the defined areas of your chart).

Understanding your open centers will help you be happier, more balanced, and more successful in your life. Awareness of the open centers of others can help you interact with them more effectively than ever before. Check your chart and the charts of family and friends. You will learn about each open center in Chapter 16. Also, see the Resources Page to learn more.

Channels

Between each of the centers you will see at least one set of two connected gates which form a **channel**. A channel indicates a potential flow of energy between the two centers. When a channel is fully colored in, whether red, black, or a combination of red and black, it is defined, and it represents a powerful flow and important theme in your chart.

When a channel is defined, it causes the centers at both ends of the channel to be defined. There can never be only one defined center on a chart. There must be at least two, created by one defined channel. Most people have several defined channels, creating multiple defined centers on their charts. Only Reflector Types have no defined channels and therefore no defined centers.

Profiles and Lines

Lines are the small numbers associated with each gate in the columns of gate numbers on your chart. The lines appear as exponents or superscript numbers. These six numbers, 1-6, represent different nuances of how the gate energies are expressed.

The six lines combine in very specific pairings to form twelve possible **Profiles**. Each Profile describes a primary conscious and unconscious personality trait. Your Profile and its implications for your life and your relationships are best explored in a private reading where the explanation can be tailored to your chart and your experiences in life.

This very brief introduction to Human Design is enough to get you started and to support your getting the most value from this book. Much more information is available from me and other qualified Human Design teachers and practitioners. Please visit the Resources Page to learn more.

PART ONE

PROJECTOR IDENTITY

Who We Are and Why We Are Here

When you know who you are and why you are here,
your paths and destinations can be consistently correct for you.

You cannot have a happy ending to an unhappy journey.
~ Abraham-Hicks

PART ONE

Projector Identity

Introduction to Projector Identity

This book is about becoming an empowered Projector, but what does it mean to *be empowered,* especially as a Projector? What is *empowerment,* and how does one get it, have it, and keep it?

Here is a helpful way to look at it: Empowerment is a process and a journey, not a fixed destination. So it isn't that "I have arrived at empowerment and there is nothing more to do." There can always be a new journey, a new challenge, a new path, and a next process that takes us further.

We can always step more deeply into:

- feeling good about ourselves.
- trusting ourselves.
- feeling confident.
- knowing at our soul level that we aren't broken.
- standing clearly in our power and setting healthy boundaries that not only protect our energy but that bring forth the fullest and most generous expression of who we are.
- making a difference in the world, in our own very unique way.
- being unfettered in our ability to thrive in this world.

These are good touchstones for feeling empowered. Here is another useful perspective: Being empowered is a state of being and a state of mind. You are empowered because you say you are, and because you choose to be.

With all of that said, there is much we can do together to clarify this empowerment journey. We will look at the mile-markers of progress, the detours and potholes, the joys of our discoveries along the way, and the exuberance of our movement through time and space towards a destination worth reaching—empowerment—knowing we can always start a new journey from there. This is my *why* for writing this book: to help you on your journey to thriving as a Projector, no matter where you are starting.

We begin with knowing who we are as Projectors, so we can know why we are here. This knowledge will help us set paths and destinations in our lives that make sense, that allow for a joyful experience, and that resonate with us to our very core. These are destinations not only worth reaching, but totally aligned with our energy and the truth of our nature.

Chapter 1

Projector Role and Aura

The role of the Projector is to guide. In the language of Karen Curry Parker's *Introduction to Quantum Human Design* book, we are Orchestrators[1]. In general, those who orchestrate are guiding and directing whatever they are arranging or coordinating. Orchestra conductors guide those who are playing the instruments but do not play the instruments themselves.

We are the only Human Design Type designed for this guiding and orchestrating. Generators and Manifesting Generators are here to respond, create, and be busy. They are the Alchemists[1] and Time Benders[1], respectively, who make everything happen. Manifestors (Initiators[1]) are here to start things and initiate others into action.

Someone needs to guide all that activity!

Our lovely Reflector Types are Calibrators[1], here as the barometers of our world, showing us how we are doing collectively.

Karen's terms for identifying the Types, and her terminology for all other aspects of Human Design, are an up-leveled version of the original labels from Ra Uru Hu, founder of Human Design, bringing the vibration of Human Design to a new, more empowering level. For simplicity and familiarity, I will refer to our Type simply as Projectors, and the other Types as their original names, throughout this book.

When all pieces of a puzzle are in their right places, the puzzle is complete and creates a beauty that transcends the contribution of each individual piece. So it is with humanity! When each Type plays its role to the fullest, the result is a highly functioning collective of human beings that can, if they choose to, create sustainable peace, harmony, compassion, equity, progress, and meaningful and fulfilling lives. They function together as a differentiated yet coordinated whole for the benefit of all.

We Projectors are designed to guide the energy of the other Types in this coordinated whole, and usher in a new consciousness in the evolution of humanity. This is a powerful and vital role, yet many Projectors struggle in today's world. We feel disempowered, invisible, unproductive, exhausted, and even broken. But the world needs for us to be powerful, wise, empowered, and thriving.

So, how do we do that? How do we make that shift? This book guides you through that process. The best place for us to start is by diving into what it means to guide and exactly how our energetic wiring enables us to do that.

What Does It Mean to be a Guide?

True guiding is not doing. It is the offering of guidance. Guidance can include suggestions, advice, directions, illuminating questions, corrections, next steps, etc. That sounds rather passive because it is. Guiding is not the implementation of guidance; it is the delivery of guidance. Delivery in this case means communicating, not doing.

Be careful with phrases like: Projectors are here to manage, guide, and direct others. First, people don't like to be "managed" even if they have asked for your help. Second, managing and directing are often active functions which require sustainable energy (more about that in a moment). We are not even here to be leaders of others, although we can be and many of us are. Simply providing the guidance is the truly correct role for us.

This does not mean that we never take action. We have bodies and lives and need to function in this busy and complicated world. Of course we take action. When we are able to do that in the way that is right for us, life is much easier. An entire section of this book (Part Two - Decisions, Actions, and Success) is devoted to how Projectors can take action correctly, effectively, and sustainably.

But let us stay with the role of guiding for now. What do we need to know and be able to do in order to fulfill this role and guide well?

Imagine a local resident giving guided tours of Paris. They need to know the history of the city as well as current and upcoming events. They need to know their way around and which roads and museums are closed. It helps if they speak your language well and also know your particular interests. They need to be able to answer questions, even the difficult ones. They need to shepherd the group efficiently to get everyone back safely and on time, with the group having seen what they were promised to see. It is an extra bonus if the guide knows the best off-the-beaten-path places that the standard tour books miss. Their job is to enhance your experience of visiting Paris.

We can see that being a high-quality guide like that requires knowledge, awareness, communication skills, people skills, curiosity, and maybe a little bit of intuition for good measure.

Projectors naturally fulfill most of those requirements. We are blessed with an innate awareness of others which provides the deep knowledge needed to guide correctly. We are also blessed with curiosity about people and the world, but our communication and interpersonal skills are influenced by the rest of our chart and may sometimes need deliberate attention for improvement. For guidance to be accepted and effective, it must be delivered with sensitivity and tact.

We easily see how others can improve what they do and maximize their potential. This is *our* creative energy—our superpower. This creativity is not for the *doing* of actions but for the gentle *guiding* of actions and the choreographing of the flow of energy. We are powerful when we are being our naturally wise, insightful, and knowledgeable selves and guiding others from that place.

The easiest and most productive way for us to accomplish all of this is to recognize and observe the systems and patterns that surround us. Then, we may bring our keen awareness of those to others—when they ask. We are an amazing resource for others because we know so much and can see the bigger picture of how things are working now and how they could work better.

How is it possible that this is our natural way of being and seeing things?

Our Basic Energy Configuration

All Projectors share the same basic configuration: an open/undefined Sacral Center and a non-motorized Throat Center. Four of the nine centers on the Human Design chart provide energy for taking action and are called "motors." When a motor center connects to the Throat Center through one or more defined channels, the Throat is "motorized" making it easier to make things happen in life—to manifest action. Only Manifestors and Manifesting Generators have motorized Throats. Everyone else has a non-motorized Throat.

Because Projectors have an open Sacral Center, they do not have the sustainable energy that is available to Generators and Manifesting Generators, who have defined Sacral Centers. Generators and Manifesting Generators are the "super-doers" of the world—they generate action. They are not inexhaustible, but they have a full tank of energy when they wake up every morning and are supposed to go to bed with an empty tank, which recharges overnight. We call that sustainable energy.

There are two other Types who share the Projector's open Sacral configuration: Manifestors and Reflectors. This means approximately 30 percent of the population is not here to do sustainable work! All of us in this category must manage our energy, which is quite baffling to the super-doers with their defined Sacral Centers.

Projectors handle this "unsustainable energy" situation by connecting into the energy of others. Please don't despair, though. In Chapter 14 we specifically redefine and address Projector sustainability. We Projectors are not doomed to be completely dependent on others or to never have our own energy!

When we find the people who want and need our guidance, their attention and invitations give us an opening through which we tap into their energy. It is a symbiotic relationship where all of us benefit and none of us are diminished.

In this mutually advantageous scenario, the other person wants and likes the attention and guidance from the Projector. The Projector gets energy from that person along with the satisfaction of helping them. It is truly a win-win when it is a correct interaction for each of them. Both parties can feel the shift when that interaction ends or the relationship itself is over. The Projector no longer has a source of energy and flow of resources, and the other person no longer has the attention and guidance from the Projector. It can feel like an energetic disruption for each of them.

If the Projector was the one who pulled away, the other person may feel deflated, disappointed, ignored, or offended. If the other person was the one who pulled away, the Projector may feel abandoned, depleted, or rejected. However, if the disconnection was mutual, both parties can come out of it feeling fulfilled and empowered.

As Projectors we often work harder than others—believing we must—to be recognized for our efforts and accomplishments and rewarded for our results. But that level of effort is not sustainable for us in the long term, which is why so many of us experience burnout during our lives, sometimes multiple times. There is tremendous pressure from our culture's expectations, and often from specific people around us, for us to have the *doing* energy of Generators and Manifesting Generators and the *initiating* energy of Manifestors. This is exhausting for us because it is not correct for our energy. We are simply not wired for the consistent hustle and nearly tireless action of those other Types.

Our Complexity and Conditioning

Because we are here to guide, we are *designed to be conditioned* by others and by the world around us. Conditioning is the influence of other people's energies on us through our openness. As we absorb their energy and influence, we gain awareness that helps us guide them. Every Projector has at least one open center—the Sacral Center. We take in and amplify the motor energy of that center, plus we absorb energy through any other open centers we have. Wisdom resides in open centers because of the unlimited opportunities they provide for experiencing the full range of human expression in those energies. The energetic input we receive through our open centers gives us a broad range of vicarious experience that enhances our ability to guide the energy of others.

Conditioning itself is not bad or something to be avoided. It is an integral part of the human experience and our personal growth. It is how we are influenced by and interact with the world around us. Openness exposes all of us to unlimited ways of expressing energy—it is where we explore, learn, and expand who we are. It is also where we get to know and interact with others because we experience their energy. Openness is the playground of humanity! This includes not only our open centers but also our open gates and channels.

Conditioning becomes problematic when our openness, particularly open centers, pulls us away from following our correct decision-making process and from correctly expressing our defined energies (our definition). The related result of this hijacking of our decisions away from our True Self is the expression of the **not-self** of our design. The not-self emerges when we operate in ways that are out of alignment with the defined aspects of our design and instead focus on the open (inconsistent) aspects in our chart.

When we don't know that we are taking in and amplifying the energy of others in our open centers, we mistakenly identify with that energy. Because this experience is variable and not under our control (because that energy is not ours), we can feel off balance and confused about what is happening. In response, we develop predictable behavior patterns to help us cope with that confusion. Those patterns are rarely healthy for us in the long term.

While we will always be conditioned by the people around us and by the transitory movement of the planets (the transits), there is a process called **deconditioning** that helps us recognize and release this energy. The deconditioning process is discussed more fully in Chapter 16. Just know that we are not stuck with this energy or those unhealthy patterns!

Traditional Human Design teaches that it takes at least seven years to decondition our open centers. It truly is a process and a practice, but you can and will see immediate benefits as soon as you begin to apply this knowledge to your life. Remember that lifelong patterns are being shifted, so proceed with gentleness. Acknowledge and celebrate your progress and be patient.

As we move through this process and understand our openness, we make better choices and move toward the wisdom available to us. This simultaneously moves us away from the confusion, overwhelm, and not-self expressions often associated with our openness and allows us to become clear about which energies are *our* energies and which are from other people. This clarity reinforces our correct decision-making process and supports our alignment with the truth of Who We Are.

How Our Aura Works

Each Human Design Type has its own aura configuration which establishes the nature of how each Type interacts with the world. The aura is the holistic energy field that surrounds and emanates from a person. From a quantum perspective, it is the mental and emotional field around us that contains our identity, our definition, and our conditioning.

The aura of Generators and Manifesting Generators is open and enveloping, reaching out from them in every direction and wrapping others in their inclusive energy field like a big warm blanket. This is not a personal interaction—their aura envelopes everyone within aura-distance: in front, behind, beside, above, and below.

The Manifestor's aura is closed and self-contained, distinctly not warm and inviting. This doesn't mean Manifestors cannot be warm and inviting. They can be when they choose to be, but the nature of their energy field keeps people away so they can do their initiating and manifesting with as little interruption and interference from others as possible.

The nature of the Reflector's aura is to reach outward and sample the auras and energies of other people. This sampling allows them to be the mirror and barometer they are here to be by giving them little bite-size tastes of what is happening around them. In this way, Reflectors can accurately reflect the people and groups surrounding them without taking in the energy of those people and groups.

Reflectors are specifically designed to *not* be conditioned by people and groups, despite the Reflector's extreme openness of nine undefined centers. Instead, they are influenced and conditioned by the transits, those constant movements of planets, sun, and particularly the moon through the 64 gates of the Human Design mandala wheel. This conditioning from the transits gives them further input about the status of what goes on around them, without being overtaken by the energy of other people.

As you can see, each aura is quite different from the others. The Projector's aura has its own very distinct configuration and purpose.

The Projector aura is penetrating and, in this way, it is very personal. This aura is naturally focused on the person in front of them which allows the Projector to experience and take in the energy and essence of that person. This process of absorbing the other person's energy gives the Projector the "data" they need to be able to guide that person, if invited. The Projector receives and can use energy from that person while being conditioned by their energy. This can lead some people to view Projectors as energy parasites, but this is not accurate. Energy emanating from definition in the chart is limitless and is not diminished by others taking in that energy. Someone's energy can be "sucked dry" by another person only when that person allows it to occur at an emotional or mental level; that is not what happens at the energetic level.

It is important to understand that the Projector is not projecting their own energy into the other person. It is quite the opposite, the other person's energy flows back toward the Projector. However, the Projector's penetrating aura can still be uncomfortable for the other person. The other can feel naked and exposed by that concentrated and keen inquiry and observation by the Projector. It is also possible for the other person to love that attention and focus from the Projector, and they can even feel jealous when the Projector shifts their focus to someone else.

Because of the singular focus of the Projector aura, our best interactions with others are one-on-one. This further supports our ability to know the other's energy and grasp deeply who they are, enabling us to provide them with wise guidance. This focused attention on the other person is our greatest asset. Most people want or need attention (for example, those with an open Throat Center), and Projectors have an abundance of attention to give.

However, because we take in so much energy from others, we need to be selective about whom we focus on. Not everyone wants our guidance. In fact, each Projector has just a small number of people who are correct for their guidance. It is a bit like a mating dance for the Projector and the other person to determine if they are the right match for each other. Each will apply their own Strategy and Authority to the interaction for entering into the relationship correctly.

When your aura projects into the other person, you need to wait and see how they respond. If your aura feels good to them and they see the value in interacting with you, they will (hopefully) respect, recognize, and invite you to interact. Then you get to apply your personal Authority to determine whether the interaction is correct for you.

You protect your energy as a Projector by connecting with and tapping into only those people who are specifically correct for you. When you interact with and focus your attention on those who are not correct for you, you risk being manipulated or used by them.

When Projectors trust the power and wisdom of their own auras, they draw to them the correct attention, recognition, and invitations. In this case, "correct" means attracting attention, recognition, and invitations from those people who see and value the Projector's abilities and welcome their insights.

One other consequence of our penetrating aura is the ability to know others far better than we know ourselves. We are not able to penetrate ourselves with our own aura. Our aura moves outward from our energy field to the other person's energy field. This leaves us relatively unaware of our own energy, which explains why so many Projectors are hungry to know themselves and are attracted to the self-awareness that Human Design provides.

How All of the Types Fit Together

Now that we have seen the nature of our role within human interactions and how our aura supports us in playing that role beautifully, let's look at how the puzzle pieces of the five Types fit together in the sphere of human functioning.

There is a vital, interdependent, and synergistic relationship between Projectors as the guides and Generators and Manifesting Generators as the "do-ers." Both sides of this equation give and receive something from the other side. It is a true win-win, at least in the ideal and most respectful version of this relationship.

The Projector gives guidance and receives energy. The Generator or Manifesting Generator receives attention and guidance and applies it to their own actions. Their Sacral energy, which broadcasts nonstop from their defined Sacral Center, provides energy to the Projector doing the guiding. Neither side of this equation can truly fulfill their purpose without the other. This healthy exchange of energy describes how approximately 90 percent of the population is designed to interact, with Projectors making up around 21 percent and defined Sacrals close to 70 percent.

Projectors are configured to perceive the energy of the Sacral beings, recognize their potential, and be of service by guiding them. Often, the best (and most well received) guidance from Projectors takes the form of insightful and profound questions. These give defined Sacral beings the optimal stimulus to which they can respond and thereby access their own internal truth. Projectors do not necessarily know what is correct for these other people, but they can guide them to discover their own answers.

When Sacral beings recognize that the Projector can help them, they open themselves to the aura penetration and guidance from the Projector and are happy with the exchange of energy.

The Manifestor operates just outside of this dominant dynamic but influences both sides of the equation. In the Manifestor's role to initiate others into action and initiate projects into existence, they stimulate the Generators and Manifesting Generators to respond and can recognize and invite the Projectors to guide. By remaining just outside the sphere of all that activity, the Manifestor is not drawn into the swirl and is mostly left alone to do their initiating, which is usually all they want to do.

Our beautiful Reflectors are outside of this broad realm of activity where 99 percent of humanity operates. From that outer edge, they bless us with their sampling aura and their ability to view with such clarity how well the overall system is working including the relative health of the organizations, groups, and families within the system. They are here to help us make course corrections based on their accurate reflection of where we are, what we are doing, and where we are headed.

Here is a diagram that depicts this entire dynamic.

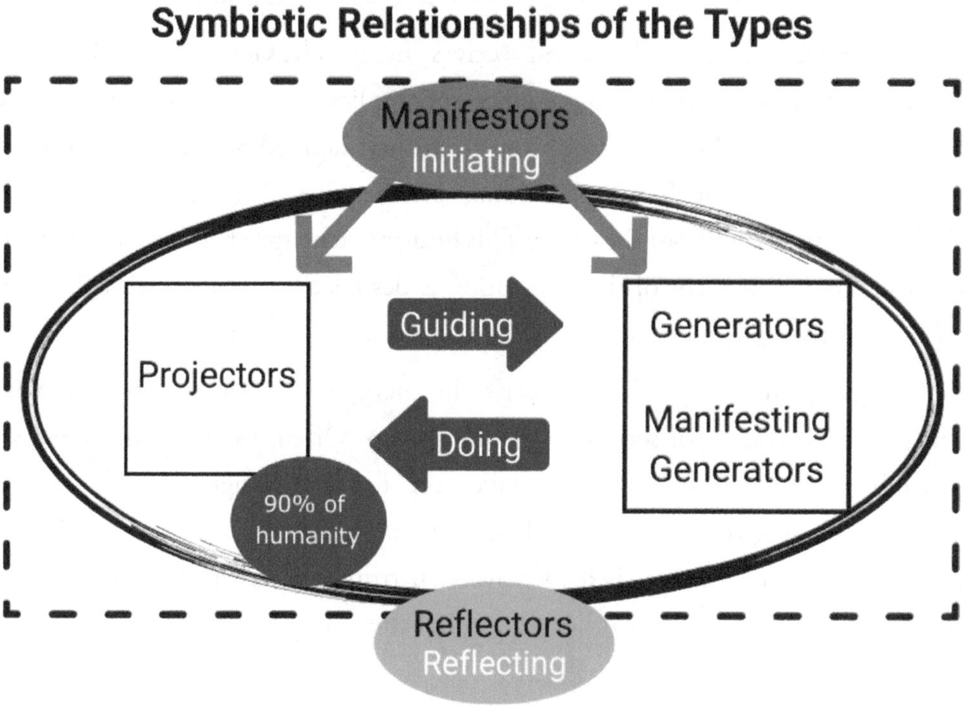

Symbiotic Relationships of the Types

Ra and Lynda Bunnell, in *The Definitive Book of Human Design*, state that Projectors are "taking leadership in a new direction," and "As Manifestors are freed to initiate processes, and Generators begin to realign with their own natural power as creative builders, Projectors will emerge as the administrators of the new order."[2]

We Projectors are naturally skilled at administration and diplomacy and can be good politicians because of our knowledge, awareness, grasp of other people, and understanding of systems and processes. But there is more to the Projector's role than merely earthly interactions with other Types. There is a larger context for humanity, and we Projectors have a vital role there, too.

Chapter 2

Our Cosmic Purpose and 2027

In the earthly scheme of things, the guiding role of Projectors is taking on greater importance. Manifestors used to be the leaders of the world because of their initiating capacity and ability to create momentum. We needed that energy to help us survive, and then to move us forward to innovate and improve the basic quality of human life. Over many thousands of years, this included advances in agriculture, trade, science, medicine, transportation, construction, creating nations and governments, as well as territorial warfare and bombs, along with many other innovations.

Things are changing now. Despite the turbulence of the last few hundred years, the softer skills of diplomacy, cooperation, and compromise are coming more to the forefront. Conflicts, battles, and wars still exist but we need them less and we are finally realizing that they do so much more harm than good. With advancements in every aspect of life, we no longer need as much physical strength to survive. We need brains now more than brawn. Projectors are exquisitely designed to take advantage of this greater need for cognitive development and awareness. This is what Projectors offer in exchange for the attention and energy of others. The muscle needed now is for global and humanitarian advancements more than survival, and these advancements require a new level of guidance.

Ra Uru Hu's Human Design teachings include a detailed description of this major shift in the evolution of humanity which is changing the bodygraph itself as well as the way we interact with one another. It is called the 2027 Solar Plexus Mutation. While the intention for this book is not to go into details about this shift, I will give a brief description of what is coming (and has already started to happen) so you have this broader context for understanding the bigger role of Projectors.

The 2027 Solar Plexus Mutation

The earth spins on its axis, measured in days, and rotates around the sun, measured in years. It also experiences a wobble in the tilt angle of its axis over a very long period of time—approximately 25,772 years. This is called the Precession of the Equinoxes and it is caused by "the gravitational influence of the Sun and the Moon acting on Earth's equatorial bulge."[3]

Even ancient cultures in human history were aware of this slow-moving shift. That very long cycle of time is now viewed as six epochs which are further divided into eight spans of about 400 years each. These 400-year periods represent global cycles of our earthly evolution and growth. According to Ra, each cycle is expressed through a specific configuration of four Human Design gates that make up an Incarnation Cross.

The Incarnation Cross for each cycle defines the themes and challenges of that era, which prepare us for the next stage in our evolution. This information helps us know what we need to learn and work through at our collective level as well as personally. These are the cycles of growth and change that fuel the expansion of our human consciousness.

The current cycle started in 1615 under the Incarnation Cross of Planning, which is determined by the Gates 37, 40, 9, and 16. This cross contains Channel 37-40 which is the energy for community, agreements, belonging, resource allocation, peace (or lack of peace), and hard work. During this cycle, humanity went through the Scientific Revolution, the Industrial Revolution, the Information Age and Technology Revolution, many wars, the building of new nations and new forms of government, and too many innovations and discoveries to name. We have also experienced a huge shift in the autonomy of individuals based on our growing ability to intentionally calibrate and direct the manifestation of our intentions and desires.

With all of that, we created stable societies, economies, political systems, currencies, trade, and more—except that they are not so stable anymore.

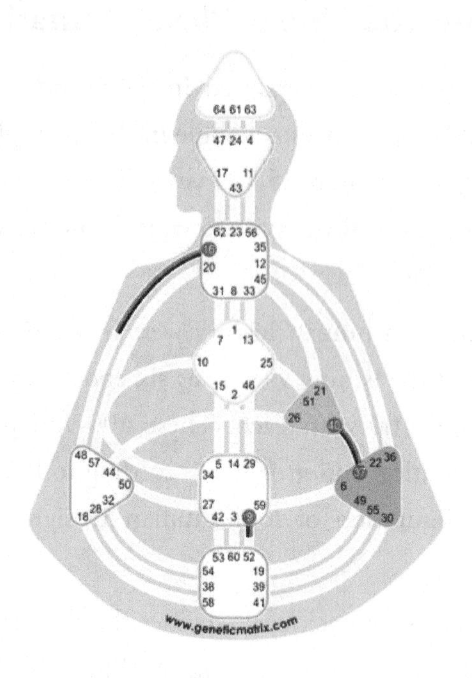

Incarnation Cross of Planning

The Cross of Planning taught us to value community, business agreements, peace, and hard work. Channel 37-40 gave us great potential and high aspirations for peaceful coexistence, the emotional energy to create it, and the willpower to enforce it. But as we fail to use our collective will for the good of all and fall short in cultivating inner peace and harmony as the necessary foundation for outer peace, we are diminishing our inner resources and resilience as we deplete our outer resources. We are allowing greed and power to continue to dominate.

And now we are bumping up against the next evolutionary cycle. In 2027, the planet shifts into the Cross of the Sleeping Phoenix with Gates 34, 20, 59, and 55. As we move toward the transition into this next cycle, we are called to reexamine the ways we value money, wealth, and material resources that have underpinned our growth for the past 400 years.

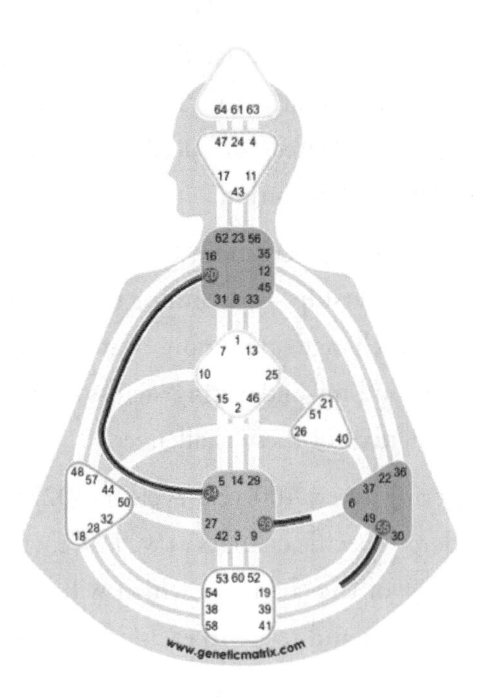

Incarnation Cross of the Sleeping Phoenix

The Cross of the Sleeping Phoenix will hold lessons for us in sustainability (Gate 59) and in our connection to spirit and the abundance that flows from faith (Gate 55), though not necessarily connected to religion. Channel 34-20 will give us unparalleled energy, power, responsiveness, and (surprisingly) patience to sense the right timing and right actions to unify us, moment by moment.

Our actions during our current cycle have led us to the brink of an unsustainable use of natural resources and an inequitable distribution of wealth and power. This new cycle can give us the tools we urgently need to course-correct and establish new values and new priorities. We will learn to use quality of life and the sharing of sustainable abundance as measures of success, instead of bank accounts, ownership, and dominance over others.

While some predictions of what the next cycle will look like sound dark and pessimistic, there is a sound basis for optimism but only if we step up to the challenges, release old ways that no longer serve the greater good, and embrace new approaches and whole new paradigms for defining and guiding our collective growth. We are leaving behind the material consciousness that got us here and moving into quantum consciousness that values every being equally. The writers of the U.S. Declaration of Independence in 1776 declared "all men are created equal" in a very bold departure from reality up to that point. They defined a new path that we have been navigating (with varying degrees of success) ever since, and that has been preparing us for our next stage of evolution.

The values of collaboration, co-creation, caring, and diplomacy—traditionally the more feminine styles of leadership—are coming to the forefront as the global level challenges we face (climate change, pollution, water quality and quantity, etc.) demand new ways of responding and acting across cultures and countries. We Projectors are perfectly designed for these challenges.

Not only are we entering a new 400-year cycle in 2027, but the Human Design bodygraph itself will undergo specific changes as well. We will have different circuitry underlying the energy flows of the channels, which will create dramatic changes in many areas of how we function and relate to each other. Life as we know it is about to transform.

For a more complete exploration of this evolutionary shift, including the specific mechanics of the changes to the circuitry of the bodygraph, see Karen Curry Parker's book *The Quantum Human.* (Find the link through the Resources Page.)

Our Bigger Role in This Changing World

With these broad and dramatic changes, humanity faces an extraordinary array of challenges to meet and problems to solve. Ra said that Projectors are here to align the generative force that creates the world. I believe he largely meant that we are to guide the creative workforce energies of Generators and Manifesting Generators. But there is something more here. The forces that create the world and these major shifts are bigger than that. And the imminent changes are global in scale and affect every living thing on this planet—either directly or indirectly.

I believe that Projectors are here to guide humanity into this future and help shape it for our collective highest good. Not only do we focus the energy of Generators and Manifesting Generators and hone the creative initiative of Manifestors, but we also hold and align the entire energy field of the planet.

Projectors scrub and polish the energy template of our collective consciousness. We anchor and guide the energy grids that heal, clear, and transmute negative energy, collective pain, and wounds. I deeply believe that we are helping to usher in a new paradigm for humanity, one of love, compassion, cooperation, and creating a planet where everyone has what they need to live a happy, productive, and fulfilling life. Not only having food, shelter, clothing, and safety but also dignity, respect, fair compensation, and real opportunities for personal growth, love, community, contribution, and global citizenship.

This is a big job and a big responsibility. No wonder we are tired much of the time. Even when we are hanging out with friends, reading a book, watching a movie, or sleeping, we are simultaneously busy at this bigger job on the etheric level.

In her book, *Introduction to Quantum Human Design*, Karen Curry Parker says that the spiritual purpose of Projectors is "To anchor the energetic template of what we are here to create, to align the energy of the world and heal the energy of the planet."[4] I know Projectors who consider this work to be their job and who embrace it fully.

As our direct role on this planet expands, primarily guiding the energy of Generators and Manifesting Generators, we also have this big vital role of shepherding and anchoring the 2027 energy shift into being. The world has never needed us more. The energetic mechanics of this shift will happen without us—the cosmic forces are in play and there is no stopping them. But with our attuned and aligned guidance, I believe Projectors can make a huge difference in shaping, embracing, and guiding the changes in positive and impactful ways.

An important yet often overlooked implication of all this is the need for Projectors to take excellent care of themselves, to remain aligned and inspired, to rest as much as needed, and to have as much fun as possible—to balance the seriousness of this work. We may look like we are resting but we may be very active and busy on a different energy plane. So, please don't judge or criticize yourself if you don't have much energy for daily life. Honor and respect your various roles and manage your energy accordingly.

A Personal Note

I share this perspective about the larger role of Projectors because this information resonates deeply with me. I first heard it from Karen Curry Parker and my internal Splenic Authority immediately vibrated powerfully. This information had the resonance of truth for me. It has also resonated powerfully with the many Projectors I've talked to about it and shared it with. I hope you find it helpful, too. Although it is not part of the original teachings of Human Design and direct confirmation of it may not yet be available, I encourage you to consider it. See if it has a resonance of truth for you and helps explain our importance in the larger scheme of things.

Chapter 3

Who Are You? (and Who Is the Not-Self?)

It is one thing to understand who we are as Projectors at a generic level, and that is a vital place to start. It is quite another challenge to understand yourself at a personal level. The best way—bar none—to learn about your details, nuances, behavioral tendencies, strengths, vulnerabilities, themes, and much more, is through a private Human Design reading. Qualified practitioners offer a variety of readings, and it is best to find a practitioner with whom you resonate.

In the meantime, let's explore what you can do now to begin to gain an accurate and empowering sense of yourself on a personal level.

Who Are You?

Humans are complex beings, as indicated by the many gates, lines, channels, circuits, centers, and definition in a Human Design chart, plus Profile, Type, Strategy, and Authority. That is a lot of moving parts, with a nearly infinite set of possible combinations. It can take a while to have an integrated understanding of all those parts, yet we crave quick answers. Especially as Projectors, we often seek outside help in knowing who we are because self-awareness is frustratingly elusive for us.

Although you may want a clear and concise description of yourself, be very careful of defining yourself too quickly and too narrowly.

If you have a defined G Center (also called the Self or Identity Center)—the yellow diamond shape on your Human Design chart—you may have a strong sense of self and clarity about your identity and direction in life, and that's great. If your G Center is defined but you do not have that clarity yet, don't worry. It will emerge when you are ready for it, and you really cannot help but be who you are anyway—unless you are forcibly suppressing your True Self.

If you have an undefined G Center (white diamond shape), who you are and where you are going are moving targets. You literally are designed to be fluid and open in this aspect. When you stop trying to define yourself and stop forcing yourself to identify a single clear mission in life, you will be able to relax and stop grasping at identities and directions that do not really fit you.

The beauty of having an undefined G is that you don't have to choose or decide who you are. Your sense of self and your direction will come from outside of you through recognition and invitations, and you need simply to apply your decision-making Authority to get clarity about which opportunities and identities feel right for you at the time. This can (and usually does) change over time, so relax, go with the flow, and enjoy the ride. It is much more fun when you enjoy the people you are with instead of trying on their identities in your quest to see if you should be more like them (or even *become* them).

With an undefined G, it is quite easy to adapt to and adopt the identities and directions of others. Then you may feel lost and not know who you are because those identities and directions probably are not right for you, and you sense that something is off. Before making important or expensive decisions, make sure you are alone for a while and away from the aura and influence of others so you can tune into what feels correct for *you*.

This brings us to the other challenge we Projectors have in knowing who we are: We are designed to know others and not really designed to know ourselves. This does not mean that we cannot know ourselves. It is just more challenging for our Type than for other Types. Our penetrating aura delves deeply into the other person, and we have an innate sense of who they are and how they can use their energy better and more efficiently. We sense them and we *know* them. But we don't know ourselves in the same way.

This is why so many of us search fervently for answers all of our lives, explore many modalities, and participate in countless self-help systems, courses, books, retreats, etc. We are trying to figure out who we are, and we are baffled that this self-knowledge seems so elusive.

Who Are You Not? (The Not-Self)

Sometimes an excellent way to know who we are is to identify who we are *not*, so we can narrow down the options. But that is not quite as simple as we might hope. As previously emphasized, we all experience all of the chart so even the not-self is part of our experience, although it is not our True Self.

The not-self is shaped by the undefined areas of our chart and is expressed when we operate in ways out of alignment with the defined aspects of our design. Our not-self expression emerges from the open or inconsistent aspects of our chart, which is where we are constantly receiving and amplifying energy from others. We predictably tend to identify with those energies, because we don't know they are not ours, and we build our sense of self and expectations about ourselves around those not-self energies.

That bombardment of energy from others through our openness can leave us very confused about ourselves and each other. You may be able to spot a fellow Projector simply by observing them briefly and recognizing common characteristics. But if a Projector is trying hard to be a Manifesting Generator (in other words, actively being their not-self), you will not easily recognize their Projector-ness.

As we saw earlier, having an open G Center can add even more confusion into the mix. When we don't know who we are, we either don't trust ourselves at all or we try to fit in where we don't belong and end up putting trust in the parts of ourselves that are not our True Self.

Recognition and invitations help us step into our True Self and avoid our not-self behaviors. When we try to initiate significant actions in the absence of invitations, we are likely operating from our not-self. While specifics will vary from Projector to Projector, some descriptions of Projectors acting from the not-self include pushy, needy, desperate, bossy, know-it-all, dependent, clingy, bitter, resentful, ineffective, lazy, and exhausted.

The not-self Projector often feels invisible and incapable of making things happen and slips into the perilous downward spiral of bitterness. Much of our exhaustion comes from paddling upstream against a strong current, as we try so hard to make our lives work.

It is important to explore the not-self, so we know what we are up against. Here are some of the ways that our not-self distances us from our True Self.

- We compare ourselves to others.
- We judge ourselves, often rather harshly.
- Others judge us, and we take it personally.
- We take on (or try to take on) the identity of others so we can be successful like them.
- We try hard to please others and to be what they need, so we can feel useful and appreciated.
- We feel purposeless and pointless when we are not helping others, especially when we are not being invited or recognized by others.
- We feel different from others, so we isolate ourselves or we stay around others and try desperately to fit in.
- We feel like we fall short or don't measure up so often that we feel like giving up.
- We think we are who we are not.
- We overwork to earn the recognition that we seek.
- We expend tremendous energy maintaining our not-self identity and keeping our not-self functioning.
- We feel shame about any or all of the above.

While the not-self is a product of the amplified energy of others and the resulting confusion that causes, it is the mind that coordinates the not-self expression. Your mind seeks purpose and identity and grasps at whatever it thinks might work. But your body, your vehicle in this life, inherently knows who you are and will live out your true purpose and identity as long as the mind doesn't interfere. (I know, that's the hard part. We will dive deeper into this challenge and how to overcome it a little later in the book.)

My favorite mantra for supporting the True Self and avoiding the not-self is "Our minds may be really smart, but our bodies are much wiser."

Our bodies hold the truth of Who We Are, as formulated by our chart's definition and augmented by the wisdom from our chart's openness. Trusting and applying our decision-making Strategy and Authority will consistently put us on our true path and navigate us away from our not-self expression.

The not-self craves confirmation and approval because of the fundamental insecurity of an identity based on something that constantly changes and is beyond our control. The resulting lack of self-confidence drives the not-self behaviors listed above. The not-self (or mind) will grasp at anything it thinks will provide consistency. The emotional, spiritual, and even physical pain from living life from the not-self can be devastating, creating deep wounds and paralyzing self-doubt. This pain and the healing of these wounds will be explored in-depth in Parts Three and Four.

If your G Center is open (white diamond shape), know and trust that your True Self is designed to be changeable. When you embrace that variability, you can release the not-self patterns of doubting yourself and grasping for confirmation, and finally enjoy the flow of your exquisite adaptability.

Whether your G Center is defined or open, you will most clearly find your place and identity and feel aligned and fulfilled through correct recognition and invitation from others, *not* by trying to be a Generator, Manifesting Generator, or Manifestor, and certainly not by trying to please others so that you get recognized.

So, Who Are You Really?

The most reliable place to find the specifics of YOU is in the definition in your chart, which are the colored gates, channels, and centers. But it is hard to start with the details and build up the big picture of Who You Are from there. The good news is that the definition in your chart also determines the broader aspects of you: your Type, Strategy, Authority, and Profile, and these are the best place to start so you can discover your True Self from the top down.

Your **Type**—Projector—gives you the role you are designed to play in this lifetime. As a Projector, you are here to guide and optimize the flow of energy and raise the vibration of the earth's energy grid.

Your **Strategy**—wait to be invited—gives you the most successful approach you can use for making decisions and taking action. Since your life experience is the direct result of *all* the decisions you make and actions you take, using your Strategy correctly is crucial for creating a life that you love and that works for you.

Your **Authority** gives you the specific instructions for how you are designed to apply the Projector Strategy of waiting to be invited. This added level of detail gives you access to the incredible power and accuracy of exactly how you can trust your body to guide you to fulfill your potential. Even Mental Authority (also called No Authority) Projectors use their bodies to trust the resonance and alignment of their decisions before making them. Projector Authorities are fully explained in Chapter 6.

Your **Profile** illuminates the personality style you bring to your role in life. The first number of your Profile shows your dominant conscious personality trait; it is the one you are always aware of and can use deliberately whenever you choose. The second number shows your dominant unconscious trait, which you are often unaware of and are not able to intentionally leverage. However, this unconscious trait does express through you, and the people in your life are often more aware of it than you are.

These foundational aspects of your chart give you the big picture of the truth of Who You Are. But that is just the beginning. Your **channels** are complete flows of energy sometimes referred to as your superpowers. They highlight key themes and focused potentials that weave through your life. Any defined gates that are not part of a completely defined channel are called **hanging gates**. They represent aspects that are a consistent part of who you are but only become fully activated by others. The **positions** of the sun, earth, moon, and planets relative to your defined gates indicate the specific ways the gate energies operate in your life. Of course, your **centers**—both defined and open—speak volumes about your behavior patterns, your strengths, and your potential for wisdom.

Two more vital parts of understanding why you are here and how to fulfill your purpose are found in your chart. The first is your **Incarnation Cross**, which is determined by the gates activated by your sun and earth positions. It represents the path you are *designed* to follow. It is the "plot line" of your life. This is a higher-level understanding of your chart so be sure you grasp the basics of your chart first. The full expression of your cross becomes activated only when your decisions and actions are aligned with your True Self, so start by following your Strategy and Authority consistently.

The other higher-level vital part of your chart is found in your **Chiron** gates. The planetoid Chiron (also spelled Kiron, Kyron, or Chyron) is called the Wounded Healer in astrology. In Human Design, these gate energies represent what your soul came into this body to learn and then help others with, including healing the wounds of these soul-level challenges. These gates reveal the broader backdrop of your life that is your soul's mission in this lifetime. Not all charts show the Chiron energies, so if yours does not, you can request your free chart that includes Chiron from the link on the Resources Page.

Putting It All Together

That is a LOT of information! Many people research all these different aspects of themselves and amass a huge pile of bits and pieces. I was one of those people. But without proper training and a grasp of the entire system and how the parts affect each other, it is impossible to formulate a coherent and useful understanding of your whole self.

Nothing comes close to the value of a completely personalized interactive reading that helps you integrate and apply all you can learn from your chart. A comprehensive reading will also address your not-self tendencies and how to decondition them. Remember, your openness is part of your design too, and understanding it is vital for getting the full picture of yourself.

Have a basic or foundational reading first then spend time experimenting with what you learn. Listen to the recording of your session(s) and review your notes multiple times. Each time you do, you will get more value from them because you will be at a more experienced level of understanding and application of that personalized knowledge and self-awareness. Learn more about available readings on the Resources Page.

The Vital Non-Chart Aspect of You

There is one more key aspect of you that you need to know, and it is not contained in your chart. It is your mindset. This is what determines how you approach, receive, and interpret everything that happens to you and around you.

While aspects of your chart will influence your mindset, how you view the world is actually a choice.

The classic example of our attitude towards the world is whether we see the glass as half full or half empty. This divides us into optimists and pessimists. While mindset choices have a broader range and deeper complexity than that, it is a good place to begin. Most of us hold a default belief that says we cannot change our mindset—we cannot upgrade how we perceive the world, but we absolutely can.

When we understand the power of our mindset not only to affect every single aspect of our current lives but also to determine our future, we begin to see the value of exerting deliberate choice in the matter. Most of us are on automatic pilot as we move through much of our lives. We function more from habits than from choices.

People do not decide their futures, they decide their habits and their habits decide their futures.
~ F. M. Alexander

Becoming aware of our habits is the first step in being able to change them. To learn about your habits and mindset, all you need to do is listen to yourself. What do you say about yourself, as internal self-talk or out loud? What do you say about your life? Your setbacks? People who have wronged you? Do you spend more time complaining about what you don't like and don't want, or more time talking about and planning for what you do like and do want? Do you view the world as hostile and scary, or do you see it as an amazing place to live with abundant opportunities?

Your mindset drives the stories you tell about yourself, your life, your experiences, and your challenges. Your stories reflect, set, and perpetuate the tone of your life. Is it a happy vibe, or a fear-based, angry, resentful, or depressed vibe? I encourage you to listen to yourself and take inventory of how you express yourself and where you put your energy and attention. If you're not sure, ask your closest friends and loved ones. They will describe your vibe.

Your stories and their underlying mindset are one of your greatest points of leverage for changing your life for the better. In reframing what you say about something that happened in the past or is happening now, choose a slightly more empowering point of view. Do not lie to yourself, because you will reject the lie, and nothing will change. Find a true statement that is in the direction you desire. Instead of saying, "I hate my job, but I'm stuck in it," you could say, "My job is not a good fit for me, and I'm actively working on ways to get myself out of it." Same situation, different perspective. A more optimistic and empowering perspective can shift your whole vibe and open new possibilities.

Having an empowering view of yourself includes embracing your uniqueness, standing in the importance of your vital role, and shifting the disempowering stories about yourself and your life. In later chapters, we will address Projector pain and help you heal wounds, restore balance and resiliency, expand possibilities, and step into a more empowered version of yourself so you can thrive sustainably.

From what we have covered so far, it is easy to see that we Projectors have several challenges. Our energy is not sustainable, we don't have much self-awareness, and a negative mindset can bring down all aspects of our lives. What is a Projector to do? We will begin to answer that in Part Two, but before we get there let's meet some of our fellow Projectors in the world. We are not alone in our challenges and, in fact, are in great company! It is encouraging to see that there are so many famous Projectors who have figured out how to thrive despite our common Projector challenges.

Chapter 4

Famous Projectors

You are in great company being a Projector. Collectively, we have made and will continue to make a major difference in the world. Below is a list of famous Projectors. Of course, they are mostly actors, politicians, and athletes, because those are the people who tend to be famous. Rest assured that there are many non-famous Projectors who also make a huge difference.

It is encouraging to see that so many Projectors have figured out how to thrive, how to live a fulfilling life, and how to make meaningful contributions to the world.

We are designed to make a difference, but to do so through subtle guiding, not through direct impact or force. Sometimes Projectors do use force when operating from their not-self, but that does not seem to be the norm.

Many on this list struggled before they succeeded, then went on to live life and achieve success on their own terms. You may be surprised—and inspired—when you learn of these famous Projectors.

Abraham Lincoln*
Albert Schweitzer
Amelia Earhart
Andrea Bocelli
Arianna Huffington*
Barack Obama
Barbra Streisand
Bernie Sanders
Brad Pitt*
Brigitte Bardot
Bruce Springsteen
Candice Bergen
Demi Moore
Denzel Washington
Diana, Princess of Wales (Lady Di)*
Diane Keaton
Douglas MacArthur
Elizabeth Taylor
Fidel Castro
Frank Sinatra

Garth Brooks
George Balanchine
George Clooney
Goldie Hawn
Halle Berry
Hugh Hefner
Jay Leno
Jeff Bezos
John F. Kennedy*
Jon Bon Jovi
Joseph Campbell
Karl Marx
Katharine Hepburn
Lance Armstrong
Marilyn Monroe
Mick Jagger
Nelson Mandela*
Osho
Pablo Picasso
Queen Elizabeth II
Ralph Nader
Ringo Starr
Rodney King*
Ron Howard
Salvador Dalí
Sandra Day O'Connor
Serena Williams
Shirley MacLaine
Steven Spielberg*
Tony Blair
Ulysses S. Grant
Wayne Dyer*
Whoopi Goldberg
William Shatner
Woody Allen

*Starred names have a Celebrity Chart Review on my blog. See the Resources Page for links.

Now that you have seen some of the famous people you share your Type with, I would like to introduce you to one of them in particular. He is a man who changed the course of history as the sixteenth President of the United States.

Meet a Projector - Abraham Lincoln

Abraham Lincoln was the ideal leader for the United States during a very turbulent time in our history. His natural abilities as a Projector to guide and inspire people resulted in his election as our sixteenth president just when the southern states were attempting to separate and create their own union. He not only succeeded in reuniting the country but also in abolishing slavery, though he had to wage a bloody civil war to do so.

We often ask ourselves what one person can do, especially against powerful forces moving in the opposite direction. While we can't all be Abe Lincoln, we can learn from his example that one person *can* make a difference, an enormous difference.

As a Projector with significant openness in his chart, Lincoln took in the energy of other people deeply. He felt their feelings and resonated with the pain and struggle of many for equality as well as survival. Then he steadfastly moved in the direction that he knew was right despite tremendous opposition.

He instinctively knew as a young man that he was not made for hard physical labor (he was what we call a no-motors Projector), so he turned to books, the study of the law, and eventually politics. His chart shows that he was designed for leadership and, literally, to create a revolution based on principles. The U.S. and the world are better places because he fulfilled the potential of his design.

Learn more about Lincoln and details of his Human Design chart in my Celebrity Chart Review of him on my website. Find the link from the Resources Page.

Name:	Abraham Lincoln
Birth Date:	12 February 1809, 06:54
Birth Place:	Hodgenville, KY, United States
Type:	Orchestrator (Projector)
Inner Authority:	No Inner Authority (No Inner Authority)
Profile:	5/1 - Visionary Leader / Resource
Definition:	Single
Strategy:	Wait for Recognition and Invitation
Themes:	Success / Bitterness
Incarnation Cross:	LAX Revolution 1
Channels:	0463 - Potentiality (Logic)

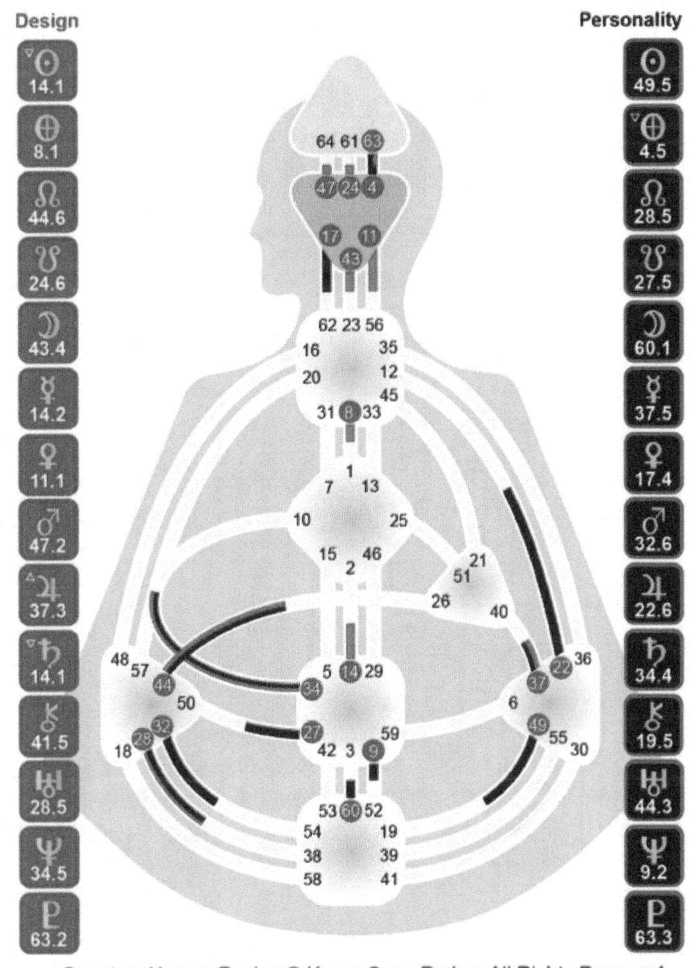

PART TWO

Decisions, Actions, and Success

Doing it Your Way

Only you can know what is correct for you, and
making decisions the right way for you will change your life.

The standard of success in life isn't the things. It isn't the money or the stuff—it is absolutely the amount of joy you feel.
~ Abraham-Hicks

PART TWO

DECISIONS, ACTIONS, AND SUCCESS

Introduction to Decisions, Actions, and Success

Now that we understand we are here to guide the energy of others, and the nature of our aura supports us in playing that role beautifully, we look into how we can fulfill that role consistently without losing our way. In this part of the book, we deeply explore how we are designed to make decisions and take actions correctly for our energy as Projectors, and how each individual is specifically designed to apply their decision-making process.

Life seems to be a dynamic combination of the Human Design chart we were born with, which is somewhat fixed, and our free will as human beings, which is not fixed.

We cannot change the chart we were born with—it is the energetic blueprint for our life—so most people consider it fixed and unchangeable. I think of the chart as somewhat fixed because we have the freedom (free will) to ignore it. We can live as our not-selves our whole lives and pay no attention to our inborn energy configuration. That does not make our configuration go away. It is still there, governing our attributes, tendencies, and choices, but we can pretend that those are not who we are. We can think we are someone else and behave as that someone else.

There are two other ways in which the expression of a chart is not completely fixed. First, there is a range of expression possible for each defined aspect of the chart. In simple terms, every gate, channel, Profile, Type, etc., has a high and low expression and the full spectrum in between. The terms *high* and *low* are not judgments of good or bad; they simply refer to the relative vibration of the expression. For example, the expression of Gate 10 can range from blame and victimhood to self-love and self-empowerment. We have control over where on the continuum we are expressing each aspect of our chart and can deliberately "move up the scale" on each one towards fulfilling all of our highest potentials.

Second, as we do our personal development work and evolve and grow in our emotional, spiritual, and mental maturity, we broaden our understanding of how everything works, and we become more patient and compassionate towards others and ourselves. This allows us to experience all of our chart energies more fully—those that are defined and those that are open.

In fully experiencing *all* the archetypes and energies contained within our human potential, we are able to transcend our personal charts to some extent. We become more of a fully expressed human and less constricted by our specific definition. We begin to trust ourselves completely and go wherever the flow takes us. We stop paddling so hard upstream, turn our kayak around, and let the current take us downstream where we can enjoy the ride without so much work. Then we can process and allow what comes our way instead of trying to force things to happen (which rarely works anyway).

As to free will itself, we have the freedom to make choices as we wish. When we make choices that align with our personal energy configuration, things are simply easier and go better. That is the path of least resistance and most success for each of us. But we are not forced to take that path. According to Abraham-Hicks, we are so free we can choose bondage. But with so much freedom available to us, why choose bondage?

As we explore how Projectors are designed to make the best choices, you will learn something crucial that will guide you through the rest of your life. This is the key to understanding your process of achieving success and living a life you love, on your own terms: **mastery of a system brings the recognition and invitations needed to be effective and successful in life**.

Chapter 5

Our Decision Strategy

As humans, we make decisions in nearly every moment of every day, and the decisions we make determine the life we have—pure and simple. Life today is the cumulative result of all the decisions both made and avoided. Not making a decision can have as many consequences as making a decision.

Every single aspect of life is affected by decisions past and present, and by those to come moving forward. Making decisions correctly is pivotal for having a great life, because our decisions either align us with our True Self or they don't.

For Projectors, wise and energetically aligned decisions are even more critical than for other Types. Our choices determine which people we let into our lives, interact with, receive energy from, and attempt to guide. If they are the wrong people for us personally, we are connecting into energies that are not correct for us and we are far more likely to have a bad experience and end up drained, or worse. Ra Uru Hu said that without good decisions, as Projectors we can become stuck, enslaved, and bitter by having the wrong people in our lives. Good decisions literally protect us from wrong people and wrong energy.

The beauty of the decision-making processes described for all of the Human Design Types is that they take us out of our minds and into our bodies for making decisions. This is completely opposite from what most of us are taught (and rewarded for) in life. We have been trained to use our heads for our decisions. Analyze and weigh the options. Make a list of pros and cons. Do the research. Get advice from others. Use a decision tree or other linear process. Choose the best (or least bad) option from the possible choices. Use logic.

What Human Design teaches is that our bodies are the fertile ground and appropriate place for our decision making, not our minds. The mind is variable, judgmental, defensive, inconsistent, critical, and confrontational. It is easily distracted and persuaded. It tries to second guess, gets confused, seeks confirmation and approval, and probably does not know the truth of Who We Are or where we are going. It usually wants proof even though there often isn't any. It does not trust our sense of knowing, and it wants to protect its own power over directing our lives.

When we use our Projector Strategy and specific Authority for our decisions, we naturally align our choices and actions with our own energy, mostly by using our bodies and paying attention to energy resonance. In this way, we are able to experience and discern whether or not the people and invitations in our environment are compatible with our energy, without relying on our variable mind which is mostly out of touch with what is actually right for us.

You can think of your Strategy and Authority as the horse, and you are riding in the cart (your life) pulled by the horse. Let the horse do the work of moving you down the road in the right direction. It knows where to go. Please don't let your mind talk you into climbing down and pulling the cart yourself.

Living life as a different Type or trying to be something you are not—whether intentional or unconscious—is exhausting. The gift of having a Strategy to follow is that it makes your choices easy (or at least, easier). You do not have to figure it all out. When you trust your Strategy and Authority, you leave your mind out of the process, which is a good thing. You can still make a list of pros and cons to occupy your mind and keep it happy, but your actual decision making is a different process. Following Strategy and Authority frees you from your mind's erratic control of your decision making.

Our Projector Strategy

The official Strategy for Projectors is to **wait to be invited**. This phrase does not give us the full picture of how we are designed to make decisions, but it is the starting point. The first word is *wait*. This seems to mean we are not supposed to be overtly active in our decision process, which sounds quite scary at first. Are we literally at the mercy of waiting for others before making any decision or moving forward to make things happen? Not exactly. Then there is the rest of the phrase, *to be invited*. This also suggests passivity and can leave us feeling powerless. It sounds like we must wait for someone else to do something, over which we seemingly have no control, before we can make decisions and function in life.

No wonder most of us are disappointed (even horrified) at learning we are Projectors.

A more recent statement of our Strategy says, **wait for recognition and invitations**. This is a little better but still not complete.

We will explore recognition, invitations, and waiting in much greater depth in Chapters 7 and 8, but for now let's simply say that an invitation must be specific and personal. It is not a generic email, an online sales page, a news article, or Mom suggesting you do something that she has no authority over. A real invitation is someone saying or writing, "[your name], would you like to do [the task or opportunity you are being invited into]?" It is a specific opportunity, and it is being offered specifically to you.

These are the basic pieces of the Strategy. You may be wondering at this point, "How the heck am I supposed to make sense of this Strategy in a way that is less passive and hopeless and more empowering?" Glad you asked. It starts by seeing the fuller picture of the Strategy. The piece that gets left out of the official phrase—but that is crucial to the correct use of this Strategy—is that waiting to be invited is only meant for big, life-changing decisions.

The Big Decisions in Life

What constitutes big decisions? These are the decisions that have major life impacts on our livelihood, environment, and relationships. These are decisions about our education, career, and specific jobs or money-generating opportunities. They are decisions about where we live and with whom. And they are decisions about romantic and business relationships and close friendships.

The next question is: Why do we need to wait for invitations for these big decisions? The answer relates to our energetic wiring which is designed for knowing and guiding others rather than for making things happen. Projectors do not have the energy configuration for easily starting and sustaining actions and events. Our Throat Center, the center for making things happen, does not get energy from any of the motor centers. Our Sacral Center is undefined, so we don't have the sustainable access to energy that Generators and Manifesting Generators enjoy. It is hard for us to make something happen out of nothing, especially something big.

Because that is hard for us, we must use extraordinary amounts of energy, focus and usually time, to make things happen. This can leave us exhausted before we even face the big task itself, like moving to a new home, starting a career, choosing a mate or partner, and establishing a relationship.

The beauty and benefit of waiting to be invited into these major life choices is that we do not have to do all the work around making them possible in the first place. We can simply choose to accept the invitation or not. This highlights the tremendous advantage of invitations for Projectors—we can step in and be our brilliant selves without having first to create those opportunities. Once we accept an invitation, there may be plenty of work to do to fulfill what we have agreed to take on, but then we have the recognition, attention, and flow of resources and energy that come with the invitation to support us in the fulfillment of it.

Here are some examples of how being invited can work well for these big life decisions.

Let's say you need to move—maybe your lease is up and cannot be renewed—but you are having trouble finding a place or maybe have not even started looking. A friend calls and says her landlord is looking for a tenant for an apartment in the same building where your friend lives. She talks to the landlord for you. He interviews you and offers you the lease. You use your specific Authority for making the decision which results in a yes. You still need to pack and move, but the initial work of finding a place to live was facilitated for you.

Another example: You want to start your own business as an energy healer, but it feels overwhelming to get started and build a business from nothing. Maybe through connections made when getting your training, someone invites you to work with them. Or you let people know in your community and someone tells you about a new wellness clinic that is opening and looking for practitioners. Or you contact local massage therapists and healing centers to see if they need what you offer. Yes, you are making the first move, but if they invite you then you have an invitation that you can accept or not.

Here is something that happened to a Projector colleague of mine. She applied for a job she thought she wanted. She did not get that job, but her resume was passed to someone else who called her and offered her a different job. She checked it out and waited through her emotional wave (that's her Authority). It still felt good, so she said yes, and it turned out to be an excellent job for her. She excelled in it, completely enjoyed it, and it boosted her career significantly.

Relationships can be tricky for Projectors, especially male Projectors. We will explore being empowered in relationships in Chapter 19, but here is a personal story for inspiration. People often wonder how two Projectors get into a romantic relationship with each other if each Projector needs to be invited. Here is how it happened for me. This was many years before I knew about Human Design or knew that we are both Projectors. I was invited to give a swing dance demonstration by a social activities club organizer, and I could choose my partner. I invited the guy in my dance class that I had my eye on for several weeks. He said yes, and we did the dance demonstration and started to get to know each other. Then, he invited me to visit him and his nine-year-old daughter at their place. I visited, we kissed, and we've been together since. That was more than twenty-six years ago!

As you work with your Strategy, it is important to experiment with how it works in general and specifically how it works for you. If you have a 3 or 6 in your Profile—you are a 1/3, 3/5, 3/6, 4/6, 6/2, or 6/3—you are experimental by nature, so it is correct for you to try things and see how they go. Even if you do not have a 3rd or 6th line Profile, don't be afraid to experiment a little. You won't know if you don't try. Just know that without an invitation, what you are trying may not go well. If you have the energy to take that risk and it feels correct and enlivening, then give it a try. If my colleague had not applied for that first job, she would not have gotten the other job. If I had not invited my partner to dance with me, we might not have gotten together.

Just don't be surprised—and don't take it personally—if you try something without an invitation and it does not succeed. Mostly, Projectors find that it is worth waiting for the right invitations and opportunities. When you make this shift, waiting no longer feels like a burden or prison sentence. It feels like an exquisite sensing of right timing and an opportunity to be happy and productive (in your own way) while waiting. You trust that waiting will bring you the best opportunities that no amount of forcing, stressing, or worrying could bring.

Your Strategy and Authority will naturally (and automagically!) align your choices with your fundamental energy structure, creating flow, synchronicity, and correctness in your life—which feels like magic!

The Little Decisions in Life

A common mistake made by Projectors and non-Projectors is assuming that Projectors need invitations for everything. We don't. In fact, it completely gets in our way to wait for or try to coerce invitations for little things. Plus, it makes us feel powerless and unsure of ourselves.

We don't need an invitation to do our laundry or grocery shopping, to take a class or pursue an interest. We can invite a few people over for a dinner party or invite a neighbor to go for morning walks with us. Invitations go both ways. Projectors like to invite as well as be invited.

Projectors can even start a business, offer a class, put up a website, or write a book without an invitation. There are no "Projector Police" who will arrest you for doing so. But here is what you need to know: Those bigger efforts will usually go more smoothly and produce better results if there is an invitation first.

Although not technically necessary, when operating in day-to-day life you will benefit from paying attention to the little invitations and "energetic openings" along the way. Trust your instincts when driving. Follow where the energy flows when shopping. Notice and appreciate when someone invites you to get in line in front of them because you only have three items in your cart, and they have thirty. Obey your body when it wants a nap or some down time. Trust your response to a dinner invitation or a suggestion to organize a dinner party or event. But remember, a suggestion is not an invitation.

Most importantly, wait to be asked or recognized before you speak. If you initiate a conversation, you may be uncomfortable and/or make the other person uncomfortable, which is not a great beginning for an interaction. If you speak up at a meeting without being asked or recognized first, you probably will not be heard or understood, or your contribution will not be valued. It's not personal! It is simply the mechanics of the energy and the nature of our basic energy configuration. Often people will resist our energy and anything we say unless they have initiated the conversation or asked for our input first.

This will seem completely counterintuitive: The way for us to be seen, heard, recognized, and invited is to be quiet and wait. *What?* It's true. Our power is in our wisdom and our observations of what is going on with the people around us. The best way to wield that power is to wait for others to ask. Wisdom and advice are rarely valued by someone who is not looking for them or ready to hear them. Do not "cast your pearls before swine." You have pearls of wisdom and guidance. Save them for those who will value them and, thus, benefit from them.

This points to the win-win nature of our correct interactions with others. The others get the benefit of our wisdom and guidance. We get the benefit of their attention, energy, recognition, appreciation, and perhaps, an invitation. If both parties are not coming out ahead, then it wasn't a good interaction. Minimize those and maximize the winning ones.

So, how do you orchestrate a win-win exchange if the other person is not asking or even recognizing you? Here is a popular, and very effective, technique that I teach all my Projector clients. If you have an insight or some guidance you would like to share with someone because you believe it would benefit them, but they are not asking, you can say something like:

"I have some insights about your situation that I would be happy to share with you. Would that be all right?"

"I have some experience with this issue. Would hearing about it interest you?"

"I have some information that might be very helpful to you. Would you be open to it?"

You get the idea. You are basically asking for their permission to speak. This does several things. It gets their attention without forcing something on them. It allows you to see if they are interested. It asks a yes/no question which is the best way for 70 percent of the population to respond (Generators and Manifesting Generators). If they say yes, it gives you an energetic opening to speak into where they are far more likely to hear and value what you say. It also lets you know if they are not interested, or if now is not a good time.

This can apply even with friends and family members who already value your input. One time I was walking with a close friend, who is also a Projector, and she was describing a problem she was dealing with. She was not asking for my advice; she was processing the issue and how she felt about it. (Her Authority is Emotional.) I listened and waited until she seemed complete in talking about it. Then I asked, "May I make a suggestion?" She stopped walking, so I stopped walking. She faced me and looked me right in the eye and said, "Thank you for asking!" It meant a lot to her that I had the courtesy to ask first, before just blurting out some advice. Honestly, her reaction took me a little by surprise. We have the kind of relationship where she would be perfectly comfortable with and welcome my advice, even if she had not asked for it.

What happened was that she felt honored and respected by my asking first. This taught me how valuable it can be for Projectors to soften their advice and nurture their relationship with the other person by asking first if it is okay to give that advice. If you are a manager, supervisor, service provider, or in a similar position where you are being paid to give direction and/or guidance, the situation is a little different, but you may find that a little courtesy and being sensitive to whether the other person is ready to hear you or not can go a long way.

The one thing to be careful with when you ask for permission to speak is whether the other person is just being polite when they say yes, or if they are truly interested in what you have to say. When you pay attention to their energy, you will feel the difference. If they are just being polite but are not really interested, you do not have an energetic opening to speak into, so adjust accordingly. What you say may not be received as well as you hope.

If you are in a group or attending a meeting, it can be very challenging to be recognized and heard by the group—even if you are being paid by them to be there and to give your advice. If you do speak up, don't be surprised (and again, don't take it personally) if they don't hear you or if ten minutes later someone says the same thing you said but gets all the credit for it. It is usually best to wait until you are asked to speak—even though that may be one of the hardest things to do. When they do ask, they will hear and value your contribution, and you will experience the gift and benefit of waiting for the right timing.

If they do not ask for your input, it is their loss. Seriously. If they do not recognize the brilliant resource that you are and that you could be for them, then they are not ready for you and they do not deserve your wisdom. Wait for the person or group who is ready. That waiting is SO worth it. Remember, you are not here to guide and advise everyone, just the ones who want and are ready for your guidance. Everyone else can go elsewhere for guidance.

This does require something important from you: the courage, trust, faith, and self-confidence to know that waiting works and that you are too valuable to waste your efforts on those who are not correct for you. When done with honesty, humility, and compassion, this is not arrogance. It is wisdom and self-respect.

We will dive more deeply into recognition, invitations, and waiting in the next two chapters, but right now here is a fun exercise and a list of tips for helping our decision making be as easy as possible.

An Invitation Inventory

It is common, upon learning about their invitation Strategy, for Projectors to look back at their lives and pick out the big invitations they have had in the past. It is like seeing with new eyes. When I did that, I realized that my best jobs and pivotal career moves were the result of specific and personal invitations. I had never noticed that before.

If you have not done this yet, I invite you to do it now. Think back to each job you have had, and whether you were specifically invited into it. Then recall how it turned out. Is there a pattern? Where did things go really well, and where didn't they? Where did invitations make a difference? How much of a difference?

Think about your education and career choices. Did those have invitations? If they didn't, that's no problem. It's just fun and illuminating to take this different view of your past. What about moves? What about relationships? Into which were you invited? Where did you do the inviting? How did things turn out?

As you might imagine, it can be challenging for men who are Projectors to enter relationships correctly. In Western societies, men are expected to be the inviters—not wait for invitations from others. If you are a Projector man, think about how your relationships started and how they turned out. You can invite a person into a relationship, but it makes a big difference if you are also invited by them, especially for deepening that relationship.

Take a serious look at what worked and what didn't work in your past. This can give you confidence, or at least curiosity, about invitations and the difference they make.

Let It Be Easy

At this point, it's time to explore how to have the Projector Strategy work for you in the easiest ways possible. Let's face it, waiting for invitations can be a challenge, and being a Projector can feel really hard. But it can be easier than it might seem when you know a few tricks and nuances about invitations. I guess we can call these *Projector hacks*.

First, **do not say yes to every invitation** just because you finally get one. Only say yes to the ones that feel truly delicious and correct for you. You will use your specific Authority for making this assessment, which we will cover in detail in the next chapter, but for now focus on your body's reaction to the invitation. Also know that sometimes you may need to say yes even though it does not feel correct. Sometimes you "gotta do what you gotta do." If you need to put food on the table and keep a roof over your head, you may need to take the job you don't really want. Be grateful for the job offer and do the best you can in it but know that it is not ideal and also keep looking for what would be a better fit for you.

There are Human Design purists who would say "don't take that job" if you haven't entered it correctly—through an invitation that feels aligned with you. I don't know about them, but I live in the real world, and you probably do too. If the majority of the world today knew about Projectors and the importance of inviting us, and knew that we are not here to work, just guide, then we could be much pickier about accepting or rejecting invitations. But the world is messy and unpredictable, and it does not know how to properly honor and leverage our wisdom and guidance. So, we do the best we can with where we are.

Once you accept an invitation using your Authority to guide you, you can **take whatever action is needed** to fulfill the task or responsibility you agreed to. You do not need to wait for further invitations within that task. This is critically important. You can now operate like a Manifestor or Manifesting Generator within the parameters of that invitation/opportunity/responsibility. Most Human Design descriptions of Projectors make it sound like we are not capable of initiating actions or manifesting anything. This is simply not true. Once we know what is correct for us, through invitation and applying our Authority, we are incredibly powerful, effective, and able to manifest as needed. It still may not be easy, but it is possible for us to take action and make things happen, and it is correct for us to do so within the context of a correct invitation.

Let's use the President of the United States as an example. There have been many Projector presidents, most notably John F. Kennedy and Barack Obama. Once invited into that position and responsibility by virtue of being elected—which is a very clear, personal, and specific invitation—they can (and must) take all the actions required to fulfill that role.

While you wait for invitations, **rest** as much as you need, but you don't have to be idle unless you want to be (and can be). Waiting is a great time to **hone your skills**, so you are completely ready to step into the invitations you really want when they show up. Take classes, practice, get a degree or certificate, perfect your craft, and develop your expertise. Be ready for the right opportunity.

Also, while you wait, make it **easy for people to find you** and invite you. I call this stacking the deck in your favor. Find ways to let people know who you are, what you do, what you are looking for, and how to contact you. It is possible for you to sit at home reading, napping, or watching movies, and have the doorbell or phone ring with the perfect invitation for you, but your belief system would need to be strong to allow that to happen. Instead, choose the activities you are willing to do, like attend networking events or MeetUp groups, volunteer, participate in community activities, put up a website, hand out flyers. Do such actions in a non-pushy way (pushy does not work for Projectors) but do whatever you can to facilitate the right invitations to come your way.

Speaking of facilitating, it is correct and very **helpful for others to facilitate** opportunities for you to be invited. Ask a friend to introduce you to someone she knows in your field. Let someone make a call on your behalf to "grease the skids" for you to get an interview. Allow others to help you, and graciously receive their help. It may be correct for Manifestors to just go out and make things happen, but not for Projectors. We are not weak or less-than, our energy is simply different and designed for a different purpose. Let others help make things easy for you. This is the sign of a powerful and empowered Projector, who knows how to leverage things to their advantage while conserving their energy.

Here is an excellent question you can ask yourself about anything that feels hard or overwhelming: How could this be **as easy as possible**? Then imagine and envision it unfolding effortlessly. Hold the idea of that as being completely possible. No contradicting or disparaging thoughts allowed. Seed the universe with those ideas and look for ways to allow and encourage the easy path. Things are not supposed to be hard for us. You can go with a flow that is already going or help a positive flow get started. Just don't try to do all the heavy lifting yourself.

Another hack worth noting is becoming **invitable**. Have an attitude, hold a vibration, and have a demeanor that is pleasant and easy to relate to. Even though bitterness is a common theme for Projectors, it is not helpful for attracting invitations. Who wants to invite someone who is bitter? Take good care of yourself, rest, have as much fun as you can, focus on gratitude, and raise your vibration in any way that works for you.

Invitations only work when they come from someone who has the **authority to issue the invitation**. Here I refer to authority as responsibility and power, not in the Human Design meaning. I know a Projector whose mother encouraged him to submit articles he had written to magazines so they could be published. He explained to her that he needed an invitation to do that, he couldn't just submit his articles. She said, "Okay, I invite you to submit your articles." He laughed and, correctly, said the invitation needed to come from the magazine, not from his mother.

When one of the cofounders of GracePoint Publishing approached me to write this book for Projectors, she followed up our conversation with an email that simply said, "Evelyn, I invite you to write a book for Projectors." Bingo. Specific, personal, and from the person with authority to issue that invitation. My Splenic Authority response was a clear, resounding "yes!"

One last tip in this section about decision making: An **energetic opening** is an acceptable substitute for an actual invitation. A personal, specific, and formal invitation will always be the most powerful way for Projectors to engage correctly with others, but it is not the only way. When things begin to fall into place easily, when the right people show up at the right time with the right resources, and the path seems to flow easily for you in a particular direction—I call that an energetic opening. Be sure to apply your Authority in choosing whether to step into that opening. Consider it a second-level invitation. These may not work as well as top-level, formal invitations, but it makes no sense to ignore these energy flows. They could lead to the right people and the right invitations.

You will find more ideas and clarity in the chapter on invitations, but now let's turn to the decision-making Authorities of Projectors so you can learn exactly how YOU are designed to apply the "wait to be invited" Strategy.

Chapter 6

Our Decision Authorities

When first learning about Human Design, some people resist it because it feels restrictive, especially when it comes to following the "rules" of decision making using Strategy and Authority. That is understandable. But these are not rigid external rules, or restrictions dictating what you should or shouldn't do. They are guidelines that put you in touch with your inner authority. They are simply a reliable mechanism that allows you to access the wisdom within you. Only you know what is right for you. No one else.

The Authority shown on your Human Design chart specifies how your energetic wiring is configured for making decisions within your Projector Strategy of waiting for invitations. Your Authority helps you decide to accept or reject an invitation, and helps you feel where the energy is flowing and where those energetic openings are. It clarifies your timing and your approach to using your Strategy. It *influences* and refines your Strategy but does not change it. Ra called Authority "body-centered intelligence."

Your Authority gives you direct access to your internal guidance and inner wisdom. There is a deep part of you that knows Who You Are and where you need to go in life to fulfill your role and mission, and it wants to help you get there. Your job is to learn how to listen for it and feel into it, and eventually trust it and rely on it. It is your personal "decision hack."

Authority serves you even when you don't have an invitation to consider. You will want to apply your Authority for all aspects of your life and for most decisions. You probably don't need to wait through your emotional wave (if you have Emotional Authority—see below) to decide whether to go grocery shopping now or later. But you will want to wait through your wave (or apply *your* Authority) for as many decisions as you can.

Your Authority is not randomly assigned. It is determined by the defined centers in your chart. There is a hierarchy to the structure of Authorities. The specific configuration of each one is explained below, along with a description of how to use the Authority and a celebrity chart example of each.

Projector Authorities

Projectors have five possible Authorities, more than any other Type. Find yours below and begin using it right away. Keep in mind that different software programs for Human Design charts may have different ways to name or describe the Authorities.

All Projectors can benefit by talking through their decisions, problems, and issues with others, but for some Authorities that is their primary decision-making approach. Whatever your Authority, don't be afraid to verbally process your decisions!

Authority: Emotional Solar Plexus

Configuration:

If the Emotional Solar Plexus Center is defined, the Authority will always be Emotional. No matter which other centers are defined, the Emotional Solar Plexus takes precedence. This is true for all Types, except Reflectors who never have a defined Solar Plexus.

Description:

You have emotional energy which operates in waves, sometimes up, sometimes down. To make a correct decision, you must wait through at least one complete cycle of your emotions to see how you feel about the decision at various points on your wave. The length of an emotional wave, as well as its intensity, can vary widely and there is no way to predict a person's wave. There are three different kinds of waves, which can be fully described and explored with you during a private reading. In general, simply pay attention to how you feel each day to begin to identify the pattern of your personal wave.

When making a decision, if you feel consistently positive or consistently negative about the choice or opportunity at different points on your wave, then your answer becomes quite clear. If your feeling changes as you move through your wave, then you need more time for clarity.

You are not designed for spontaneous decision making—your clarity comes only over time and by *feeling* your way through the decision, not thinking your way through. When faced with a decision, it is important to give yourself enough time to sleep on it or take as long as needed. Big decisions may require several emotional cycles to reach your point of clarity. Even with small decisions, including what and when to eat, you will benefit from giving yourself time to feel through whether you are truly ready for it. You simply don't know your Truth in the immediate moment, whether the decision is big or small.

You may never feel 100 percent confident about a decision, and that is all right. If you have leapt into decisions in the past and then regretted them, you may feel especially hesitant. You will want to wait for the feeling of an internal click or the sensation that you have reached a comfortable, or at least reasonable, level of calm and clarity. You are here to enjoy life in your deeply passionate and creative way, so take your time.

I invite you to experiment with this general guideline for Emotional Authority decision making: If your feeling about something isn't a "hell yeah!" consistently through your wave, then it is probably a no.

You are encouraged to keep a record of your wave, how your decisions feel, and the outcomes of your decisions so you can develop trust and confidence in your decision-making process. This is a tricky Authority to learn, but once you do you will consistently make much better decisions for yourself.

Example:

Former U.S. President John F. Kennedy was a Projector with Emotional Authority. This beloved leader, known for his humor, charm, intelligence, and mental vigor, needed to take his time in making decisions, so he could arrive at the clarity he needed. This was especially crucial for national and global level issues. The channel that defines one's Solar Plexus Center determines the nature of the emotional wave. His Channel 37-40 is in Tribal circuitry, so he had a Tribal wave. If you have multiple defined channels to your Solar Plexus Center, you may have multiple kinds of waves which can make decisions a little more challenging. Give yourself as much time as you can.

Name:	John F. Kennedy
Birth Date:	29 May 1917, 15:00
Birth Place:	Brookline, MA, United States
Type:	Orchestrator (Projector)
Inner Authority:	Creative (Solar Plexus)
Profile:	3/5 - Explorer / Visionary Leader
Definition:	Single
Strategy:	Wait for Recognition and Invitation
Themes:	Success / Bitterness
Incarnation Cross:	RAX Planning 2
Channels:	3740 - Administration (Community)

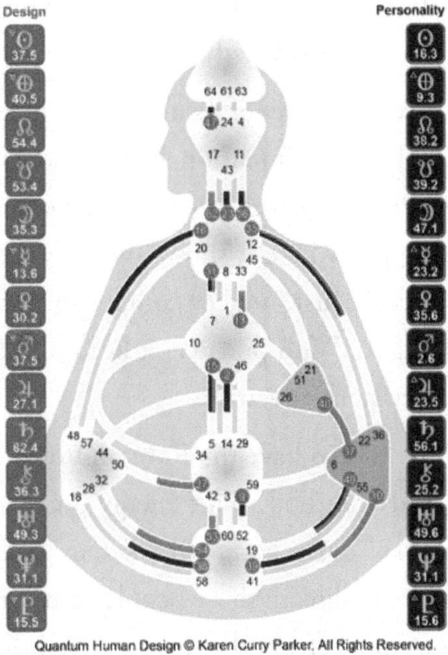

Quantum Human Design © Karen Curry Parker. All Rights Reserved.

Authority: Splenic Awareness Projected, or has the word Splenic

Configuration:

This Authority always has a defined Spleen Center and an undefined Emotional Solar Plexus Center. It doesn't matter what other centers are defined. Of course, the Sacral Center is never defined for a Projector.

Description:

You have intuition/gut instinct to guide your decisions. You are designed to make decisions in the moment with the benefit of this intuitive awareness. Your intuitive "hit" always happens in the immediate moment, only speaks once, and is usually very quiet so it can be missed if you are not "listening" for it. Because it is a primal instinct, it usually shows up as a fear or concern about your safety or well-being.

For example, you will have an instant intuitive awareness about whether a situation or opportunity is healthy and safe for you. You will also sense whether a person is healthy and safe for you, with penetrating awareness into the truth about them. You know whether that person is lying or can be trusted.

Because many of us are taught to ignore intuition and trust the mind instead, you will need to intentionally tune yourself to listen for or feel for your intuitive hits. Most Projectors feel this in their bodies, often in a specific area of the body. Pay attention to where it shows up for you, so you can recognize and value it when it happens. At first, it takes courage to trust your splenic awareness if you are not used to doing so. With practice, it becomes easy to trust this intuitive Authority to guide your decisions and actions.

If you also have the Root and/or the Will Center defined, these motor energies will feed your body with energy but also may distract you from the clarity of your splenic awareness about whether an invitation is correct for you. You will need extra vigilance to discern those people who simply want to use your motor energy for their own purposes from those who recognize your true value as a guide and provider of wisdom.

All people are potentially subject to the fears associated with Spleen Center gates, called the Fears of the Spleen. When your Authority is Splenic, the defined gates attached to your defined Spleen Center provide you with clues about which fears to watch for as you make decisions. Splenic fears are in-the-moment and need to be pushed through, though they can feel so dangerous or threatening that they can stop you in your tracks. See the Resources Page to access my Fears of the Spleen series of blogposts, which details each gate's fear and how to handle it.

My personal experience as a Splenic Authority Projector confused me at first. I sometimes do not have an instant sense of whether something feels right and safe for me. Through paying attention to this, I realized that I don't get a splenic hit about everything, just the ones that are very clear. I feel a strong yes as a powerful vibration in my whole body. I can get a powerful no as well, but those are less common. If I don't have a clear yes or no, I keep looking at other options. When I find a yes, I know it. The Projector's Splenic Authority is not like the Sacral response of

Generators and Manifesting Generators. Their defined Sacral Center will usually give them a yes or a no about anything and everything they focus on. Splenic Authority to me feels like it doesn't waste energy on responding to everything, just the things that are important and that are clear in the moment.

Example:

Nelson Mandela was a Projector with Splenic Authority. This world-changing leader knew instantly what was right for him, even though his choices (for example, his political activism which led him to twenty-seven years in a South African prison) may not have seemed wise to others. Although it was very hard on his physical body, he knew it was the way to gain world attention for his cause and bring forth major changes for his country.

Name:	Nelson Mandela
Birth Date:	18 July 1918, 14:54
Birth Place:	Mvezo, Eastern Cape, South Africa
Type:	Orchestrator (Projector)
Inner Authority:	Mastery (Splenic)
Profile:	5/1 - Visionary Leader / Resource
Definition:	Split - Small (17,23,56)
Strategy:	Wait for Recognition and Invitation
Themes:	Success / Bitterness
Incarnation Cross:	LAX Obscuration 1
Channels:	1648 - Mastery (The Wavelength) 2461 - Cosmic Perspective (Awareness) 0731 - Egalitarianism (The Alpha)

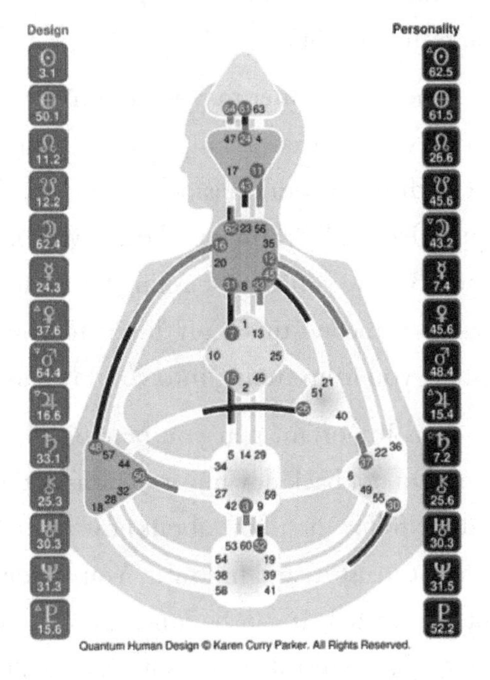

Authority: Ego Projected

Configuration:

With this Authority, the Will Center is defined to the G Center through Channel 51-25, and no centers below the Will are defined. This is the rarest Authority for Projectors and is only found in Projectors.

Description:

You are your own Authority; whatever your ego-self wants is usually correct for you. You can make decisions in the moment if you follow your Strategy for big decisions. Small decisions can be based purely on what you want and what you have the willpower to do. Your energy is precious, so only commit to things that you really want. When you hear yourself say that you "will" do something, you have already decided. This shows up most powerfully when your will is challenged; that is when you really dig your heels in.

The Will Center may waver on the options you are considering before it finds its own clarity. Take as long as you need to feel certain about your choice. It can help to talk through your decision with others. This allows you to hear (in your words and your voice) and feel (in your heart) what is clear for you about your choices and what is not. Be sure you are not asking for advice from others; what you need is a sounding board—someone to simply listen to you. Their advice, while well-meaning, may distract you from tuning into your own awareness.

It is important that you be radically honest about what you want and do not want. Do not back down just to please others. An Ego Projected friend and colleague said the following to me about how to use this Authority: "Be brave enough to hear it, feel it, trust it, and follow it. You are designed to be the first one on a path that is not yet created. It can be lonely sometimes and others may think you're crazy but doing what you truly want is not as selfish as it sounds at first. You just need to take the leap."

Channel 51-25 is in the Individual Circuitry which means you are here to be different and not fit in with how others do things. The beauty of forging new paths for yourself is that you also open paths for others.

Example:

Bernie Sanders is an Ego Projected Projector. This well-known politician is a powerful force in U.S. politics with surprising sustainability. His defined Channel 51-25 gives a deep spiritual underpinning to his policy proposals which attempt to guide us to universal love and compassion. He happens to have no defined centers above the G Center, but someone with this Authority could.

Name:	**Bernie Sanders**
Birth Date:	**08 September 1941, 12:27**
Birth Place:	**New York, NY, United States**
Type:	**Orchestrator (Projector)**
Inner Authority:	**Resource (Ego - Heart)**
Profile:	**5/1 - Visionary Leader / Resource**
Definition:	**Single**
Strategy:	**Wait for Recognition and Invitation**
Themes:	**Success / Bitterness**
Incarnation Cross:	**LAX Dominion 2**
Channels:	**2551 - Higher Purpose (Initiation)**

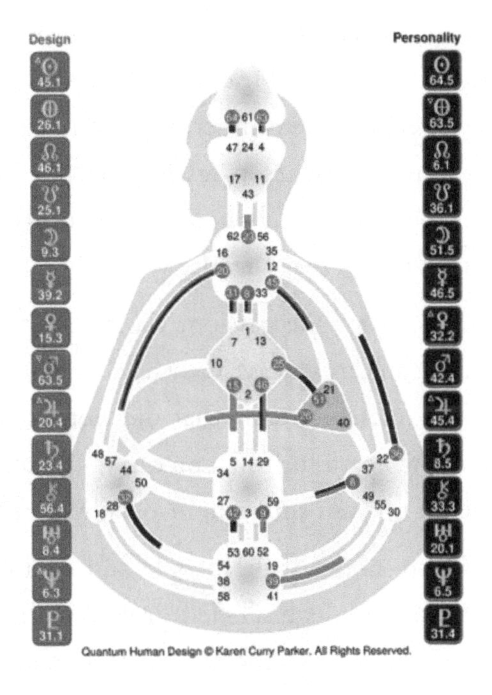

Authority: Self-Projected

Configuration:

Here, the G Center is defined to the Throat Center by one or more of four possible channels—10-20, 7-31, 1-8, or 13-33. No centers below the G Center are defined. Only Projectors can have this Authority, although it is not as rare as the Ego Projected Authority we just saw. Projectors with this Authority and the Mental Authority described below are always no-motors Projectors which means that they have none of the motor centers defined—Will, Solar Plexus, Sacral, or Root.

Description:

Your internal guidance is based on what feels resonant with you at your soul level as well as in your human form. You gain clarity about what feels "like you" and comes from your heart by talking about it with others—not for their advice but so you can hear yourself speak about it and feel whether it resonates in your body. You are looking for what feels aligned with Who You Are which then helps you express your True Self in the world.

As invitations come your way, process them by listening to yourself talk about them. Invite trusted friends to be your sounding board so you can sort through the issues verbally. Remember, you are not looking for advice. You are creating a space for hearing what resonates for you from your own speaking. You usually will not know how you feel about a decision or issue until you verbalize it. What you say and how you say it may surprise you.

Listen for the passion, clarity, and resonance of your words and tone as you speak. You can also ask your listener about what they heard from you, what had the ring of resonance and what did not. If you do not have someone willing to be a sounding board for you, you can try to talk out loud to yourself or, better yet, record yourself on your smartphone or other device and listen to the recording.

Also, notice if the people and environment feel right for you regarding your decision. Although all Self-Projected Projectors have a defined G Center, which means you are less affected by what is around you than someone with an open G, this can still be a useful factor in processing your decisions. Since you have many open centers, all of which are influenced (conditioned) by the energies of others, it is best for you to be away from others to find your own clarity before making a decision.

Example:

Mick Jagger is a Projector with Self-Projected Authority. This rock and roll legend and leader of the Rolling Stones has had amazing longevity and sustainability in the music world. He is designed to use his body and his voice to assess what feels like the right fit for his inner self and for who he is in the world. He is very driven, often exhausting himself during tours, and he realized long ago that to manage his energy he needs to go to his dressing room after concerts to restore his energy instead of partying with his band mates. He also waits until he is called out to the stage for a performance and then takes in energy from his audience to sustain his tremendous energy output.

Name:	**Mick Jagger**
Birth Date:	**26 July 1943, 02:30**
Birth Place:	**Dartford, Kent, United Kingdom**
Type:	**Orchestrator (Projector)**
Inner Authority:	**Calibration (G - Self)**
Profile:	**1/3 - Resource / Explorer**
Definition:	**Single**
Strategy:	**Wait for Recognition and Invitation**
Themes:	**Success / Bitterness**
Incarnation Cross:	**RAX Unexpected 2**
Channels:	**1333 - Collective Consciousness (The Prodigal)** **0731 - Egalitarianism (The Alpha)**

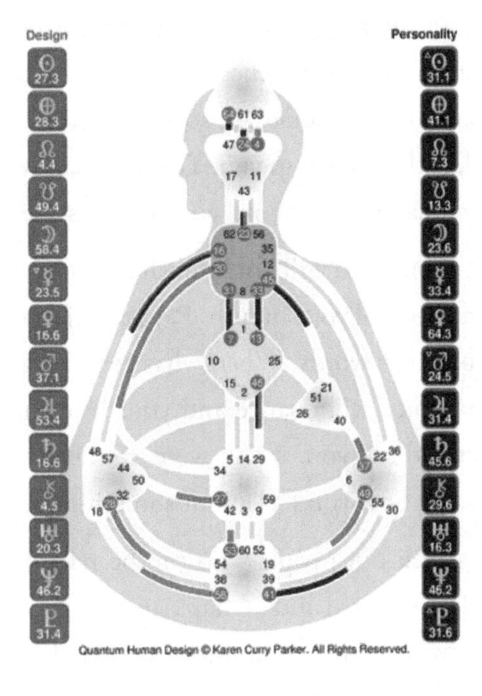

Authority: Mental Projected, or None

Configuration:

This Authority has at least two of these three centers defined: Head, Ajna, and Throat, and has no other defined centers. This configuration has a lot of mental energy but no energy from motor centers lower in the chart, which are all open (Will, Solar Plexus, Sacral, Root). This can mean challenges in getting things done; however, I know quite a few Mental Projectors who have a tremendous amount of energy. Even before knowing their Human Design, they figured out how to tap into the energy of others and into their own personal drive.

Description:

You have the most mentally focused Authority. You, even more than all other Projectors, are specifically designed to provide valued knowledge and guidance to others from your strong mind and piercing awareness. But, because you rely so much on your mind, it is challenging for you to accept that you cannot (must not) use your mind for your own decisions.

You gain clarity for making your decisions by talking about them with others—not for their advice but so you can learn how you feel by hearing yourself speak about your choices. You generally do not have direct access to your feelings regarding your decisions on your own, so you need people around you and your environment to reflect them back to you. You will hear what is right for you when you talk it out and it resonates throughout your body as the right choice for you to make.

You often will not know how you truly feel about something until you hear what comes out of your mouth. Pay attention not only to your words but also to the energy behind the words. When what you are saying resonates deeply for you, the quality of your voice will change and your listener will hopefully be aware enough to discern that and tell you, if you were not able to hear it for yourself. Sometimes, what you say and how you feel about something may surprise you.

Seek out people who can be reliable sounding boards for you, people who are willing to listen and perhaps summarize what they are hearing, but who are not trying to give you their opinion or advice. Because you have an open G Center, you are deeply affected by the people and environment around you. So, take into account their impact on you as you process your decision.

Because you have at least six open centers, you have many ways to be influenced by others—including by your sounding board people—so it is best for you to talk to several different sounding board friends for each decision so you can reach your truth.

Your clarity is within you, but you do not have direct access to it. If you do not have trusted listeners in your life, you can try talking to yourself out loud or, even better, record yourself talking about a decision or issue and then listen to the recording. As you get used to listening for your truth as you speak, you'll become more aware of it in the moment of your speaking.

Example:

Amelia Earhart was a Mental Authority Projector. This extraordinary woman was not only an aviation pioneer and adventurer, she was also a nurse, author, poet, social worker, and fashion designer. In 1932 she was the first female aviator to fly solo across the Atlantic Ocean. Her significant accomplishments and broad range of interests exemplified the high expression of the strong mental energy in her chart.

Name:	Amelia Earhart
Birth Date:	24 July 1897, 23:30
Birth Place:	Atchison, KS, United States
Type:	Orchestrator (Projector)
Inner Authority:	No Inner Authority (No Inner Authority)
Profile:	1/3 - Resource / Explorer
Definition:	Single
Strategy:	Wait for Recognition and Invitation
Themes:	Success / Bitterness
Incarnation Cross:	RAX Unexpected 2
Channels:	2343 - Innovative Thinking (Structuring)

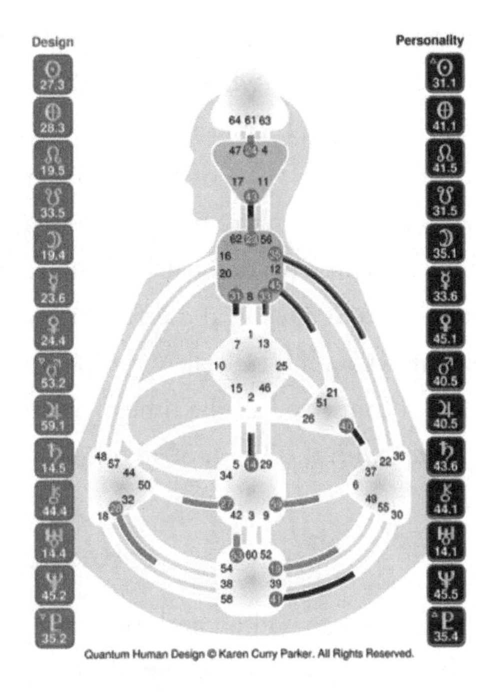

Applying Your Authority

Details of exactly how to apply your personal Authority with your Strategy would be explored in detail in a Human Design reading, but the information above is enough to put you on your correct path for now. If you are not already doing this, please begin to apply and rely on your Authority as you make decisions and take actions. You will probably find that it feels comfortable and natural for you. If it doesn't, keep experimenting with it. You have been making decisions in a particular way all your life. Remember that your mind is not going to easily relinquish its power over you and your decisions. You are instilling a new habit, and that can take time and practice. The results are totally worth it. Learn to trust your body more than your mind. If it helps to reassure your thinking mind, you can keep notes about your decisions, whether you applied your Authority, and the outcomes, so you track your process and see patterns as you learn.

Making decisions with our Strategy and Authority is a natural and, in many ways, automatic method for aligning our choices and actions with the truth of Who

We Are. We don't have to "figure it out" anymore. We just have to follow our Strategy and Authority.

I have put a lot of emphasis on trusting your body, not your mind, which is a vital step in improving your decisions. If you are ready to go beyond this step, I invite you to consider that what feels good and resonates within may not actually have to do with our bodies. You might consider it to be your soul or spirit, or the piece of us that is part of the whole of the intelligence of the universe. You see, our perceptions about our bodies are still being processed through our minds. But the part of us that is from the fabric of All That Is (Source, God, Cosmic Intelligence) is the part of us that has direct knowing and direct knowledge. It is creative, not reactive. Expansive, not contractive. It is eternal. We are not separate pieces, scattered about the universe; we are all connected all the time. That is the part of us that knows our Truth and is connected with the Truth of all others.

Reality Check

I do want to add a check on reality here. All the Authority information above sounds great, but it is not always as easy to implement as it sounds. Your life will probably not suddenly and miraculously become problem-free when you begin using your Strategy and Authority, with everything proceeding easily and swimmingly for the rest of your life (although it could!). What is more likely is that you will gradually ease into this new way of moving through life, with a few bumps and turns, challenges and setbacks. You will see what works and doesn't work for you. We learn more from what doesn't work than from what does work, so don't be afraid to try. The only way you will not get better at navigating your life is if you do nothing.

Also, do not be too quick to judge whether something is working or not. Sometimes what looks like a dismal failure is exactly what you need to get you on a better path. When we accept that, at some level, we have something to do with everything that comes our way, then we can embrace the lessons, let go of any pain or disappointment, and move on. It is when we resist the lessons and our role in those lessons that we get stuck and fail to move forward.

As you experiment with using your Authority and see exactly how it best works for you, you will refine your decision-making process. Be patient and pay attention to how the process feels and how things turn out, so you can adjust and fine-tune as needed.

Now that we have covered the basics of Projector Strategy and Authorities, it is time to dive deeper into the role of recognition and invitations in our lives. It is easy to misunderstand these and get confused about what they really mean and how to work with them. Let's look at how to attract and then step into the right recognition and invitations for you and bust a few myths about them along the way.

Chapter 7

Why Recognition Matters

Recognition is not just a nice thing for Projectors to have; it is our life blood. It is our mechanism for experiencing outward success in the world. But as we will see, it is not related to how we experience inner success and self-worth. Understanding and managing this difference is vital to thriving as Projectors.

The first thing to know about recognition in the Projector world is that it goes both ways. We are designed to recognize others. This is what gives us power and the ability to contribute something valuable to them. We are also designed to *be* recognized by others. This is what gives us energy and the opportunity to contribute.

The whole point of making correct decisions, which we explored in the last two chapters, is to determine which recognitions and invitations will bring us the right energy, the right opportunities, and the right people. If you do not know what is correct for you, you put your precious energy, vitality, and intelligence into recognizing things and people that don't bring you the rewards and recognition you deserve.

Being recognized by someone is the step before being invited by them. Someone needs to know at least a little about you (your name and how to contact you, for instance) before they can issue a personal and specific invitation to you. They probably also know, or assume, that you might be the right person for the invitation. Maybe they think you have the right skill set, relevant interests, useful information, or perceptive insights. Maybe someone else told them about you, they observed you, or they know you from something you have in common.

Somehow, they know at least something about you. Whether that something is accurate or not is a different issue!

That initial recognition opens the door to your next possibilities, and to your success or lack of success from that initial recognition. The more accurate and relevant the recognition is, the more likely the invitation will be appealing and correct for you. It is easy to (mistakenly) think that recognition is something that simply happens to you, that you have no control over it, or that you are at the mercy of the vagaries of life, the whims of strangers, and the randomness of luck when it comes to being recognized. Nothing could be further from the truth.

How Others Recognize Us—Our Expertise

As stated in the introduction to this part of the book, the expertise we achieve through **mastering a system** brings the recognition and invitations we need to be effective and successful in life.

The word *mastery* has multiple definitions. When using this term, I am referring to this definition from the Oxford Dictionary, the "comprehensive knowledge or skill in a subject or accomplishment."

Mastery for Projectors is different from mastery for Generators and Manifesting Generators. Those energy Types tend to master skills through their sustainable energy and their response to what interests them. Projectors tend to—and need to—master a system. And we need to understand that system more deeply than anyone else.

Projectors have a natural ability to sense the flow of energy and how to improve and optimize processes. Mastering a system gives the Projector a realm of expertise that brings appropriate and desired recognition. It also puts the Projector in the right relationship to work: having the knowledge to guide the work rather than actually doing the work.

Of course, there is usually a set of skills that comes along with mastering a system, so some "doing" can be involved as well. But it is the system that matters. Any body of knowledge, system, or process will do. Develop *your* expertise in ways that feel natural and correct for you and are based on your chart. You may have the energy for details defined in your chart, or you may not. You may have a strong focus on logic or intuition or have a big picture perspective, to name just a few other examples. There are many ways, and many combinations of ways, to achieve and express mastery.

Recognition alone, even without an invitation, brings us energy and activates us. Think of when you have been recognized for something you are proud of. How did it make you feel? Did it boost your confidence and give you a sense of achievement beyond the mere accomplishment or quality being recognized? Were you beaming and feeling that you could just burst with excitement and pride? Were you ready to do more? That's a lot of energy embodied from that recognition!

Of course, we Projectors can and do get recognized (and invited) without mastering a system. It is not a requirement or prerequisite. Primarily we get recognized when we are being our True Self—expressing the defined parts of our chart which are where we have consistent flows of energy. We can also be recognized for knowledge, wisdom, and insights outside our areas of expertise or proficiency. So why master a system? It positions us to attract and receive recognition—especially the right recognition—while leveraging our time, energy, and effort.

How should you choose which system to master? Your Strategy and Authority will guide you to what you are designed to be recognized for. If your mind insists on getting involved, think about what would feel completely logical for you to master. We often make this harder than it needs to be. Look at what you are naturally good at. What do others ask you for or about? What intrigues you and feels like fun to learn? What would you love to help others with? What are you being invited into and where is the energy opening up for you? Explore that system and its related set of skills. You can always switch later or simply expand your mastery by adding more systems when ready.

Ideally, the system you choose will allow you to peer into the truth of others, so you can best guide them. Human Design is a perfect system for Projectors, as are the many healing modalities and human potential systems in the world, such as astrology, energy healing, Myers-Briggs, psychology, coaching, and counseling, among many others. No wonder Projectors are disproportionately drawn to these. A deep understanding of one or more systems can help you be recognized and activated so you can bring out the best in others. By mastering the right system for you, you will attract the right people who want, need, and recognize your expertise.

Mastery takes dedication to the study of a particular system and, along the way, to the study of how the world works in general because systems do not exist in isolation. This dedication translates into our success over time. Rarely does a

Projector have overnight success. Developing expertise takes time and honing our awareness of others takes patience. Conventional wisdom says it takes seven years to master anything, which includes systems. So, use the gift of your Strategy and Authority to guide you to the right system for you, and dive into learning it.

Let's lay this out in its full equation so it is completely clear: mastering a system brings recognition, which brings invitations, which bring energy and activation, which bring an arena in which to play/operate and a place/person to connect into, all of which allow us to be the fullest expression and make the highest contribution we possibly can.

How We Recognize Others—Our Penetrating Aura

Our penetrating aura may make others uncomfortable, but it is the brilliant and reliable mechanism through which we gather information and awareness. This then allows us to guide others wisely and with deep insight. We build the *knowledge* we need through skillful proficiency with a system and gain the *insight* we need through our penetrating awareness. This helps us to recognize others in a truly profound way, which is the gift we bring to the world.

The way our aura works explains why Projectors usually excel at one-on-one interactions. Our aura penetrates deeply into the other person's aura and energy flow. This gives us keen insight into how they could use their energy more effectively.

What we recognize in others is their potential and what could be possible if they lived up to that potential. We also recognize the potential in a system and what could be possible if it were fully optimized and used correctly. We are "potential-recognizers"!

The information gathered from our aura penetration gets synthesized by the mind. While it is best to not use the mind for our own decision making, recognizing others is the *best* use for the mind. Our minds are brilliant at observing, measuring, and analyzing, but not at guiding our own lives.

Once we recognize the potential and possibilities of someone, how can we call those forth from them? The simplest and most effective way is through asking the right questions. Evocative questions can awaken and transform a person. These questions arise from our deep awareness of that person through our focused aura which observes them both individually and within the context of the bigger picture, or perhaps the system, in which they operate.

We are most impactful when we simply ask powerful questions. This opens the door for improved human productivity and invites the other person to step through the door. If we try to push or pull them through that door they will probably resist, but we can open the door and gently beckon them through with focused and transformative questions. This is guidance at its finest.

How We Identify a Correct Recognition—Our Authority

Now, we can really put the details together. The way we correctly recognize the right opportunities for us is by waiting to be recognized and invited by the right people, and then using our personal decision-making Authority for whether to accept the invitation or not. Ideally, we have already paved the way for these opportunities with our proficiency in a system that is the right system and right proficiency for us.

When we receive the wrong recognition but think it is the right recognition, we can mistakenly put our energy into something that ends up draining us instead of empowering us. Wrong recognition comes from the wrong people in our lives. They are not bad people, just not the right people for us. These are people who do not truly know and value us for who we are, as we are. They want us to be and do what is not correct for us, either for self-serving purposes or from their lack of awareness.

When you find the right people for you, whichever specific Authority you have will light up with the feeling of rightness. You will know it. You may need to wait for that clarity, depending on your Authority, but you will know it unmistakably.

A Projector does not need to have many people in their life, just the right ones. The right people are those who recognize the Projector's brilliance, value their wisdom, and see the Projector as someone who can help them to change their life for the better. Our gift of guidance is not meant for everyone, just for the right ones.

It is to your advantage to be choosy about whom you allow into your life. Most people need guidance, but you are not here to guide everyone. When a person recognizes you as their guide and invites you to guide them, and that invitation feels correct for you, then you have a truly correct relationship that will benefit both of you.

To be clear, you are not supposed to look for the right people for you. You just need to recognize them when they show up. When you are waiting for the right people and right timing, following your bliss, developing expertise in the right system(s) for you, managing your energy, being invitable, and doing the other Projector hacks discussed previously, you will attract them without any effort. This is the magic of correctness.

Life isn't supposed to be hard. We make it hard when we push against what we do not want, pull on what we do want, and try to force things to happen. There is a grand design, and we are an integral part of it. When we play our part well and correctly, the whole story unfolds naturally and elegantly.

Where We Get into Trouble with Recognition

There are several places where we can get on the wrong side of recognition and suffer the consequences.

When we are recognized for what we *do* for others, rather than for our insight, knowledge, wisdom, and guidance, we set the stage for more *doing*. Even if the person is correct for us, that recognition is not. If we agree to do more of that *doing* (because we like feeling recognized even though it is the wrong recognition), we will attract people who want us to do more of that *doing* or to do similar *doing*, and we have a prescription for burnout and misery.

That example illuminates a central issue for Projectors: Recognition feels so good that we want more of it, even when it is not the right recognition. We are willing to put up with wrong-feeling recognition because it seems, in the moment, better than no recognition. But here is what is driving that—we are using recognition from others as an indicator of our value.

When we are not feeling properly or sufficiently recognized, we begin to wonder if we are even worthy of recognition. If we were worthy, people would surely see that and recognize us accordingly. Wouldn't they? Isn't that how it is supposed to work?

Several things happen from this scenario. We judge ourselves negatively because we feel that others are judging us or not noticing us at all (which is almost as bad). We work harder, usually *doing* more, and we give more of ourselves trying to earn the recognition and praise of others. This burns us out and brings us the wrong recognition, if any. All of which leads to more lack of self-value, more hard work, more burnout, and more pretending to be who we are not, just to please others and get the recognition we crave.

Then, we feel insecure, confused, exhausted, and broken, and we look to the self-help world for answers because we sure need the help. We read the books, take the courses, attend the workshops, go on expensive retreats—whatever promises to give us answers. We will do anything that can help us fix whatever is wrong with us.

We think we know what is wrong: We are not good enough, strong enough, smart enough, hardworking enough, energetic enough, sustainable enough, worthy enough, valuable enough, loved enough, lovable enough, or loving enough. But those are NOT what is wrong, so fixing those will never fix the problem anyway. We are simply not getting the right kind of recognition.

It is no wonder so many Projectors are drawn to Human Design—they are looking for answers about themselves. Their self-awareness is already hampered (being designed to know others deeply but not themselves), so any glimmer of understanding or glimpse of self-knowledge is like a drop of water to the parched.

Another place we bump into trouble with recognition is believing that it is selfish to want recognition, so we hide our gifts and maybe ourselves and try to NOT be recognized.

I wrestle with this issue myself. I want to be recognized for my contributions but then feel guilty or worried that my motivation is not pure and that I am being self-centered to want to hear some praise and feel some appreciation. Then, fortunately, I remember that I am a Projector and that it is correct for me to want, need, and receive recognition, as long as it is the right recognition. But without knowing my design, I would really be in a mess about this.

Our need for recognition as Projectors is real and legitimate, but when it drives our sense of self-worth, there can be a very high cost. Cultivating a healthy respect for and relationship with both outer recognition and inner self-worth will have lifelong benefits.

A Healthy Relationship with Recognition

How do we have a healthy relationship with recognition from others and with our self-value at the same time? We make sure to separate the two.

Recognition brings energy from outside of us that activates us and leads to invitations. Self-value is an inside job that is not dependent on recognition from the outside.

When you stand fully in your self-value, allowing it to be self-sourced, it does not matter if you are recognized or not. That has no impact on your sense of worthiness and the value of your presence in the world. Not being recognized will impact other aspects of your life, but not those.

When you disconnect recognition from self-worth, you restore your healthy relationship with recognition and are no longer driven to get it at any cost. You are free to attract it correctly and determine whether it is good for you. Then, you can easily avoid engaging with the wrong recognition. This preserves your precious energy, attention, perception, and wisdom for the right opportunities.

You become so self-confident that you naturally attract correct recognition like a magnet. It is not forced. You are open to unexpected recognition that allows for new possibilities you may not have considered or even noticed before. You take time to move forward correctly for you, using your Authority to tap into your body and your own guidance. You say no to the people and the recognitions that are not correct for you.

But recognition is only the first part of the equation. Invitations are the next part, and there are many myths and misunderstandings about them.

Chapter 8

Myths and Truths about Invitations

Invitations are of paramount importance to Projectors. A correct understanding of what they are, what they are not, how they relate to recognition, and how and when to use them is key to unlocking Projector success and empowerment.

We explored recognition in the last chapter, noting that it comes before an invitation in the "formula" for Projector success. Put succinctly: Recognition activates *your* energy; an invitation allows you to connect into a *source* of energy.

We also defined an invitation as "specific and personal," not a vague suggestion or a generic broadcast asking for participation. The most powerful and most correct invitation for a Projector is a truly formal one—on embossed letterhead or on bended knee. There is no mistaking those invitations. We also further distinguished big decisions, for which invitations are of greatest benefit, from small decisions, for which invitations are usually not needed.

But how do you know which invitations to say yes to? Use your Authority. It will guide you to the answer that is aligned with your energy and your True Self. Whichever specific Authority you have, look for a reaction and body resonance that translates into something like: "OMG, are you kidding, I would LOVE to do that!!!"

A correct invitation, coming through correct recognition from a correct person, feels delicious! Those are the ones to say yes to.

Remember to disconnect your sense of self-value from whether you are receiving recognition and invitations. Only from a place of strong and consistent self-value can you correctly discern and accept the right invitations for you.

With this foundational understanding in place, let us now reveal some truths and bust some myths about invitations. It is easy to assume that we know everything about them. After all, invitations in general are widely understood. But there are important nuances in the arena of invitations for Projectors that make all the difference in leveraging them wisely and effectively.

Truths about Invitations and Waiting

In addition to what we have covered about invitations throughout this book so far, here is a list of some specific applications and explorations to deepen your grasp of invitations and enhance your ability to use them as the vital tools they are for your empowered success.

- Waiting for an invitation is not a passive sport. You do not need to, nor should you, sit on your hands and feel restricted or constrained while you wait. Waiting does not mean that you must do nothing while you wait. We will explore this further in Chapter 11 - Hating to Wait. In the meantime, consider what it would look like and feel like to wait actively, patiently, and productively—which for Projectors can include lots of sleep, naps, rest, and fun.
- When you wait for an invitation, you receive the gift of seeing who shows up and what that person recognizes you for. You get to see what the invitation is calling forth from you, and how it activates your defined energy and engages your wisdom. You also allow time for your Authority to operate correctly. When you are impatient and not waiting, none of these get to happen.
- Getting a correct (for you) invitation activates and gives you access to your energy. It wakes you up.
- Stepping into a correct (for you) invitation gives you access to the energy and resources of others for the fulfillment of what you step into, without you needing to do all the work involved in making the invitation available and possible in the first place.
- You need to manage your energy while waiting for an invitation and manage your energy while fulfilling an invitation.
- The correct recognition helps you feel validated and successful, even without an accompanying invitation.
- Just say "no, thank you" to incorrect invitations, until and unless the inviter recognizes and respects you. Then you can still say "no, thank

you" if the invitation does not feel correct. Always use your Authority for these decisions.

- Receiving an invitation helps you avoid the not-self approach of trying to force something to happen.
- We are not dependent on others. They are dependent on us if they want guidance! Energy is available to us through the mechanism of an invitation, but we are not dependent on that energy. The invitation brings with it the energy for fulfilling that invitation. Without invitations, we just go about our own business with our own energy, being wise, brilliant, and curious about life.
- Some invitations are subtle, and you may not even recognize them as invitations, especially if they are unexpected or outside your normal sphere of functioning.
- An invitation from someone indicates their recognition of your value and their willingness to invest in you—in your skills, talents, wisdom, and insights. In exchange, you invest in yourself—your energy, time, and focus—when you accept.
- Waiting to be recognized and invited to speak before offering advice or guidance, even in a casual one-on-one conversation, is very respectful and almost always appreciated by the other person.
- It may seem like a paradox, but the best way to be heard, recognized, and invited is to be quiet and wait. The silence of waiting gives others time and space to align their own energy then correctly recognize and invite the Projector in the right timing.
- The lighthouse is a helpful metaphor for Projectors: Like the lighthouse, we are designed to send out a powerful beacon of light (and enlightenment) to guide those looking for our guidance. The purpose of the lighthouse is to guide ships safely into a harbor, so they avoid the rocky shore or any other dangers or obstacles. It stands strong and centered and puts out a powerful beacon that draws the ships toward it. The ships that want the guidance of a particular lighthouse will follow its beacon in; those that aren't interested will keep going. Our purpose as Projectors is to guide the energy of others, to help them achieve their objectives and avoid the pitfalls and obstacles that we can see clearly but

they cannot yet see. We put out a powerful beacon of energy—our aura—that reaches out to others and naturally draws to us the people who want our guidance. But, what if instead of standing strong and centered and purposeful, our lighthouse takes a marketing course about how to draw in more ships and starts running up and down the shore shooting off fireworks instead of its beacon, shouting, "I'm over here... hey, now I'm over here"? This would cause great confusion and probably more than a few crashed ships because the lighthouse would not be doing its job of being a steady, guiding force. When you as a Projector stand in your power and beam out your aura that reflects the truth of Who You Are, you will be an attractive force for the right people to find you and use your guidance.

- When you walk into a room (even a virtual room), let your aura do the speaking. Have the confidence of a lighthouse calling the right ships to you. Trust that the right people will be drawn to you. You don't need to push, prod, or position yourself assertively.
- It is correct for you to be visible and findable—so people can invite you. Let people know, in a non-pushy way, who you are, what you do, what you are looking for, and how to contact you. The right people would probably find you anyway, but this gives you something to do while waiting that feels productive, and it may help. This could be done in conversations in which you are more interested in the other person than in talking about yourself, but as a courtesy you share a little about you. It could be through a website, social media profile, listing in a directory, or free introductory class about your services or knowledge. There are many in the Human Design community who would say these actions are not correct for Projectors, but I say that we live in a world that is not correct for Projectors so we need to do whatever we can. It is best to have invitations or energetic openings for the actions mentioned, but if the action feels correct for you—not at a mind level but at a body level and according to your Authority—then give it a try. Don't expect too much from it. But if it gives you an opportunity to hone your skills, refine your message, deepen your knowledge, or strengthen your confidence, then it might be worth it.

- Forcing or manipulating an invitation never works. The magic of a genuine invitation is in the other person's recognition and respect for you as they request your help or participation. Invitations can be facilitated by others for you. And you can help an invitation along in gentle ways, but it must truly come from the inviter.
- Be careful of false invitations. There are two categories: politeness and manipulation. With politeness, the other person may feel obligated to invite you or feel it is the "right" thing to do, but it is not coming from their heart or from genuine recognition. With manipulation, the other person has an agenda to fulfill regardless of whether you are truly the right person to fulfill it. When you tune into the other person's energy and your own visceral reaction, you will feel if it is a genuine invitation or not.
- With a true invitation, there are no negative consequences, like punishment or retaliation, if you say no. If there is retaliation of some kind, then the invitation was actually a request or demand.

Myths About Invitations

We've looked at some powerful truths about invitations, but there still may be some incorrect assumptions and misunderstandings about them. Let's articulate a few common myths and misconceptions about invitations and clarify them.

Myth #1 - If you say no to an invitation, you will not get another one.

I hear this often. As we develop our understanding of energy and the Law of Attraction, we worry that saying no to an invitation will send the wrong signal to the universe, telling it that we do not want invitations. This is not accurate. If you are saying yes to wrong invitations, you are encouraging more wrong invitations—and not encouraging the right ones. Only say yes if an invitation feels GREAT in accordance with your Authority. When you say yes to the right ones and no to the wrong ones, you are sending the correct signals and telling the universe which ones you want more of.

Myth #2 - Once you have an invitation, it stays available forever.

Invitations are situational, and situations change. Energy changes. Alignment changes. Invitations are in the moment and temporary. If someone invited you to teach a workshop at their healing center a few months ago but it was not the right timing for you, that invitation may or may not remain open. You will need to contact that person and find out. If your partner wanted to talk about your relationship last night but you were too tired, do not assume that you can launch into that conversation anytime today. That opening may not be there today. So, ask. Invite them to talk, ask when it would work for them, and let them know when it would work for you. Don't assume, be respectful, and don't take things personally.

Also, don't rush to accept an invitation just so it won't expire. If the invitation is correct for you to accept, it will wait for your decision-making process to complete so you know whether to accept it now or not. That is how the magic of Strategy works. If it expires before you can determine its correctness, then trust that it was not truly correct for you at this time.

Myth #3 - An invitation is a sign that something is the right action for you.

This is a big one. Many people love to get a sign from the universe that something they want to do is right for them. That is understandable. They believe that if something shows up related to their preference, it is a signal that means it is the correct choice. It confirms their desire. But there is a different, I believe more accurate, way to interpret the sign: It is something to respond to with your Authority. It does *not* represent an automatic yes just because it shows up. It is an opportunity to get clarity about whether your response is yes or no, using your personal Authority. This is true for invitations as well as other signs.

Myth #4 - An invitation is a guarantee that it will work out well.

Ah, we all want guarantees, don't we? Sadly, there aren't any. Following Strategy and Authority gives you the best shot at making the best choices. But it is not a guarantee. When you follow your Strategy and Authority and make a choice, go into it with confidence and positive expectations. Keeping your energy vibration high will support the best outcomes. If it does not go as well as intended, look for the useful lessons and silver linings. Sometimes, an opportunity not going well is exactly what is needed and is completely correct. So, don't be too quick to judge, doubt, regret, give up, or get bitter. Re-frame the experience, pull the lessons, and move on with more wisdom and greater discernment. Remember to source your self-value from within, not from how things go externally. Correct invitations are how your G Center guides you to your correct path, even if it isn't always smooth, linear, logical, or observably successful.

Myth #5 - As Projectors we need to project strength and power, so we are seen as worthy and get invited; asking for help is a sign of weakness.

The best way for Projectors to project strength and power is through strong self-value and unshakable self-trust, which includes knowing when you need help and standing in your power when requesting it.

Projectors are wired for a give-and-take, win-win relationship with 70 percent of the population—the Generators and Manifesting Generators. Because we are designed to guide them, by definition we need to interact with them to fulfill our role. Because we are not designed to initiate actions on our own, it is appropriate to get some help when needed, especially to get things started. Ask for help. Accept help. Also, give help. When giving help, offer and ask, do not just tell others what to do. Also, do not do things *for* them unless that is totally appropriate. Stick to your guiding role. Each Type is unique and has their own expression of power. Ours is subtle but substantial.

Myth #6 - The more invitations you get, the better.

You are not waiting for a bunch of invitations. You are waiting for a specific invitation, a correct one. For you. The success factor here is quality, not quantity. You certainly do not want a bunch of wrong invitations. The big, correct invitations do not come often, and that is normal. They are worth waiting for. Follow your bliss while you wait. Of course, small invitations are more common, for example an invitation to dinner, a party, or a boat ride. Use your Authority to assess those and choose correctly. Receiving too many invitations, even correct ones, could lead to burnout. Be discerning. Go for quality, fit, and alignment.

Myth #7 - If you are always waiting, you will always be ready for the invitation.

That depends on how you wait. If you are in joy, bliss, fun, rest, creativity, exploration, enjoyment, enthusiasm, skill development, knowledge building, and love while you wait, then you are ready for whatever shows up, and you will attract awesome invitations. If you are frustrated, angry, bitter, impatient, anxious, or insecure, then you are not ready and will not attract the awesome invitations. You will just attract the not-awesome ones, if any. Feeling that you are constantly waiting, or that you must be constantly waiting, is not a prescription for success and empowerment.

The best possible approach is to be so busy BEING happy, joyful, skillful, enthusiastic, creative, rested, and renewed that you have no focus on waiting. When it does not feel like you are waiting, then you are in the right space for invitations to be drawn to you. You do not want to fill your waiting time with worry, anxiety, impatience, or bitterness. You also do not want to fill it with a lot of *doing*. Of course, there are always life-based things to do—shop, cook, eat, do laundry, pay bills, etc. But don't try to be a "doing machine" that is busy-busy-busy all the time. Projectors are not designed for that, and you won't get the right invitations from that kind of waiting activity. You will get the busy-based invitations, which are not correct.

All of this leads us into needing a new definition of what success looks like and feels like for Projectors. It is very different from success for the other Types.

Chapter 9

Redefining Success

More than any of the other Types, Projectors are here to *have* success and experience the sweet *feeling* of success. That may surprise you. For many of us, it feels like we have the most challenging energy configuration for being successful. No other Type needs to wait for specific and personal invitations. That is hard in today's fast-moving, response-driven world. It partially (but not completely) takes us out of the driver's seat of success in our lives.

So, how can we achieve sweet success when creating *any* success seems so hard for us, and how can we possibly do it without burning ourselves out?

Glad you asked. This is, understandably, a major topic for Projectors and one that influences the judgments we make about ourselves and our lives. In other words, this issue of success deeply affects how we feel about ourselves.

Signature Themes of Each Type

Each Type has a **not-self theme**, which is a low vibration expression of that Type's energy, and a **signature theme**, which is a high vibration expression of their energy. Most of us are somewhere in the middle most of the time. As we go through the natural deconditioning process that results from knowing our Human Design, we move up that scale and express more and more of the signature vibration of our Type.

When we are expressing our not-self theme, it serves as an indicator that we are not focused on our highest expression. Our openness (which is the source of the not-self) can also have a very positive effect: It helps us develop and access our wisdom throughout life. Distinguishing the benefits of openness from the low expression of the not-self will support our movement toward the higher expression of our signature theme.

To understand our Projector themes, let's first look at those of the other Types. By knowing their themes, we can easily distinguish them from our own, plus we will know what our fellow humans are dealing with.

Generators and Manifesting Generators are here to experience **satisfaction** but not necessarily success. Satisfaction is their signature theme. Their inner satisfaction exists separately from outward success, and while some Generators and Manifesting Generators are ambitious and seek that outer success (ambition lives primarily in Channel 54-32), their true sense of achievement comes from inner satisfaction. They do not need recognition from others and often do not even want it. When not following their Strategy and personal Authority, they will tend to experience their not-self themes of **frustration** (Generators) **and impatience** (Manifesting Generators).

Manifestors are here to experience **peace** (their signature theme) which calms their **anger** (their not-self theme). They have no interest in recognition, don't care about satisfaction, and don't like to be asked questions. They want to be left in peace to pursue the creative flow of their initiating energy and to have an impact on the world around them. When comfortable that they will not be interrupted, they experience an exquisitely serene peace while totally absorbed in their pursuits. Their anger flares when that peace is disrupted.

Reflectors are designed to experience **delight and surprise** (their signature theme), as a counterbalance to their tendency toward **disappointment** (their not-self theme). They sample the auras of everyone around them, like they are tasting a little bit of everything at a buffet table, and they love to be happily surprised by what they find. As keen observers, they are adept at seeing the potential of everyone and they experience disappointment as they watch people not live up to that potential.

The Projector's signature theme is **success** and the not-self expression is **bitterness**. You can see that these are very different from the others' themes. This brings us back to the question of how to define success for Projectors and specifically how to understand our high-expression signature theme.

The Big Shift in Success

The old-school measures of success were based on numbers, material wealth, and prestige, such as size of bank account, amount of salary, value of house, advanced degrees, schools attended, club memberships, and position at work. All of these involve what people *do* and what they *have*. And most of these things don't actually make people happy.

These measures have been gradually losing meaning as more people focus on how they *feel*, who they are *being*, and how their actions *impact* others and the planet. We are seeing the environmental movement, the tiny house movement, and so many back-to-the-land choices. There is a growing fascination with artisans and craftspeople and niche markets; millennials and newer generations are opting out of the so-called rat-race and making choices that do not fit our old paradigms.

As guides and facilitators of change, Projectors are at the forefront of redefining these measures of success and transforming the world's ideas of what is worth doing, having, and being. We are perfectly positioned to guide humanity toward a new set of values as metrics for assessing happiness and a new version of wealth. These new metrics also happen to be compatible with our own design for success.

Success for Projectors

Let's bring our focus to you personally, as a Projector. How have you defined your success, or lack of success, in the past? If you're like me, you unquestioningly bought into the paradigm of our time and used the long-standing metrics of money, job, education, awards, etc. as measures for evaluating progress and celebrating success. Those accomplishments felt good in the moment; however, they quickly felt hollow as we faced climbing the next mountain, jumping the next hurdle, and adding the next zero to the bank account. It felt endless, unsatisfying, and exhausting. At least, that is where I was around age forty, which happens to be when many Projectors burn out. I was on the verge of it. I didn't realize that burnout and disillusionment were nipping at my feet, but I felt empty. I knew there was something more that was possible. There had to be. *But what?*

Your journey was probably a little different than mine, maybe significantly different, but the result was likely very similar—*there must be more, why is it so hard, and this can't be all there is.*

These existential crises in our life's trajectory are not only important, they are also necessary. They cause us to pause, reevaluate, ask new questions, and seek new answers. They cause us to re-define success for ourselves.

At some point, sometimes at a young age, Projectors realize that we are different from others and just can't seem to do things the way others do them. When we are rewarded along the way for taking action and *doing* things, it feels good temporarily but brings more demands for doing more—*bigger and better*—and we eventually burn out. Instead, if we are rewarded for being smart, wise, helpful, kind and/or generous, that feels much better and is rarely associated with exhausting demands and burnout, but sadly that recognition is rare when compared to the rewards we get when we step into the *doing* aspects of life.

We learn, sooner or later, that ACTION is not the cause or measure of our true success. But we are embedded in a Generator-driven, action-based world, and it is hard to make a living by simply being wise and generous! What we are designed for—wise guidance—is not what counts in today's material world.

That's the bad news. The good news is that the world is changing. What we value as a species is changing, and the metrics for success are beginning to change along with them. As Projectors we are leading the way and demonstrating with our own lives what the new values and metrics look like.

A good place to begin defining these new values is to distinguish between outer success and inner success. **Outer success** for Projectors looks like appropriate recognition, correct invitations, and successful fulfillment of our responsibilities within those invitations. Outer success also looks like deep wisdom and good guidance given to those who are ready and asking for them. It looks like helping to improve the use of human energy and other resources, the alignment of the energy grid, the choices people make, the development of innovative solutions, and even to soothe irritations and smooth out relationships.

Inner success feels like valuing ourselves no matter what is happening (or not happening) around us. It feels like an eternal inner wellspring of healthy self-confidence mixed with strong self-worth and genuine gratitude. It feels like trusting ourselves and taking excellent care of ourselves because we recognize our own value and the transformative potential of our contributions.

Here are a few useful parameters for measuring our success as Projectors:

- Recognition from others is not a measure of our value; it is a measure of the value that others perceive about us—which may or may not be accurate. Even if their perception is accurate, it is not a measure of our true value, it is just an indication of how well we are being perceived (and it is filtered through the others' issues anyway).
- The size, shape, and frequency of the invitations we receive are not measures of our success. Again, they are a reflection of the accuracy of how we are perceived, and they are based on the needs and desires of others, not on us or our needs.
- Similarly, money, rank, salary, and other numbers are not measures of our value or our success.
- The actions we take, especially not-self actions, are not related to our success. When we attempt to tie our success, both external and internal, to our actions we lock in more of our not-self expression and increase our chances of bitterness, burnout, or both.
- Receiving correct and appropriate recognition reflects our success in following our Strategy and Authority, which automatically puts us in the right places at the right times with the right people where our brilliance is noticed and valued.
- Attracting excellent (correct) invitations to ourselves is an indicator that we are accurately portraying ourselves to the world, are findable, invitable, and we are also expressing our True Selves.
- When you feel little or no resistance from others to your energy and you receive correct invitations with no effort on your part, you know you are in the "Projector zone" of being your True Self and not trying to be anyone else.
- Feeling good about yourself is the most fundamental measure of how well you are doing in life. Nothing else is as important as that. Self-value outranks external recognition, every time, and is completely within your control.

- When you do not feel bitter and have nothing in your life that you are inclined to feel bitter about, you know you are succeeding as a high-functioning Projector.
- When you are correctly recognized and invited, actively appreciated, generously compensated (not just with money), and you feel good about yourself, you know you are truly successful.
- We can be brilliant in the actions that we do take, and I'm not suggesting that we can never or should never take actions. But we are not an energy Type. They are the ones designed for making things happen. Generators and Manifesting Generators have a defined Sacral Center for sustainable energy to *take action*. Manifestors have a defined motor center connected to the Throat Center for energy to *initiate action*. We have neither; we are here to *guide action*. Doing that is what brings us the sweetness of success that we seek.

New Success Metrics for the World

Joseph Campbell, author of many books on mythology, captured the concept of Projector success best when he said, "Follow your bliss." Little did he know that he was a Projector! When we do what we love and what calls to us, we bring to it an energy that attracts more energy and opportunities in a positive feedback loop. When we live our lives this way, we contribute to the bliss, success, and upliftment of the entire planet.

"A rising tide lifts all boats." Every positive thought, action, energy, and intention adds to the growth and enlightenment of the whole. Even those who are not actively participating in this consciousness evolution of humanity will benefit from what you and I think, say, do, and believe. Everything matters.

Having a clear vision of where we are going also matters. It is hard to steer a good path forward if we do not know exactly where our destination is. It is harder yet when we do not have ways to gauge our progress and get back on the right path when we have strayed from it.

So, by what can we steer our path and measure our collective progress? What values and guideposts are useful for this?

New and important emerging themes we can use include faith, abundance in spirit, sustainability, enoughness, creative flow, compassion, and the power to get things done tempered by the wisdom and patience to wait for the right timing. What becomes possible is a world of justice, equity, balance, peace, prosperity, abundance and dignity for all people, and respect and honor for all living things. This occurs by promoting the values of cooperation, co-creation, alignment, and fulfillment. And, in the terminology of humanity's signature themes: satisfaction, peace, delight, and success.

But do not expect a smooth path. Disruption (which often looks like chaos and calamity) is part of the evolutionary process. Old systems, institutions, beliefs, and identities begin to crumble before we have new ones to take their place. Within this gap lies the opportunity to shape and guide their replacements. It is a chance to redefine and retell the story of humanity as a fresh narrative that describes our new potential, our new path, and our new identity.

We must clear the old to make room for the new, but this does not mean throwing out everything. It means being thoughtful, deliberate, and conscious in our choices. It means keeping what does work and integrating it with new innovations and approaches as we move forward, creating as we go.

We may long to return to the known, to what is comfortable. Some of us may cling to the old and fear the unknown of what is coming. This is understandable and normal, and it fills the vital function of ensuring that we do not wildly and recklessly create a new normal that is not grounded and functional. Resistance to change provides necessary checks and balances in our evolutionary process.

The evolutionary mechanics of the 2027 global cycle shift are in place and inevitable. But the realities that emerge from these changes are malleable. We can influence, shape, guide, and nudge the path of humanity. We can determine the results of this transformative process by defining what we want, personally and globally, every day and in every way. We get to write the story of who we are becoming and of living the highest versions of ourselves.

Remember that words are powerful, and stories are even more powerful. Let's craft the new story of humanity through the story of our own lives, every day. Let's create on a small scale what we want to be, do, and have on a big scale.

Bringing It Back to the Personal Level

Shaping reality is all about the stories we tell. I don't mean made-up stories and fairy tales, although those have their place. I mean what we say about ourselves and our lives. What we say about our family and our jobs. What we say about our relationships, our communities, and those "other" people out there. To shape our personal as well as our collective reality, we need to be deliberate in what we say about what we want, where we are going, and what is possible.

Start to pay very careful attention to what you say about yourself, others, and life. Also, pay close attention to what you want and what you think is important. How are you measuring your success? What would make you feel successful? Is that actually aligned with YOU, with who you really ARE, and with who you truly want to BE?

Now that you know what you know, what does true success mean to you? What do you want in life? What do you want to be recognized for? What do you want to achieve? Where do you hold back? Where do you compromise? Where are you hard on yourself?

Remember to experience and enjoy the sweetness of life every day. It can be as simple as looking someone in the eye with compassion and understanding and seeing their grateful reaction. It can be smelling a flower or appreciating a tree. It can be holding your child or your lover, petting a purring cat, wrestling with your dog, or being there for a friend in need. It can be sitting quietly, breathing deeply, and feeling grateful for your life and all the blessings you have received.

It is exceptionally helpful to spend one day a month away from your normal routines, to change your perspective, review your life, and feel into what is *really* important in the bigger scheme of things. This is more than a mental health day. It is a mental, physical, emotional, and spiritual health day. It is a *life* day. It can be a stay-cation or a getaway. If it is with others, make sure you have enough alone time to ponder, reflect, and tune-in to yourself, your True Self, so that you may create your life from that authentic place.

You may find that you have more "success" in your life than you give yourself credit for. Savor every moment you can. You can even substitute a different word or phrase for success because that word can be so heavy with expectations, judgments, disappointments, regrets, and pain. Maybe "sweet life" or "sweet Projector-ness." You've got this!

But, if you also have wounds to heal, those need to be addressed. Before we ever reach a place of feeling successful in life, especially as Projectors, most of us have experienced a considerable amount of Projector pain. Let's explore that next. The more we know about our challenges, the more effective our efforts will be to remedy the problems, stop the pain, heal the wounds, and emerge stronger, more resilient, more empowered, and more successful.

On our way there, let's meet another inspiring Projector—an epically successful film director and producer. You've probably heard of him.

Meet a Projector - Steven Spielberg

Steven Spielberg is one of the best-known and most influential Hollywood directors of our time and has been called, by some, the greatest film director of all time. This prolific and multi-talented Projector has woven together his natural ability to guide others with his inborn talents and passions, creating a world-impacting career spanning several decades.

Spielberg has significant openness in his Human Design chart and is what we call a no-motors Projector. How has he been so consistently productive in his career? He knows who he is (defined G Center), loves what he does, uses his energy wisely, takes breaks, and understands the power of recognition, invitation, and leveraging his influence. He started exploring his creativity and honing his skills early and was still quite young when invited to direct four movies for Universal Studios. The rest is history.

While not all of us are designed for leadership, he has several aspects of his chart that clearly point to and facilitate this capacity. His only defined channel is the Channel of Leadership, the 7-31, from the G Center to the Throat Center. Plus, his Profile is 5/1 which is an ideal configuration for leadership. His openness makes him sensitive and aware, and he is designed to have strong values and to break rules that no longer serve the greater good (Gate 50.4). Plus, with his defined creative self-expression (Gate 1), he does everything in his own unique way.

Learn more about Steven Spielberg and details of his Human Design chart in my Celebrity Chart Review of him on my website. Find the link from the Resources Page.

Name: Steven Spielberg
Birth Date: 18 December 1946, 18:16
Birth Place: Cinncinati, OH, United States

Type: Orchestrator (Projector)
Inner Authority: Calibration (G - Self)
Profile: 5/1 - Visionary Leader / Resource
Definition: Single
Strategy: Wait for Recognition and Invitation
Themes: Success / Bitterness
Incarnation Cross: LAX Education 2

Channels: 0731 - Egalitarianism (The Alpha)

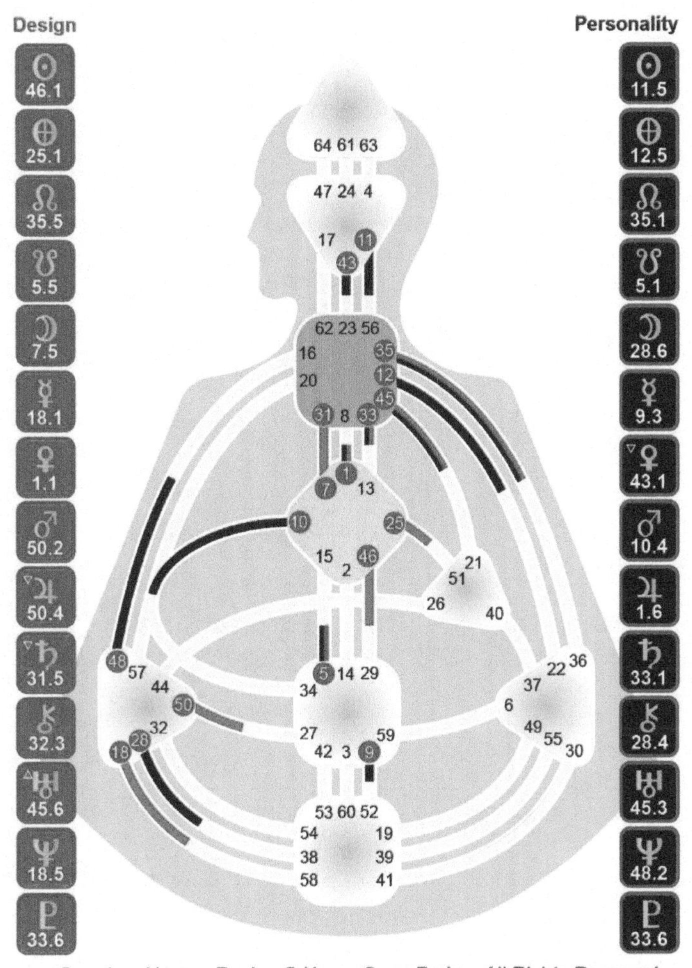

PART THREE

PROJECTOR PAIN

Where We Struggle

Projectors are challenged by being a non-energy Type in an energy-dominated world that does not understand them.

I am a teacher of enlightened selfishness. This is what we're here for. You would not be here unless you were already different and trying to find a way to live with your difference with dignity.
~ Ra Uru Hu

PART THREE

Projector Pain

Introduction to Projector Pain

What we have covered so far sounds great in theory, but down here on the playing field where life really happens, it isn't always easy. You probably can relate. When you have no income, cannot find a job, cannot buy groceries or pay rent, and nothing you try is working, you are in Projector hell. When you feel totally alone, rejected, ignored, judged, burned out, and bitter, you are in the deep end of the Projector pool of misery.

We are literally like square pegs trying to fit ourselves in the round holes created by the energy Types. This world is not designed *by* us (yet) and not designed *for* us (at all). We are stuck in a Generator-led and Manifestor-inspired realm in which precious few people understand our role, our value, and how to activate our gifts and contribution. It is so simple. Just recognize us and invite us. But they rarely do. They don't know. It is not their fault but not ours either. It is just how things are right now, and how they have been for a long time.

But we—specifically you and me—are here at this particular time for a reason. We are here to change all of this by guiding the change (not by doing all the work!). But we cannot do that when we feel isolated, rejected, bitter, and burned out. We cannot do that when we are unable to support ourselves financially, are in the wrong work for us, or cannot get out of a dead-end we find ourselves in. When our light is dim and flickering, our hope waning, and our faith in tatters, we have no wise guidance to give.

We must heal ourselves so we can step into our power and fulfill our crucial role in humanity. No one can or will do that for us. All healing is an inside job, no matter what Type you are. But for Projectors, living in today's world is like trying to play basketball with both hands tied behind your back. You can show up and you can move up and down the court, but you cannot dribble, pass, or score. You certainly can't win the game. More importantly, you can't even play the game.

Precisely because the deck seems perpetually stacked against us, we tend to suffer from a near-universal affliction: a profound lack of self-love. While healing this will go a long way toward solving many of our personal issues, by itself it will not change the world. Fortunately, the world is already changing. Our best move would be to ride that wave of change and actually lead the charge. But we need to be in good shape to do that.

Before we can focus on healing our wounds, rebuilding our strength, rebalancing our lives, and stepping into our power, we need to fully understand the depth and breadth of our pain. If we just bandage the surface wounds, we will miss the infections raging beneath the surface. We need a complete assessment to identify where the problems are, so we can know what specific areas need attention.

We will look at the pain of Projectors in four broad areas. These cover the bulk of our common issues and provide us with some structure for going in deep.

Chapter 10

Brokenness and Shame

Aside from the specific Projector issues of waiting, burnout, and bitterness, there is a whole constellation of sources of pain, struggle, and disempowerment for Projectors which I group together under the title of Brokenness and Shame. These issues seem to underlie, amplify, and lock into place the other issues that follow in the next chapters. So, these are—potentially—the linchpins that can release those other sources of Projector pain.

The title of this grouping indicates the one-two punch of these issues. First, there is the searing pain of feeling broken and in need of somehow being "fixed." Then, there is the added trauma of experiencing deep shame around the pain and brokenness.

There is a spectrum of brokenness that spans from mild twinges when things don't quite turn out as expected to deep despair that you are hopeless, helpless, unfixable, and irredeemable.

There is, of course, also a spectrum of shame from mild embarrassment to the total self-loathing that results from feeling completely humiliated and mortified.

How awful. How does this happen? We are so brilliant and vital to the world. We have so many gifts and talents and such a strong drive to help others. How do we get so tangled up and fall so far?

Brokenness

Many Projectors come to Human Design having already experienced deep fears that there is something wrong with them, that they are in some way broken or defective. They have repeatedly noticed that they are not like everyone else, and often felt (or were made to feel) that they simply do not measure up. Many have a lifetime of questioning their own "okayness."

Now that we know how we are energetically wired as Projectors and that we *are* different from others, we know that our perceptions (about being different) are correct.

For many of us, discovering that we are Projectors truly explains a lot, at least at the cognitive level. It may ease some of the hurt and help with self-acceptance, but it does not take away all of the pain or its effects. We may still be carrying the wounds of all those years of comparing ourselves to others and coming up short or being criticized for the ways in which we are different.

And for some, learning you are a Projector actually makes things worse, at least initially. You may feel doomed, fatally flawed, and totally hopeless.

The number one reason my clients and students identify for feeling different or ashamed is related to their **energy level**. We Projectors are not designed to have sustainable workforce energy. In a world where Generators and Manifesting Generators are the large majority, we may be called lazy or unmotivated, and feel like failures. The truth is, Projectors can be very productive when we know how to leverage our energy in healthy ways. We are not supposed to keep up with the energy Types of the world, but the pressure to do so is real and often very compelling.

To make matters worse, our sense of brokenness goes far beyond our energy levels. I surveyed Projectors about the themes of brokenness and shame, and here are a few of their responses.

"I feel different, don't measure up, like I'm an alien."

"I need to hide, so they don't find out I'm not like them."

"Nothing works for me the way it works for everyone else."

"Why is everything so hard for me?"

"I feel guilty when I can't keep up/need to take a rest/can't support myself."

"They said, I'm too: lazy/sensitive/bossy/pushy…"

When we choose the wrong people to have in our lives (by not following our Strategy and personal Authority), we are far more likely to experience feelings of brokenness and dysfunction. They do not see us or value us for our True Self, and we begin to think we are who we are NOT. Then we have a much harder time relaxing into our okayness and healing our wounds.

When we try to prove ourselves to others, to gain their recognition and approval, it can feel to them that we are interfering in their lives, and this causes discomfort and resistance on their part. This sets up a bad interaction that can quickly become draining and discouraging for the Projector who feels rejected and not valued.

Here are a few other ways Projector brokenness and pain can show up:

- Feeling isolated, rejected, and/or invisible.
- Feeling traumatized (by life, people, experiences, self-doubt, to name just a few sources).
- Struggling with money, energy, relationships, self-worth.
- Working harder than others to prove yourself and still not coming out ahead.
- Not trusting yourself.
- Squandering your energy, awareness, and insights on the wrong people, the wrong projects, or at the wrong times.
- Feeling guilty, lost, and confused about all the above.

You can probably add a few of your own. All of these symptoms of feeling broken are sources of Projector shame.

Shame

When we feel so different and so out of alignment, it is easy to feel embarrassed and want to hide. If we could just fix ourselves then we could feel comfortable being with people, introducing ourselves, talking about our lives, and showing pride in our accomplishments. Then it would be okay to feel good about ourselves. But until that always-elusive and never-arriving moment, we are stuck feeling isolated, ashamed, and never *ever* good enough.

Here are two quotes that illuminate the pain and damage that shame can cause.

From Brené Brown: "I define shame as the intensely painful feeling or experience of believing we are flawed and therefore unworthy of love and belonging—something we've experienced, done, or failed to do makes us unworthy of connection."[5]

From Steve Safigan: "Shame tells us that we are unworthy, unlovable, and incapable of change. Shame tells us that our imperfections make us inadequate and that our vulnerabilities are weaknesses."[6]

It is important to note that Projectors are not the only people who experience shame. There is much "unworthiness" in circulation in the world. But we do seem to have more than our fair share. There is also an important distinction between Projector shame and what is clinically referred to as "toxic shame" which arises from experiencing abuse or trauma. That calls for professional help.

Projector Shame

When we secretly (or not so secretly) believe that we are flawed and undeserving, we are in deep pain. We may lash out and want revenge at times, but mostly we just want to hide. We want to bind our wounds and figure out what the heck we are doing wrong.

The combination of feeling broken then feeling shame on top of that distorts our ability to make good choices. When you don't trust yourself, you probably won't trust your Strategy and Authority. When you don't value yourself, you won't invest in quality and will try to compensate with quantity (for example, in friendships or even with food). When you don't believe in the wisdom and guidance you are here to offer, you will focus your aura and attention on the wrong people and projects, trying desperately to prove yourself. When you feel rejected and shamed, you won't know who to trust or you won't trust anyone.

Projector Shame relates strongly to five specific Resiliency Keys out of the nine Keys identified by Karen Curry Parker in her brilliant work for helping all Types heal their wounds, the Quantum Alignment System™. We address all nine Keys in detail in Chapter 15. For now, just ponder these five in the context of brokenness and shame: Vitality, Lovability, Self-Worth, Empowerment, and Authenticity. When you do not have healthy levels of resiliency in each of these areas, you will experience some level of pain or suffering.

Exploring Your Shame

Sorting out and healing all this pain can be, well, painful. But there is no substitute for doing the work of healing your wounds and addressing the underlying issues. The questions below will help. The relief, release, and new clarity you will experience as a result will make the challenge of facing your pain totally worth it.

Even if you love being a Projector and do not feel ashamed now, you may be carrying some "schmutz" from the past that is weighing you down—those unconscious beliefs that can erode your energy and keep you from your fullest expression. Here is your chance to uncover them and clear them out!

Take a little quiet, thoughtful time to answer these questions honestly and completely. Physically writing out your answers on paper can help ground and release the energy but do whatever works best for you.

#1 What are you ashamed of (or hate about) being a Projector? What has been painful for you?

#2 What do you love about being a Projector? Why?

#3 What would you like to love about being a Projector? How could you feel proud of who you are?

#4 What gets in your way of claiming your Projector brilliance and feeling great about who you are?

Reverse-Shame for Projectors

Here is an odd but increasingly common phenomenon. After you work on accepting and living in alignment with your Projector nature, a new kind of shame can show up. I call it reverse-shame. It is shame about not being a "good" Projector.

Knowing that you are "supposed" to wait for invitations, wait to be invited to speak, not be pushy or bossy, discharge energy every day, leverage your defined center strengths, decondition your open center vulnerabilities, face the challenges in your chart, develop expertise in a system so you can be recognized, etc. puts you in a tricky position. If you are violating one or more of these "shoulds," you may feel shame that you are not being a good Projector. If you participate in online Projector groups or Human Design groups, others may do that shaming for you. "Oh, you're not supposed to do THAT without an invitation." "Oh, THIS is why your life isn't working."

Most of us want to be good and do things right. When we learn the list of what is supposed to "save us" and "fix us," of course we will try to do those to the best of our ability. Except that we're human, and those things may not even be the right answers for us.

The last thing we need is more guilt, more shame, and more feeling bad about ourselves. Enough already! Human Design teaches that only we know what is correct for us and what works for us. This system is not meant to be dogma with rigid rules. It is not meant to be another tool with which we beat ourselves up. It is meant to help us understand ourselves and navigate our lives with more joy and more success.

So, relax about the "shoulds." Ease into your understanding of yourself and figure out, as you move forward, what works and does not work for you. This is not a race or competition. The only prize is feeling good about yourself. That is an inside job.

But, before we focus on healing ourselves, there are a few more big Projector issues we need to examine.

Chapter 11

Hating to Wait

Waiting can feel like that thorn in your side that keeps you in pain and prevents you from playing full-out in the game of life, or like a lead weight dragging you down. It is easy to blame your Strategy of needing to *wait for an invitation* for all the ways your life isn't working.

Waiting implies lack of action. Lack of power. Lack of control. Being dependent. It conjures images of being idle. Sitting around with nothing to do. Being at the mercy of the others who make things happen, because we "can't" make things happen ourselves. It feels like a curse, punishment, or worse.

It is easy to HATE our need to WAIT.

But what if that view of waiting is all wrong? What if it's a blessing, not a curse? I know that seems like a really big stretch right now. Stay with me, though. Let's see if we can turn this thing around. First, we will explore waiting in general then focus on Projectors.

Nearly Everyone Needs to Wait

All Types except non-emotional Manifestors need to wait for something. That means around 96 percent of the population is waiting! This is definitely not just a Projector issue.

Generators and Manifesting Generators need to wait for something to respond to, and then become aware of their response. In the larger scheme of things, this is a relatively easy process. They can respond to anything and everything in their environment. Anything they can see, touch, taste, smell, hear, or sense, they can respond to. In fact, they are already, always responding. They were born responding. This is their beautiful, interactive dance with the world. They know what is right for them and what is not based on their response. This is how they know themselves and how they know what to do next. Approximately half of them need to further wait through their emotional wave to gain clarity for their choices.

However, many Generators balk at the idea of waiting, and Manifesting Generators even more so. They want to get busy and get on with things, but their waiting rarely takes very long. If nothing is showing up related to their decision so they can respond to it, they can have a friend ask them yes/no questions so they can directly access their internal Sacral guidance. Once they get the hang of their waiting process, they see the value it provides. It is their moment-by-moment guidance through life, used for everything from what career to choose, whom to marry, and where to live, to what to eat and whether to answer the phone. They can respond to anything including emails, billboards, social media posts, and conversations they overhear. Their responding process is not dependent on other people.

Reflectors need to wait at least twenty-nine days to get clarity before they make a decision. That is a full lunar cycle, and they need this time because they are deeply affected by the moon activating each of the 64 gate energies of Human Design during the course of that cycle. Each moon-activated gate will have an effect on their chart, with some having significant impact. Their clarity comes from waiting through all of these effects, talking to others about their decision, and finally reaching clarity over that time. For big decisions, they may need more than one lunar cycle to get that clarity.

While it is challenging in today's fast-paced world to wait that long to make a decision, Reflectors are not really dependent on anyone else for their decision process, only on time itself. Finding a trusted sounding board friend to listen as they verbally sort through their issues is the only people-related challenge for their decision process.

Manifestors are designed to be the most dynamic action-takers of all the Types, but even half of them need to wait. Of the 8-9 percent of the population who are Manifestors, at least half are emotionally defined (they have Emotional Authority) which means they need to wait through their emotional wave to get their clarity. While this can take some time and is not predictable, they are still Manifestors who are here to initiate action and make things happen. Once they have their clarity, they are good to go.

Some might argue that even non-emotional Manifestors need to wait for their internal sense of timing (unrelated to emotions). That would bring the total of everyone who needs to wait to 100 percent.

What Hating to Wait Feels Like and Sounds Like

Before we flip waiting on its head, let's dive a little deeper into the pain Projectors experience in the realm of waiting. Here are a few things Projectors have expressed about having to wait for an invitation. Please add your own versions to the list.

"I'm afraid that I'll wait and wait, and never get an invitation."

"How can I support myself if I'm waiting?"

"I never get invited."

"Waiting feels so passive; I want to be DOING things. And I see so much that needs to be DONE."

"I hate being dependent on other people..."

"I can't wait any longer, so I'll take the next offer that comes along."

"I waited and got an invitation, so why didn't it work out?"

Why Projectors Are Designed to Wait

For all Types, waiting allows them to find correct alignment and correct timing so they can make the right choices for themselves. If not waiting, they all operate from their not-self instead of from alignment with their consistent energy and their True Self.

For Projectors, waiting for an invitation has several aspects. They all involve correct alignment and timing, and they all position the Projector to give wise guidance and orchestrate tasks and projects. First, waiting stops the Projector from trying to force things to happen. Second, it gives them the time and opportunity to align with themselves and send out an accurate and coherent energy signal. Third, it allows time for the right people to find and respond to the Projector's energy and provide the appropriate recognition and invitation.

There is power in the invitation, as we have seen. There is also power in waiting for it. We are *designed* to wait for an invitation to major things in life. That is how our energy works best.

When we as Projectors wait for and accept a correct invitation, we get connected to the resources, support, and energy to fulfill the intention of the invitation. Instead of correctly waiting for an invitation, we may spend our energy trying to find one or create one. Or we may try to make things happen without an invitation. But all of those are the hard way. The easier way is *allowing* the right invitations to find us.

It does not work to finagle or manipulate an invitation. You must wait, but not passively! When it does show up, you must notice it and *recognize* it as an invitation. This is actually more of a challenge than it may sound—you need to tune your awareness to notice invitations. The subtle ones can be easy to miss.

The waiting process for Projectors is dependent on other people. That makes it unpredictable and partially outside of our control. Yes, waiting can seem painful, but only if our understanding of it and mindset about it are not correct.

A Projector student in a class I taught shared that she had discovered the power of silence thanks to Human Design. When she waited quietly during a discussion until she was asked for her input, people really heard what she had to say. Previously, she would try to speak, and the others would talk right over her and never actually hear her.

One More Time—Why Wait?

As stated earlier, recognition brings invitations, and invitations bring additional energy that we can use in the fulfillment of the accepted invitation, and so much more.

It is really smart to wait for an invitation because...

- it allows you to receive recognition (without chasing after it).
- it brings you energy.
- it can prevent you from slogging along in the wrong direction, draining your energy.
- it conserves energy: It takes a lot less effort to allow and receive an invitation than to make things happen in the first place.

- it lets you be selective and pursue only the options that feel right from among all the options that come your way.
- you are more likely to play your correct role (guiding) instead of your not-self role (doing).
- with the right attitude, you become more invitable when you are waiting.
- this "surrender" to your Strategy will let the universe and your G Center bring into your life what is correct for you.
- it allows you to step in and be your brilliant self (without exhausting yourself) and fulfill your role and purpose as a Projector with grace and ease.

Waiting is worth doing, and worth doing well. It is not about right or wrong, or someone else's rules. It is about how you can have your life work best and most enjoyably.

For fun, pick up your copy of Top Ten Reasons for Waiting for Invitations from the link on the Resources Page.

How to Wait

When you wait correctly, with the right attitude and mindset, waiting becomes a gift and a pleasure. It gives you time to observe and be curious. Time to play and to rest. Time to prepare and time to heal. Time to get other things done when the energy is there for them. Time to tune into yourself, develop your skills, pursue your interests, enjoy your relationships, and thoroughly learn a system.

If you are anxious, angry, impatient, bitter, worried, or resentful while you wait, none of the above blessings will be available to you *and* you will not attract the invitations you want anyway. If waiting feels like punishment, doom, and abject helplessness, you will be bitter and miserable and only attract more misery to yourself.

Here are a few tips to help you wait positively, productively, and as an active choice.

- Don't wait passively. Do what feels appealing, exciting, or fun while you wait for the next big invitation. Expand your knowledge, hone your skills, follow your bliss.
- Wait with curiosity and positive, eager anticipation. Shift your attitude

to view the waiting and inviting process as a collaboration between you and the other person, and between you and the universe. More than the other Types, our Strategy is a collaborative and co-creative process. It is a dance, and dancing is fun with the right partner and horrible with the wrong partner!

- Use the waiting time to heal any burnout you are experiencing. There is a natural protective feedback loop at work here: When you are burned out, opportunities dry up, giving you the time to restore your energy. The sooner you heal your burnout, the sooner the invitations and opportunities will come back.
- Use the waiting time to heal any bitterness you may be harboring. The energy of bitterness is not appealing and can actually repel invitations. I know many Projectors who deny being bitter, but their bitterness is palpable.
- Stand in your power. With the right mindset, the waiting time can be relaxing, enjoyable, and empowering.
- Work on your Resiliency Keys (we will dive into all the keys in Chapter 15). These will help you develop confidence, personal power, inner strength, and the ability to bounce back quickly from challenges and setbacks. The keys particularly related to the issue of waiting are Courage, Lovability, Self-Worth, Self-Trust, Empowerment, and Authenticity.
- Deliberately create space for the Universe and your G Center to work on your behalf and to bring what is correct to you. This means creating space physically, mentally, emotionally, and spiritually. Work on your beliefs. Meditate, muse, walk, dance, sing; use healing modalities like EFT (Emotional Freedom Techniques), flower essences, or essential oils; practice mindfulness; practice surrender (as a gift of power, not a giving up). Practice receiving and allowing. Practice patience and trust. Tap into faith. Practice gratitude. Expand your wisdom and knowledge. Find and do the things that support your highest well-being. Give love, receive love, create love, bestow love. Love yourself. Allow yourself to BE.

A Workaround to Waiting?

Although some would say that Projectors always need to wait for the invitation, there IS a workaround that can facilitate the little invitations, at least. Simply make an offer and see if there is a response. For this to work, you must have no attachment to the outcome. If you get an invitation from it, you will have an opportunity to step into it, or not. You get to choose, using your Authority. If you do not get an invitation, you have lost nothing.

Here is an example: "I would love to help you on that project if you find you need help." Then leave it at that. No desperation, assertion, pushing, or attachment. You leave the ball in their court. It is essentially an invitation for them to invite you. But you can still say no if the invitation comes but it does not feel correct. Remember, invitations do not last forever, and not all invitations are in alignment with you.

Let's end this chapter with a relevant quote about the wisdom of waiting that comes from American theologian Fulton J. Sheen.

"Patience is power. Patience is not an absence of action; rather it is 'timing,' it waits on the right time to act, for the right principles and in the right way."[7]

Chapter 12

Burnout

Burnout and the challenges of energy management are considered by many to be the Achilles heel of the Projector. This is where we get tripped up, over and over. We see others getting things done and we want to be like them. We pay for a business coach who tells us to do fifty million things to get our business on track and profitable, and we feel like a miserable failure (in addition to being burned out) when we cannot do them all. We compare ourselves to others and judge ourselves. Others compare themselves to us and judge us.

Burnout and bitterness often go hand-in-hand, but we will address bitterness in the next chapter so we can keep a clear focus on each.

Defining Burnout and Stress

Here is a simple definition of burnout: Exhaustion of physical or emotional strength or motivation usually as a result of prolonged stress or frustration.

The term originated from the healthcare field where excessive work demands were resulting in physical and emotional exhaustion leading to decreased effectiveness in health care professionals. From there, it became universally recognized as a potential issue for any person in any field (including non-work settings), causing a range of physical, emotional, or mental impairments.

Stress is a major factor in burnout. The main truth about stress is that it is relative—what is stressful for one person may not stress someone else. It is based largely on our perceptions, which are formed by our thoughts and beliefs. This means that managing stress, and therefore managing burnout, is mostly an inner game like strengthening self-worth and self-confidence.

I do not mean to imply that burnout and stress are trivial or all in our minds. They are very real and have real and sometimes debilitating physical, mental, and emotional impacts. But there is a component to managing these challenges that is absolutely within our control.

What Burnout Looks and Sounds Like

Here are some comments from Projectors when describing their burnout and exhaustion.

"No matter what I do, nothing works for me."

"They say to follow the Joy, but I don't see it anywhere."

"Nothing I do matters."

"I just can't do it anymore; I'm too tired."

"Nothing is worth this much effort—it's too hard and I'm too exhausted."

"I just can't get out of bed or off the sofa. It's like my energy source is completely cut off."

"What's the point of even being here... I can't make a difference if I can't get out of bed."

Symptoms of burnout include exhaustion, irritability, reactivity, despair, hypersensitivity, overwhelm, confusion, apathy, disengagement, hiding, feeling helpless, feeling hopeless, feeling defeated, and even wanting to die.

The Eight Factors of Burnout

Building on the work of Michael Leiter and Christina Maslach in the field of occupational psychology, here are eight factors that can predispose someone to burnout. The first six are from their research and are specific to the workplace setting. Two more factors are added that address Projector issues. Keep in mind that the workplace factors can apply to situations outside the work environment, so take a broad view as you examine which of these factors may apply to you.

These factors focus on the potential mismatch between the person and their situation. It is the mismatches that cause both internal and external stress and can lead to burnout.

Factor #1 - Work Overload – too much work, too urgent, too complex.

There is a potential mismatch for Projectors between available energy and the demands of a job or family or even social life. In the workplace, this can be made worse by instances of layoff, firing, and quitting leaving the "survivors" to do the work previously handled by those co-workers. If you have urgent deadlines or your assigned tasks are beyond your skill level, you will be under constant pressure to keep up.

Also, work often spills over into our "off" time as 24/7 connectivity and working from home blur the boundaries. If you are self-employed, it is even harder to stick to healthy boundaries between work and leisure time.

Factor #2 - Insufficient Reward – not enough money or satisfaction.

Employees often focus on monetary compensation. Feeling underpaid (and resenting that) is a fairly direct path to burnout. If you are a business owner, your focus may be on the bottom line and the pressures of paying bills, employees, coaches, and virtual assistants instead of paying yourself. If your business is not supporting you (or them), that financial pressure is relentless.

Plus, there are intangible rewards that factor into work satisfaction, such as recognition and the intrinsic reward of feeling effective. Recognition is so basic to Projector success that its absence produces tremendous stress, especially if you mistakenly rely on external recognition for your sense of self-value. Also, if the initial recognition you receive with an invitation does not continue, the situation may not be energetically sustainable for you and lead to burnout.

Factor #3 - Lack of Control – no say or control over things that affect you.

If you are not able to control or at least influence things that affect your work, burnout is more likely. The highest rates of burnout, as well as heart disease and depression, are correlated with high job demands combined with a lack of control.

For us as Projectors, this is a perfect recipe for burnout. For example, we easily see the most effective way to do things or how to set up a system to run smoothly. But without recognition and an invitation to give our input and affect the outcome, we can end up spinning our wheels, wasting energy, cultivating bitterness, and burning out.

Factor #4 - Values Conflict – mismatch between your core values and workplace or family.

Burnout is more likely when there is a mismatch between the core values embodied in your work environment or by your family or close friends, and your own core values.

For example, if you have a strong value of freedom and autonomy but are being micromanaged, you have a values mismatch that will cause stress and lead to burnout if not remedied. Or perhaps you are being asked to do things that conflict with your ethical framework, or you strongly disagree on key issues.

For Projectors, there is a predictable conflict between a personal value of self-care and workplace expectations of forty to fifty to sixty hours of work per week. If you own a business, the conflict can be between your expectations of how much you could or should get done versus how much energy you have for it. There can also be an internal conflict between a strong work ethic and commitment to your work versus family priorities, obligations, and expectations.

Factor #5 - Unfairness – favoritism, arbitrariness, secrecy, lack of justice.

This factor can easily lead to giving up and/or feeling resentment or bitterness. Research on burnout identifies an unfair workplace as a major source of stress but it can also happen in families, groups, close relationships, and even volunteer and charity work.

A common expression of the unhappy Projector is, "It's not fair!" So, there is already a sense of general unfairness for some Projectors. When adding unfairness in the workplace or family, burnout is a likely result.

Factor #6 - Loss of Community/Unsupportive Culture – not having supportive relationships or being in a toxic culture or environment.

A lack of social support, in and out of the work environment, is a significant factor in burnout, as is working in a toxic culture where disrespect or passive-aggressive behavior is the norm.

As Projectors, we need people but only the right people—those who recognize and call out our talents and who invite and follow our guidance. This includes our support networks as well as social circles. Wasting precious energy by sharing our wisdom when it is not recognized or welcomed is a risk factor for burnout. Any resulting feelings of rejection and bitterness only compound the problem.

Factor #7 - Projector's Lack of Consistent or Predictable Energy – wearing out, not keeping up, not meeting expectations of others.

Generators and Manifesting Generators hold the majority in this world, so they establish the rules and set the expectations, most of which we Projectors cannot fill consistently. Because we amplify Sacral energy from them, we can outwork the busiest Manifesting Generator… for a time. However, we cannot sustain that level of productivity indefinitely. Overworking and struggling to meet unrealistic expectations (from ourselves and others) can put us at serious risk of burnout.

The number of motor centers defined in your chart is not a good predictor of energy levels or stamina. The Will, Solar Plexus, and Root Centers are motors, all of which provide energy for taking action when defined. (The Sacral Center is also a motor but is never defined for Projectors.) Sometimes people assume that a no-motors Projector will have less energy than a Projector with defined motors. That has not been my experience. I know no-motors Projectors with far more energy than three-motors Projectors. So please do not use the number of defined motor centers in a chart for setting expectations or issuing judgments about energy levels and sustainability.

Factor #8 - Projector Pain – feeling rejected, ignored, isolated, unworthy, incapable, unfairly judged, and/or bitter.

Any of these examples of Projector pain can create an energy drain, lead to burnout or feelings of entrapment, and block the invitations and recognitions that would provide a way out.

Identifying the factor or multiple factors from this list that are causing stress is a necessary step in stopping that stress and taking appropriate action to reduce and eliminate ongoing sources of stress.

The Problem with Burnout

For some of us, being in or on the verge of burnout is such a familiar experience that we tend to ignore it as a warning signal. "It's just how things are! And there's not much I can do about it. I'm a Projector. This is my lot in life."

Burnout is a vital indicator that tells us we are out of balance in one or more areas of life, perhaps due to one or several of the factors above. We ignore it at our own peril. Feeling helpless and hopeless about our burnout just further compounds its intensity and negative effects on us and can keep us stuck there.

This may seem obvious, but it feels important to point out that burnout is not a desirable place to stay. As a friend of mine says, don't pitch a tent there.

In addition to well-documented effects of general burnout on the body, mind, and emotions, there are several Projector-specific issues that are particularly problematic and make recovering from burnout even more challenging.

Issue #1 - Lack of Invitations.

When you are in burnout, the invitations simply do not come, or the ones that do come are usually not correct for you. Maybe it is a built-in failsafe mechanism. When you are burned out, you probably do not have the energy, stamina, or resiliency to pick yourself up and step into an invitation—especially a big one. But being in burnout poses a very big problem for getting out of burnout, because recognition and invitations are key players in the process of getting back on your feet.

Issue #2 - Pattern of Not Taking Care of Ourselves.

You simply do not feel good when you are burned out. This goes way beyond the clinical and observable effects of physical burnout. Whichever factors or issues drove you into burnout are probably still in your life or have left a mark so deep that it is challenging to heal that wound and move on. Not only do you not feel well physically (exhaustion is not pleasant), but you also do not feel good about yourself and may blame yourself. When you don't feel good about yourself, it is hard to do the good things for yourself that will help you recover, especially if you did not have good habits of taking care of yourself before burnout.

Issue #3 - Not Fulfilling Our Role Makes Us Feel Worse.

Being burned out is like having a blanket over your light, smothering your brilliance and your magnificent essence. It is hard to be authentic and express your talents when you cannot get off the sofa. You cannot fulfill your vital role on the planet or help those who need your guidance when you can barely function in your own life or when you feel miserable most of the time.

Recovering from Burnout

Your first step is to embrace that recovering from burnout is your number one job. Nothing else you do or try will work well or be sustainable if you do not heal your burnout first. This means making your well-being your highest priority. This is not egocentric; initially, it is simply survival. Then, it allows you to be of greatest service to others when you have recovered. If you are not in good shape consistently, how can you fully be there for others?

According to Abraham-Hicks, "There is nothing more important than feeling good." It is truly an act of generosity to take care of yourself. Too often, caring and generous people have a pattern of putting themselves last on their list of who needs their care. You need to be at the top of your own list.

A vital part of healing is understanding what got you into burnout. What were you doing or not doing, thinking or not thinking, believing or not believing, and trusting or not trusting that landed you there? There is probably not just one but a cluster of related thoughts, beliefs, and actions that caused you to disconnect from your body and from your sense of what is right for you.

Yes, a compounding factor is the Projector's open Sacral Center challenge of "not knowing when enough is enough." But mastering that challenge is a lifelong learning process and something all Projectors need to make peace with. We get better at it over time, but it will still trip us up occasionally.

Burnout is something to learn from and commit to never repeating. It is a strong indicator that something needs to be fixed in your life. You do not need to be fixed—you are not broken (although it can feel that way). Something in your life needs to be fixed so you are not stressed to the point of burnout. Keep in mind that it could be your attitude or mindset that needs adjusting, not just external factors.

Here are a few tips to help you.

Tip #1 - Rest and restore your body and emotions; find joy again.

In full burnout, it is hard to get in touch with joy and ease and peace. But those, along with a lot of rest and a little pampering, will help your recovery. Find those things that bring even a glimmer of joy, a moment of peace, a delicious feeling of ease. Milk those for all they are worth. Savor them. Revel in them. Let your body, mind, heart, and soul relax. Do whatever you know to do for restoring your lifeforce energy and vitality. You may need to experiment to see what works at any given time. Remember to ask for help. Don't try to do it all yourself. That might be what landed you in burnout in the first place.

Tip #2 - Recognize where you went wrong; set intentions to make needed changes.

You cannot fix what you cannot identify. Get clarity. Use others as your sounding board (with their permission and cooperation, of course). Follow the clues until you find the underlying disempowering belief(s) that supported your actions and choices and get any help you need to shift them. EFT is a powerful technique that can help, and you can learn it for free online. Explore other options as well.

If there are circumstances you need to change in your life, career, or relationships, start considering new possibilities, setting intentions, and thinking through your plans. You may not have the energy right away to make needed changes in your life, but you can put things in motion energetically. Envision what you want. Feel into it, breathe into it, step into it in your mind. Relax into it. By doing this now, when your energy returns and invitations start to show up, you will know when they feel like a fit for your new direction. Be prepared to adjust and adapt as things move forward but stay focused on the essence of what you truly want.

Generally speaking, assess what works and does not work in the way you have been doing your life. You will probably notice that when you push to make things happen, not only do you move toward burnout, but you also don't even get the results you want and work so hard for. Pushing needs to be on your list of "things to let go of."

Tip #3 - Build resiliency!

Learning to build the Projector's version of sustainability into your life is paramount. This means having a core stability that allows you to weather minor challenges with grace and agility and bounce back from major setbacks with speed and strength. In upcoming chapters, we will explore the concept of Projector sustainability and address all nine of the Resiliency Keys. For now, let's focus on those Resiliency Keys that are specific to burnout.

Vitality – Managing energy wisely is critical to staying healthy and avoiding burnout. If you are low on this Resiliency Key, you are likely to ignore your body's signals that you need more rest and balance in your life and ignore the high levels of stress that are depleting your energy.

When you build strong resiliency here, you set and keep healthy boundaries, borrow energy appropriately from defined Sacral Centers (without overloading your own body), and make the most of your natural high-energy times. You are rested, calm, and sustainable with plenty of energy reserves.

Self-Worth – If you are trying to prove your value, you are going to overwork, overpromise, and overdeliver, leading you directly down the path of exhaustion and burnout.

When you have a healthy and resilient level of Self-Worth, you are not dependent on the approval of others to feel confident and secure in yourself. You make better choices and value your well-being enough to protect yourself from burnout.

Self-Trust – Not trusting yourself, and not trusting your Strategy and Authority as your best choice for decision making, can leave you without access to your reliable inner process for aligning your actions with your energy. This can lead to anxiety, uncertainty, self-doubt, not trusting your intuition, and using your fickle mind for making decisions instead of your wiser body. These can all make burnout far more likely.

When you are sure of yourself and feel connected to your inner knowing, you feel capable, trustworthy, and secure in your ability to take care of yourself and make healthy choices.

Empowerment – Feeling disconnected from your personal power and powerless to change circumstances around you are prescriptions for burnout and despair.

Stepping into self-empowerment gives you new options and choices and a renewed commitment to healing your burnout and remaining powerful and resilient.

Authenticity – When you are afraid to show up authentically as yourself, you send the wrong signals about Who You Really Are and attract recognition, invitations, and opportunities that are not right for you. You can then find yourself in situations where you must keep up the façade and cannot honor your truth or your needs.

Knowing and expressing your True Self sends the right signals and attracts people and opportunities in alignment with you and your energy. These situations increase your confidence and power so you can minimize factors that lead to burnout and maximize your healthy self-care.

Tip #4 - Focus on Transformation.

While in the throes of burnout, whether mild or severe, it is hard to imagine ever feeling *really* good again. But that is the goal, so it is crucially important to imagine it!

What might that look like? It will be different for each of us but here is an inspiring description to get you started:

You manage your energy beautifully. You say no in appropriate ways and at appropriate times. You do the same with yes. You have balanced energy, with plenty of reserves. You feel resilient, alive, and in control of what you can control in life. You bounce back from challenges and setbacks, learning lessons from those experiences. You do what brings you joy and restores you. You give to others from your saucer, not from your cup, and you know that your job is to keep your cup so full that it overflows so you have plenty of extra to give.

Final Words on Burnout... Your Story!

A crucial aspect of bouncing back and healing from burnout (whether a big, life-disrupting one or a small, annoying, and nagging one) is to change your story about it. **Change what you say about it... to yourself and to others.** If you say "I'm in burnout" then it is hard to shift it. Saying "I'm healing from or recovering from burnout" is better, but it keeps you stuck in the recovering phase. If you could say "I'm building resiliency every day" then you have shifted your story, your vibe, your aura, and your identity. I am not saying to ignore reality (well, maybe I am saying that a little!), but put your focus—your mind, your words, your actions, your values, your intentions—on where you are going and where you want to be and not where you no longer want to be.

Notice what your current stories are, and how they may be disempowering you and keeping you stuck. Play with different stories you could tell, about your situation now as well as your past. Come up with several. Pick one or a few that feel resonant for you and practice saying them, out loud. First, to the mirror, then to others. Notice and allow the shift in energy that happens as a result.

Now that we have explored burnout, the archnemesis of Projectors, let's turn our focus to the last topic in our sources of Projector pain: bitterness.

Chapter 13

Bitterness

No exploration of Projector pain and struggle would be complete without addressing bitterness. On Human Design charts, it is often listed as the "Life Theme" of Projectors, but bitterness is really our not-self theme. Our signature theme is success. This is an important distinction because many Projectors feel discouraged when they (mistakenly) believe they are doomed to experience bitterness their whole lives.

As our not-self theme, bitterness is the default emotional reaction for Projectors when things are not going well, but we are *not* fated to be consumed by it or mired in it all the time. We have more control than we think, and more control than some Human Design teachings would have us believe.

What is Bitterness?

From the field of clinical psychology, we learn from Stephen A. Diamond, Ph.D., that: "*Bitterness*, which I define as a chronic and pervasive state of smoldering resentment, is one of the most destructive and toxic of human emotions. Bitterness is a kind of morbid characterological hostility toward someone, something, or toward life itself, resulting from the consistent repression of anger, rage, or resentment regarding how one really has or perceives to have been treated. Bitterness is a prolonged, resentful feeling of disempowered and devalued victimization."[8]

Bitterness is one of those self-reinforcing energies: When you feel bitter you will attract less recognition and fewer invitations; with less recognition and fewer invitations you will likely become more bitter, further isolating yourself from others and becoming less and less invitable and attracting fewer and fewer correct invitations and recognition.

Bitterness is an end point but there is a progression that leads to it. If we can interrupt the progress at any step along the way, we can avoid what seems like (but does not have to be) the inevitable downward spiral into full bitterness. That progression starts with the common Projector refrain, "It's not fair."

It is easy for us as Projectors to experience that life is unfair. We don't have sustainable Sacral energy and may be called lazy. We must wait for recognition and invitations to get energy and take action. If we are not waiting to be asked for our guidance, we are called pushy or bossy. People do not listen to our wise (and excellent) advice. We can feel rejected, avoided, and sometimes much worse. It can seem that life is stacked against us.

That refrain, "It's not fair," may be justified but that does not mean expressing it, or even feeling it, is a good idea. It is easy to slide from there into resentment. Resentment is a little stronger and sticks around a little longer than the more transaction-based protest against unfairness. Resentment recognizes the pattern of unfairness that keeps showing up and tries to push back against that pattern. Resentment can become a theme in our lives, and it gets reinforced every time a perceived slight or injustice occurs. Like bitterness, it is self-reinforcing.

The final step is when our resentment cascades into full-blown bitterness. This becomes a vibe that we emit no matter what is going on around us. It does not have to be permanent, but while we are in it, we feel stuck and miserable.

The Many Faces of Bitterness

Bitterness and its precursors are insidious energies that may be simmering below conscious awareness. I have met many Projectors who proclaimed that they were not bitter, yet their bitter energy was very apparent. They were completely unaware (or completely in denial) about their bitterness. Like other emotions not consciously managed, bitterness may spew out unexpectedly and create mischief, betraying its existence underneath the veneer of "niceness."

A whole variety of intense personal experiences and big negative life events can trigger bitterness. Natural disasters (fires, floods, tornadoes, hurricanes, avalanches, mudslides, and the like) can leave people understandably resentful and bitter, as can being a victim of violence or trauma. Yet, there are victims of disasters and traumas who do not carry bitterness related to their experiences.

Failed or difficult relationships and failed efforts, like a business, job, or career, can also lead to bitterness. Any failure or perceived failure, big or small, can do it. So can the typical Projector issues of being misunderstood, not being recognized, not being heard, feeling rejected, and seeing others get the credit for your contribution—yet not all Projectors are bitter.

As the quoted definition above says, bitterness can be triggered by your *perceived* treatment by others as well as your interpretations of events. For example, someone may not be intending to judge or criticize you but if you perceive and interpret their words as criticism, you may feel resentment toward them. Or you may believe that your efforts on a project were a failure, but others may not see the results—or see you—that way. How we perceive things matters enormously.

Bitterness can seriously distort your view of yourself and the longer you are bitter, the worse it gets. It changes how everything feels. Whether triggered by words or deeds of others or by your own self-criticism, self-judgment, and self-condemnation, bitterness cloaks you in the not-self, keeping your True Self hidden. It is true suffering for the Projector, but it is not inevitable.

We are beginning to see a common thread here about bitterness: It is based on the conclusions we draw (about the events in our lives) and the stories we tell ourselves about them. In the last chapter, we looked at the role of the story we tell about our burnout and our recovery from burnout. It is the same with bitterness.

The Voices of Bitterness

Here are a few examples of what bitterness can sound like. See if any of these resonate with your experience and add your own versions (so you become aware of your self-talk and stop reinforcing these expressions of bitterness!).

"That's not fair."
"Nothing works, why even bother trying."
"I'll never find the place where I belong and where my contribution is valued."
"After everything I've done for them..."
"No one ever listens to me."
"I never feel recognized for who I really am."
"Why is it so much harder for me, when THEY have it so easy?"

"I was just trying to help!"

"People just want to use me but give me nothing in return."

"I'm just not good enough and never will be."

"I was just born with rotten luck and nothing I do will ever change that."

These statements can be said and believed by anyone, not just Projectors. But the difference is that while the Generator who has these thoughts may get frustrated and want to quit, the Projector can easily slide from resentment into the abyss of bitterness.

What to Do about Bitterness

Your best defense against bitterness is to start noticing your self-talk, the conclusions you draw, and the stories you tell about your struggles and pain. Pay particular attention to the *meanings* you give things. Bitterness can develop *from* these meanings or be reinforced *by* them. Here are some examples. "Nothing's working" means that I am incompetent. "It's too hard" means that I am incapable and maybe unworthy of being successful. "No one ever listens to me" means that I am not smart enough to be heard or valued. "It's not fair" means that life is not fair, so I will never win or succeed. "It's not my fault" means there is nothing I can do about it, so I won't take any responsibility or even try to fix it.

Tending to our mindset and stories is vitally important. Be deliberate in the thoughts you think, the conclusions you reach, the meanings you give to events and experiences, and the beliefs you hold.

Remember, this pattern can start rather innocently, with the simple reaction of "It's not fair." That can easily fester into resentment and get entrenched into full bitterness. It is a slippery slope.

As bitterness increases, your energetic attractiveness and invitability decrease, creating a negative spiral of proof. At the very least, you are broadcasting a "negative vibe" that is perceivable to others and is quite off-putting and repelling. While this vibe pushes away recognition and invitations, it may actually be a form of self-protection. It is like a wall or barrier that tries to protect you from further hurt and pain. It keeps others out.

This shows us that there may actually be a valid purpose for us to experience and express bitterness! When we recognize it as a protection mechanism, we can see that bitterness is telling us that we are under some "perceived attack" by others, that we are in survival mode, and that we are just trying to prevent further harm to our self-value and self-esteem.

Further, when we can see bitterness as an indicator that something is "off" in our perceptions and/or beliefs, it can serve an even greater purpose: It can help us identify and resolve the underlying issue, not just the transactional circumstances that led us there.

The underlying issue is NOT what the other person said or did or meant. The issue is with your mindset.

The Antidote to Bitterness

We humans have far greater choice in our mindset, which includes our thoughts, words, actions, and beliefs, than we think we have. You may have a default perspective that sees the glass as half-empty instead of half-full, but that default is not set in stone. It is mostly out of habit, and habits can change. Mindset can be changed. How you view and interpret the people and world around you can change. You may have a habit of taking what people say to you or about you personally, but you are not forced to do that. You are choosing to do that, although it may not feel like a choice most of the time. The trick is to bring your default pattern into your conscious awareness when it is happening, so you can deliberately make a different choice in that moment.

I admit this isn't easy at first. You may not recognize the pattern until after it has played out. But recognizing it then at least brings it into your awareness and gives you the opportunity to think about how you might handle things differently the next time it happens. This makes it more likely that you will notice the pattern earlier next time. Eventually, you will be able to catch yourself *before* the pattern plays out and make a choice in that moment (or even before that moment) to shift your interpretation and reaction to one that is more empowering. This usually means not taking things personally, not trying to correct everyone, and not letting real or perceived judgments from others take up residence in your head.

When you can separate the opinions and reactions of others from who you know yourself to be, you can stand in your own power and value, and then their opinions are just that—their opinions. Their reactions are simply their reactions. I am not saying to be rude to people, but do not let them disturb your positive sense of yourself. You can value their input without feeling hurt or resentful. You can avoid the slide into bitterness when you are unshakable in your own self-worth. It may not be easy at first, but it is SO worth getting to that place. Not only is it possible, but it is also doable. This is not only my own experience but that of countless Projector clients who have stepped into their value and are no longer willing to let others derail them. Let this new pattern become your default perspective and your new habit.

When you first started driving, you were not yet in the habit of checking the gas gauge to see if the car needed gas. Maybe you ran out of gas a time or two before you developed the habit of checking that gauge regularly and using it as an indicator of action you need to take. Once you developed this useful habit, you did not need to think about it anymore—it became automatic. You can also develop the habit of detecting bitterness in its early stages and completely avoiding it.

Let's now circle back to bitterness as the not-self theme for Projectors. Yes, it is the so-called default emotional reaction for us. But when seen in this new light, we can view the early stages of bitterness (protests of unfairness and resentment) as early warning signs that we are headed down that slippery slope and are just trying to protect ourselves, and now we can do something about it. That self-defeating downward slide into bitterness is avoidable. You *can* adjust your mindset, thoughts, beliefs, and reactions. Those are all within your control.

I know Projectors who exude no bitterness at all. Not even a whiff of "It's not fair." They have transcended the default lower expression of their Type, and you can too.

Resiliency Keys for Resolving Bitterness

We will fully explore the Nine Resiliency Keys in Part Four, but because bitterness can be such a pervasive and debilitating issue for Projectors, take a quick look here at the six Keys that are specifically relevant to bitterness.

Emotional Wisdom - If you are low on this Resiliency Key and your Emotional Solar Plexus Center is open, you may experience bitterness from feeling responsible for handling other people's emotional stuff and from being overwhelmed by it all. If your Emotional Center is defined and you do not understand your emotional wave, you may be bitter from feeling there is something wrong with you because your emotions are so changeable, so intense, and so uncontrollable.

When you are higher in the expression of this Resiliency Key, you handle everything better. This especially includes your perceptions and interpretations as well as actual criticism and judgment from others. You also better navigate your relationships and life's challenges. You are less likely to feel overwhelmed and bitter about emotions. If you are emotionally open, you know that others' emotions are not yours to manage, and you can effectively be a screen, not a sponge. If you are emotionally defined, you are not blindsided or confused by your emotional wave and the intensity of your own emotional energy.

Also, please note that emotions like anger, grief, or guilt may be linked to bitterness and may need to be released or resolved themselves. When you start to poke at your bitterness, you are likely to uncover some related issues.

Lovability - Feeling unlovable can lead to bitterness. This can escalate into feeling that "nobody loves me" or worse, "everyone hates me." Some Projectors are so prickly that they create a self-fulfilling situation: I'm not lovable and everybody hates me anyway, so I'll push people away and not let anyone get close.

When you are secure in your sense of Lovability, you can navigate through disappointments, tough times, and even rejections more easily without feeling victimized or falling into bitterness.

Self-Worth - If you are not solid in your sense of Self-Worth and you feel uninvited, unrecognized, or invisible, it is easy to feel unworthy and bitter.

When you are secure in your internal sense of Self-Worth, the judgments or reactions of others are less likely to send you into self-doubt or resentment.

Decisiveness - Making incorrect decisions (not following your Strategy and Authority) can lead to burnout and bitterness when those decisions do not work out well. You may feel you cannot do anything right and even feel hopeless about getting your life to work.

Following and trusting your Strategy and Authority can lead to conservation of your energy, greater access to resources, and a much higher likelihood of success in every aspect of your life.

Empowerment - Feeling powerless and like a victim is a classic path to bitterness. Then, feeling stuck in that bitterness is further disempowering.

When you are more secure in your sense of Empowerment, it is easier to observe life's events from a healthier perspective, not take them personally, step into your full and natural power, and tell a new, more empowering story about your life and experiences.

Authenticity - Feeling rejected for who you are or hiding because you do not feel good about yourself is another path to bitterness.

When you are being authentic and fully expressing your True Self, you position yourself to be accurately recognized and appreciated for Who You Really Are.

Transforming Bitterness

This seems counter-intuitive, but it is true: Bitterness is not bad. It is a useful indicator. It should not be feared or ignored. Just remember that it is not personal. It is a familiar path we Projectors take that tells us something is out of alignment. When you treat bitterness as an indicator, you can take appropriate remedial action, including changing your interpretations or beliefs. When the gas gauge in your car indicates that gas needs to be added to the tank, you do not want to slap a happy sticker over the gauge and pretend all is well. Similarly, you don't want to pretend your bitterness is not there. You need to acknowledge and deal with it.

So, make friends with bitterness. Notice it with compassion and detachment. Ask it, "What are you telling me?" Ask yourself, "What thoughts or beliefs do I hold that are leading to this bitterness, or underlying this bitterness, or simply keeping it activated?"

In order to heal and transform your bitterness, you need to really pay attention. Hypersensitivity is a symptom of bitterness, so notice if your awareness is tuned to pick up any hint of rejection or criticism, which instantly increases bitterness. What are your sensitivity receptors tuned to and looking for?

Notice and be careful about the conclusions you draw, and the meanings you assign.

Pay close attention to the story you tell about the reasons behind someone else's actions. It is probably a complete fabrication.

Remember that the high expression of the signature theme of Projectors is "the sweetness of success." Savor that idea for a moment. Notice and focus on what *is* working in your life and on the invitations and recognition you *do* get, even the little ones. Do not focus on what you don't get. Focus on what feels good and what you want more of. Celebrate what feels good.

Become aware of, then address and release, the thoughts and beliefs behind any bitterness you harbor. One baby step at a time, choose a thought or belief that feels a little better, a little more positive, a little more empowering.

While a little pain may be inevitable in life (it helps us learn and grow), suffering is entirely optional. Make sure you are not adding drama, blame, victimhood, or martyrdom to your pain.

Now that we have trudged through the pain that Projectors feel and have looked at a few ways to combat the different kinds of pain, we can turn our attention fully to the tools for healing these Projector wounds. But first, let's meet another Projector. She experienced considerable pain in her otherwise fairytale life.

Meet a Projector - Princess Diana

This shy Projector from royal lineage in England was thrust onto the public stage at age twenty when the world watched her storybook romance and wedding to Prince Charles in 1981. The intense public scrutiny was hard on her at first as she was not yet self-confident and secure in who she was. Charles was apparently not very supportive on that score, which did not help.

Sadly, this beautiful and gracious lady had a troubled married life despite the regal trappings. She had a very busy schedule and many royal functions for which she had to look and be at her best. It was undoubtedly demanding and exhausting, plus she was a devoted mother to their two sons.

Her Human Design chart very clearly shows her passion for family, community, and worthy causes. She was an enthusiastic and effective fundraiser for charities and causes around the world. She could speak for others with her Open Throat and communicate very effectively when asked or recognized (Oprah Winfrey also has an Open Throat). Her Open Identity Center let her take people in at a soul level—giving her the easy connection and compassion she was famous for. Her chart also shows her vulnerabilities and lower-expression potentials.

Learn more about Princess Diana and details of her Human Design chart in my Celebrity Chart Review of her on my website. Find the link from the Resources Page.

Name:	Princess Diana
Birth Date:	01 July 1961, 19:45
Birth Place:	Sandringham, Norfolk, United Kingdom
Type:	Orchestrator (Projector)
Inner Authority:	Creative (Solar Plexus)
Profile:	1/3 - Resource / Explorer
Definition:	Split - Large
Strategy:	Wait for Recognition and Invitation
Themes:	Success / Bitterness
Incarnation Cross:	RAX Tension 2
Channels:	3041 - Intention (Recognition) 3740 - Administration (Community) 0463 - Potentiality (Logic)

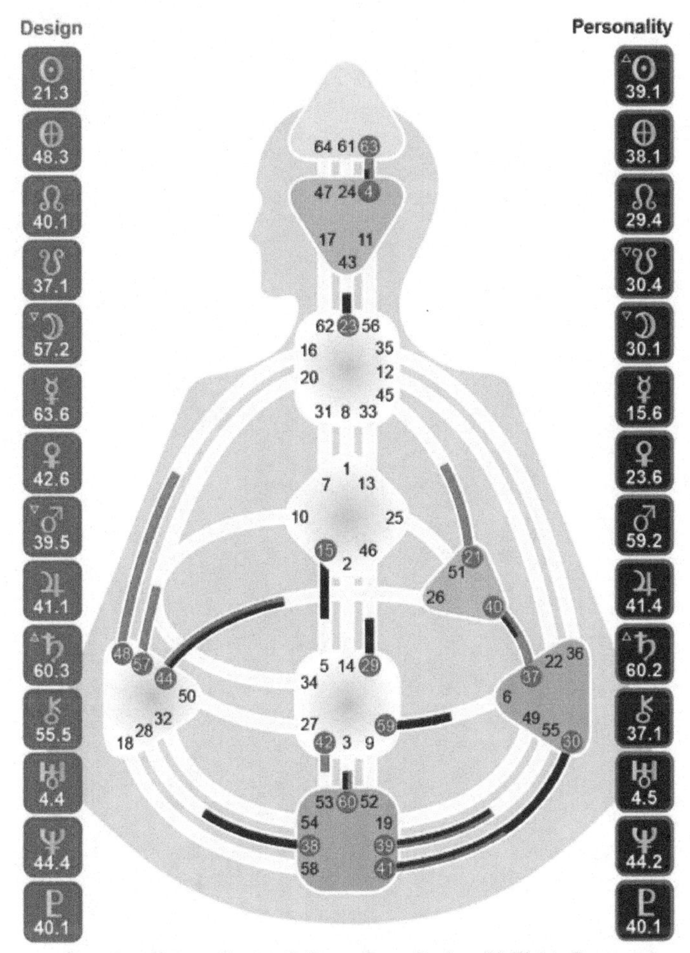

PART FOUR

HEALING THE PROJECTOR

Doing the Work

There are no shortcuts to true healing, yet it can happen quickly when you do your inner work.

Having a vision is more powerful than having goals.

~ Natalie Collins

PART FOUR

Healing the Projector

Introduction to Healing the Projector

As a Projector, what do you really want? I mean, *really*? This is a vital question, and the answers can be transformative. When we begin to heal and reach for a healthier, happier, more empowered version of ourselves, we need to have clarity about what we want our lives to be. We need a vision for what we are creating.

This is true at a global level as well as a personal level. Healing happens from the ground up, from the inside out, and from the micro to the macro. So, let's begin with your personal healing which calls for *your* clarity about the life and life experiences you want to create.

Here are a few suggestions to try on and see which are a fit for you. As always, add your own. These lists are meant to help begin your self-exploration process, not end it. Let your heart speak to you about what it truly wants.

As Projectors we want to feel:

- whole, complete, that we are firing on all cylinders.
- that there is nothing broken, nothing missing.
- relaxed, self-confident, secure.
- seen, noticed, heard, recognized.
- accepted, appreciated, that we belong and are valued.
- respected, honored, included, invited, welcomed.
- loved unconditionally by ourselves and by others.

As Projectors we want to be:

- allowed to be ourselves.
- given the time and space we need.
- invited to guide the energy of others.
- consulted for our knowledge and wisdom.

- supported financially and in all other ways, for being who we are (not for doing things for others).
- so fulfilled and abundant that we have plenty of energy and resources to give to others.

As Projectors we want to:

- live our purpose.
- express our gifts.
- contribute to the greater good.
- feel blessed, abundant, successful, and empowered.

To address our Projector pain, we want to:

- heal our wounds and recover our energy and our self-respect.
- be liberated from bitterness, disappointment, resentment.
- have the freedom to allow our lives to unfold naturally and easily.
- end the struggle, uncertainty, and despair.
- stop the shame, embrace the waiting, avoid the burnout.
- upgrade our mindset so it supports us instead of sabotages us.

How do you get to where *you* want to be? It is a journey. It could be a steep and rocky path for you, or a long and winding one. Or you could have a swift epiphany or major shift that changes everything quickly and easily. The next three chapters will give you tools and tips that will not only support your immediate healing but also give you processes and information you can use and rely on for the rest of your life. This is the work. Take your time with it, but also allow for those surprising quick shifts that can change everything.

Chapter 14

Projector Sustainability

We need a completely new definition of sustainability. Like me, you may feel beaten up and even defeated by the traditional Human Design teachings that Projectors are "not sustainable." How the heck are we supposed to function in this world without being sustainable? That feels debilitating. They might as well tie big rocks to our feet, throw us in the river, and tell us to swim. No way is that going to work.

At the larger level, all of humanity needs a new definition of sustainability because the way we are living and using/destroying planetary resources is not sustainable. While that is a big conversation for another time, it is a deeply relevant issue for us as Projectors. As we redefine sustainability for ourselves, I am confident we can guide our fellow beings into better sustainability for us all and for our planet. I believe this is part of our cosmic purpose.

Let's begin at the micro level with sustainability in our personal lives before we try to address the macro level of humanity.

Being Sustainable at a Personal Level

While we do not have consistent Sacral energy, because our Sacral Center is not defined, we still function in this world and many of us function quite well—whether others *consider* us sustainable or not. Sacral workforce and lifeforce energy are not the only indicators of sustainability. As we have seen, the number of motor centers we have defined in our chart is not an indicator of energy or sustainability. So how do we redefine and then assess our sustainability? What constitutes being sustainable?

I submit that there are two important components to consider. One is external and one is internal. The external aspect is our physical ability to function in life and have a life that works for us—meaning we can satisfy our needs and our desires. That may be safety, security, and comfort. It may be adventure and excitement. It may be creativity and contribution. It may be faith and surrender, or any combination of these and much more. It means having our basic needs met (food, shelter, safety) without constant stress about them, then having what we like most in life. It means relationships that are satisfying, work that is fulfilling, financial flow that sustains us, and health and well-being that support all we do and want to do in life.

The internal aspect is the more important of the two, as it deeply influences all aspects of the external component. For simplicity, I'll call this internal component our mindset. As we have seen throughout our time together so far, how we view and interpret the world around us determines everything about our experience of ourselves, other people, and the world at large. Our mindset is the lens through which we see and experience *everything*.

When we adopt the lens through which others see the world, we lose our way, and we lose ourselves. The world view of other Types is not the Projector's world view. My lens as a Projector is not the same as your lens as a Projector. Each person views and experiences the world differently.

A Generator or Manifesting Generator may view sustainability as their ability to keep going, day after day, consistently, no matter what. That definition does not work for Projectors, Manifestors, or Reflectors. A Manifestor may view sustainability as the capacity to pursue their creative flow of energy whenever they choose, and trust that their flow will keep showing up even though it may not be a steady stream that is always on. That is not the lens of the other Types. Reflectors may see their sustainability as being able to remain outside the main flow of busy energy on the planet, where they can sample the energy and experiences of others and follow where their own unique flow may take them.

Let's step back a little further before we get to Projectors and to you specifically. Sustainability, in general, means the ability to continue something for a long time without it being used up or destroyed. What is actually needed for such a sustained effort? **Sufficient resources.** Those could be personal energy or physical resources such as money, food, water, bandwidth, etc. The operative word here is *sufficient*, or sufficiency.

Sufficiency means having enough to meet the needs of a situation. If you have enough, why would you need more? If you have enough in each moment and each situation, then you are sufficient and sustainable. You have enough, consistently. Instead of striving for overabundance, you find the sweet spot where "enoughness" is sufficient to your needs *and* wants.

Financial expert and small business consultant Mackey McNeill says this, "Enoughness is a state of being. Enoughness is a way to live that honors yourself, brings you peace and honors the planet."[9]

Funny (or ironic) that a core issue for Projectors is not knowing when enough is enough! When we don't even know what enough is—what it looks like, feels like, tastes like—then we cannot know when we have it. We don't know when to stop, when to be satisfied, when we have reached sufficiency.

What if getting in touch with enoughness is all we need to do to redefine sustainability for ourselves? What if feeling that we are enough, *knowing* that we are enough, just as we are right now, is what can give us Projector Sustainability? We don't need to meet the other Types' definitions of being sustainable. But we do need a working definition for Projectors that supports our ongoing well-being and viability in the world, so we no longer feel less-than when inevitably compared to other Types, especially the energy Types. We need a sustainability of our own.

Tools and Measures of Projector Sustainability

What does it take, specifically, for us to be sustainable in our own unique Projector way? What does that look like?

There are several things we can do that will help enormously, and a few things we can stop doing because they do not help at all. We have talked about many of them already as we have progressed through our empowerment journey together. Now we get to pull them all into one place and assemble them like tools we can keep in our tool belt, to use if and when appropriate.

Each of the approaches below encompasses several aspects of awareness and healing, so they represent useful groupings of attitudes and actions. They are roughly in an order that has a progression to it, but feel free to use them as needed in any order. The two biggest themes weaving through these "tools" are energy management and self-worth.

Tool #1 - Setting Healthy Boundaries; Saying NO.

Your first line of defense is being clear about what is your responsibility and what is not and saying no when appropriate. Yes, this is harder than it sounds at first, until it becomes a blessing as an ingrained habit. Clearly defining boundaries and responsibilities can get tangled up with many Projector issues, such as overpromising, that we previously explored. Making decisions using Authority will help you say no to the incorrect opportunities and responsibilities that come your way.

We easily blow past healthy boundaries when we are *trying* to be seen, heard, recognized, included, invited, and valued, and also when we are trying to prove our worthiness, prove our lovability, prove that we care, prove we are wise, demonstrate our knowledge, and show how capable and competent we are. We overpromise and then must overdeliver. Most of us are classic overachievers, although sometimes we get so discouraged that we want to give up entirely.

To set and hold healthy boundaries, we need to be strong in all nine of the Resiliency Keys, which we will cover in the next chapter.

Tool #2 - Being Correct in How You Present Yourself.

When you are authentic in expressing yourself, you will attract the people who want and need what you can offer, and who will value you for who you are. This authenticity includes clarity about your role as well as your skills and knowledge. Just because you *can* do something does not mean you *should* do it or become known for it.

Emphasize your knowledge, wisdom, and role as a guide. De-emphasize your ability to *do* things and to work hard at them. Remember that we have a not-self drive to prove ourselves, so choose to stand firmly in knowing that you are magnificent and amazing just as you are and you do not need to prove yourself to anyone, not even to yourself! Also, remember your ability to amplify Sacral energy and be a super-doer on steroids and choose to use that capability frugally and wisely.

When you stand in your power as *you*, your clear signal (your lighthouse beacon) will draw the right people (and ships) to you, so you can skillfully and safely guide them to where they want to go. It is really quite simple when seen in this light. It is when we are trying to be what we are not (because we think that will get us what we want) that we send the wrong signals. Then we attract the wrong recognition and wrong invitations. When those are the only ones we attract, we get trapped and can be forced (due to circumstances) to say yes to those wrong invitations, which creates a negative loop leading to bitterness, burnout, lack of success, and lack of sustainability.

Tool #3 - Recognizing and Saying YES to the Right Invitations.

To receive the right invitations, you need to present yourself authentically and embrace an empowered version of waiting for those invitations. If you are waiting with impatience, bitterness, anxiety, etc., you are pushing them away.

Once the correct recognitions and invitations are coming your way, then you need to recognize them as correct invitations. Some may be easy to miss if you are distracted or looking in the wrong places. Once you see them as legitimate invitations to consider, then you apply your Authority to assess if they are correct for you right now.

As noted above, our not-self drive to prove ourselves by working hard can distort our ability to tune in to our Authority and sense whether an opportunity is truly aligned with our energy.

When saying yes, keep in mind that the opportunity will bring you energy and resources. You will still need to manage your energy appropriately. You need to set and maintain healthy boundaries. Invitations do not last indefinitely, so you need to check in with yourself and the others involved to see if the energy of the invitation and its flow of resources are still there.

Tool #4 - Re-framing Invitations as Collaborations.

To wait for invitations in an empowered way, you need to shift your perspective on them. If you see yourself as a victim of your Strategy and at the mercy of others, with no control at all, you will be stressed and bitter and will repel the invitations you want. That is a no-win situation.

It can take time to develop trust in your Strategy and Authority. It happens when you see them working in your life. When you can trust your decision process, trust yourself to recognize and make the right decisions, and also trust your role and place in the world, the way the world looks begins to change. You begin to see your entire life experience as an elegant dance that brings the right person to you on the dance floor at the right time with the music, and you dance and twirl together until it is time to move on. Some twirls are short. Some can last a lifetime.

When you see that the universe, the mechanics of energy attraction, and the recognizers and inviters out there are all your partners and collaborators in this dance we call life, you will have an easier time waiting and you will actually enjoy the process and the flow. You will welcome your waiting time and the fruits of your waiting. You will see the big picture of what is happening and the sheer beauty of the mechanics. You will know that the process is not personal—it's energy mechanics—but it is also deeply personal in its correctness for you.

Tool #5 - Keeping Your Cup So Full That It Overflows.

It is easy to give tips about self-care and encourage you to follow them, but if you do not have a healthy relationship with yourself or if you have deep wounds that need healing, just reading a few tips will not help. What needs to be addressed first is your fundamental sense of Who You Are and of your immense importance to the planet, along with the value of your contribution to those you are specifically meant to help.

It is hard to apply any of the tools described above if you do not believe that you are worthy of being successful, empowered, and sustainable. If you don't believe that you deserve to be treated well by others, then you won't be. We train others how to treat us by how we treat ourselves. We set the bar. It is an inside job. To repair your relationship with yourself, focus on the Nine Resiliency Keys in the next chapter and all five chapters in Part Five - Becoming Empowered.

With healing comes renewed strength and new ways to keep your cup full. The best way to protect your precious resources (time, energy, happiness, vitality) is to keep your cup of joy so full that it overflows, then you have plenty of abundance to give to others. If you give from your cup, you risk depleting your resources. When you give from your saucer, you are giving from your overflow. (Credit to Lisa Nichols for this wonderful analogy.)

Our job as humans is to keep our cups so full all the time that we have plenty to give to others and can do so joyfully. To do this successfully, we must believe that we deserve an overflowing cup. However, we don't have to earn it through hard work! Just because we are here, alive and breathing, we are deserving. Our cup of joy gets filled by *doing* the things and *being* in ways that increase our joy. Here is where self-care tips can be very useful by giving us great ideas.

Remember to use the lessons from the Projector pain chapters. Don't tie recognition from others to your sense of self-worth—they are separate. Manage your energy. Learn to rest. Believe that you are not broken. Trust yourself. Make peace with What Is. Don't compare yourself to others. Know that we are *all* born worthy and, no, you are not the exception to that.

Leading the Sustainability Shift

As we shift into new modes of sufficiency and enoughness, and new definitions of success and sustainability, we begin to carve new pathways in the world and create new neural pathways in our brains. We demonstrate to ourselves and the world what a healthy, respectful, and sustainable version of enoughness looks like, and what a healthy relationship with ourselves looks like. If imitation is the highest form of flattery, then leading by positive example might be the most powerful way of changing the world.

But what does it take to model this new sustainability? How can we feel sufficient in every area of our lives, even when we are not exactly where we want to be yet?

The first step is to relax our standards of perfection. Sustainability is a process and being "a work in progress" is perfect enough. Perfection is overrated anyway. The second step is to embrace life as a team sport, not a solo marathon. Don't try to go at it alone. Get help. Ask for support. Support others. Process together. Have friends be your sounding board and return the favor as appropriate. We learn more from what does not work than from what does, so don't be afraid to make mistakes. They are part of the learning process, especially if you have a 3 or 6 in your Profile.

Review and use the above tools which can also be self-assessment opportunities.

#1 How well are you setting and keeping healthy boundaries? Saying no?

#2 How well are you attracting correct recognition and invitations, which means presenting yourself accurately?

#3 Are you noticing the invitations that come your way and saying yes to the right ones?

#4 How well are you waiting with a healthy and positive mindset, and seeing inviters as your collaborative dance partners?

#5 Are you keeping your cup overflowing and giving to others happily from your saucer?

The online world of social media offers many opportunities to connect with like-minded people who are eager to gather into communities. These days, there are many Projector groups to join and participate with. There is nothing quite like being with a group of fellow Projectors. It feels like being able to breathe again, after holding your breath for a long time. Ask questions, share experiences, offer support, ask for support.

How to Support Planetary Sustainability

At the global level, sustainability means meeting our own needs without compromising the ability of future generations to meet their needs. In addition to natural resources, these needs include social interaction and economic resources. We need self-sustaining and regenerative ecological balance as well as compassionate humanitarian balance.

Planetary sustainability is the intersection of getting your own needs met in ways that are sustainable for you *and* for the planet. I propose that we are the ones to guide this transformation. And I propose that it begins with the embrace of enoughness. Being enough. Having enough. Doing enough. Not *more* than enough. Just enough. Enough IS enough. We need to learn how to recognize WHEN enough is enough. That is our journey. And then we must share our awareness of enoughness with the world. That is our role. To fulfill our role, each of us must trust that we are enough just as we are.

The straightforward answer to how to support planetary sustainability is to support your personal sustainability and enoughness first. We will explore how to do that in the next chapter.

Chapter 15

The Nine Resiliency Keys for Projectors

In 2013, Karen Curry Parker shared the latest evolution of her work with Human Design in the form of eight Resiliency Keys, later expanded to nine. These Keys are correlated with the nine Energy Centers of the Human Design chart, but they do not match up one-to-one with the centers. That is the beauty of the Keys. They show how different centers work together to support (or challenge) our core strengths as humans, such as Courage, Authenticity, Self-Worth.

Karen says that while vulnerability and potential pain show up at multiple levels in our Human Design chart and our lives, we cannot effectively address the deeper levels until we have established resiliency in these nine key areas. She developed these Keys to systematically help people release beliefs and patterns that keep them from living an abundant, joyful life that is aligned with their design.

The material in this chapter is drawn from the many courses I have taken from Karen and the programs I have taught using this information.

An Introduction to the Nine Resiliency Keys

Originally part of the Healing by Human Design System™ which evolved into the Quantum Alignment System™, these Resiliency Keys are the expression of certain vital qualities in our lives. They are interrelated and working on one Resiliency Key can create change in another, so be open to shifts in Keys you have not worked on yet. Each Key relates to one or more energy centers on the chart.

While these Keys are for all Types, our focus in exploring them in detail will be on the unique challenges and opportunities for Projectors within these Keys. Although there is no substitute for the depth of understanding and integration you receive in a private Human Design reading, I have found that many wounded and struggling Projectors need more than a reading to support their healing process. These Resiliency Keys are the missing piece, especially when addressed using Karen's

Quantum Alignment System™ (QAS). This system focuses on emotional clearing through EFT (Emotional Freedom Techniques) and other supportive modalities such as essential oils, flower essences, and inquiry. Visit the Resources Page for more information.

Here is a quick overview of the Nine Keys in their highest expressions:

Emotional Wisdom	You manage your emotional energy well. You understand your emotional wave or how you respond to the emotional energy of others.
Courage	You move through challenges gracefully and trust your Strategy and Authority.
Vitality	You manage your energy well. You have balanced energy and productivity, with plenty of reserves.
Lovability	You feel inherently and unconditionally lovable.
Self-Worth	You have core-deep self-confidence and worthiness, and practice healthy self-care.
Self-Trust	You are comfortable relying on your inner knowing; you feel capable and dependable (trustworthy).
Decisiveness	You make good and aligned choices, and you follow through.
Empowerment	You express personal power in healthy ways, have a connection to infinite power, and empower others.
Authenticity	You are fully self-expressed in healthy ways, creating a life you love.

How to Use These Keys for Healing

These Keys provide you with powerful access to the areas of pain and misalignment in your life so you can see them, address them, soothe them, and support their healing.

In the Healing the Projector Level 1 program that I teach with my colleague Robin Gallob, we address one Key each week on a group Zoom call. After exploring the Key, we use EFT to tap on the issues that come up related to that Key. Volunteers sit in the virtual Chair of Change (commonly known as the Hot Seat) to share their issues and tap, with Robin leading and the group tapping along. The impacts and healing are profound.

Although it is beyond the scope of this book to provide the full process that we follow in that program, you are encouraged to use the descriptions below to understand the Keys and rate yourself on your current expression of each. This will reveal to you the places where you can focus to address underlying beliefs and wounds and to heal and strengthen your expression and resiliency. With this awareness, you can apply clearing techniques that work for you. You may find it helpful to work with a QAS practitioner privately or in a group program. (See the Resources Page to learn more about QAS and the Healing the Projector Level 1 program.)

Take your time going through the information below about each Key. Especially spend time with the sample Assessment Questions. Your thoughtful answers will be deeply illuminating and healing. Be sure to rate yourself on each Key, then periodically re-rate yourself as you continue to heal, grow, and step into your empowerment.

Resiliency Key: Emotional Wisdom

Your experience of this Resiliency Key depends on whether your Emotional Solar Plexus Center is defined or undefined/open. The emotional energy of this center gives richness, depth, and creative flow to human life. We all experience this energy whether it is defined or undefined in our charts.

Emotional Wisdom with a Defined Solar Plexus

You have an emotional wave, with variable highs and lows over time. Your wave is a natural cycle and not a problem to be fixed, so embrace it. Allow yourself to be where you are on your wave. Don't fight it, diagnose it, or try to rush through it. Your Authority is Emotional, so you need to wait for clarity before making decisions.

Emotional Wisdom with an Undefined Solar Plexus

You take in others' emotional energy and amplify it, so it is easy to think those emotions are your emotions. Learn to be a screen not a sponge so you can let those emotions flow through you but not get stuck in you. You might have a pattern of avoiding upsetting others and trying to keep everyone happy, but you *can* take back your power and stand in your truth. This is especially important for Projectors who are often natural people pleasers.

The Emotional Wisdom Spectrum

Low expressions:

> Impulsiveness, paralysis (no action), despair, depression, codependency, drama, being overly sensitive, trying to keep others happy, inability to separate yourself from others.

High expressions:

> You manage your emotional energy well; you are not derailed by it. You wait for clarity if this center is defined, and you embrace the fullness of your emotional experience. If this center is open, you are aware of the emotions of others without identifying with them or becoming affected by them.

Sample Assessment Questions

If Defined:

- How well do you understand and manage your own emotions?
- What is it like for you to wait for emotional clarity? What happens if you don't?

If Undefined:

- How much trouble do you have letting go of emotions that are not yours?
- Do you feel responsible for keeping everyone else happy?

Self-Rating on Emotional Wisdom

How healthy is your expression of and your relationship with emotional energy? How emotionally wise are you?

Rate yourself on a scale of 1-10

10 = I am very healthy and wise regarding my emotions.

1 = I am not at all healthy or wise regarding my emotions.

Resiliency Key: Courage

Courage is the capacity to push through fear and take appropriate and aligned action at the right time. Courage can affect the expression of many of the other Resiliency Keys. The centers related to this Key are the G Center (aka Identity Center), Emotional Solar Plexus Center, Sacral Center, and Spleen Center. Each of these centers has its own challenges related to the Key of Courage.

Courage and the G Center (aka Identity Center)

The G is the center for self-identity, love, and direction in life. The challenges here include having the courage to see yourself and know yourself, and to face your fears of not being loved, not being accepted, and not knowing what direction to take.

Courage and the Solar Plexus Center

The Solar Plexus Center is the seat of emotional energy, which gives such depth and richness to life. Here the challenges include the courage to do what feels right, and the courage to wait through your emotional wave if this center is defined. There are also fears to be faced related to making the wrong decisions, whether this center is open or defined.

Courage and the Sacral Center

The Sacral is the center for lifeforce and workforce energy. Managing and leveraging energy is a crucial issue for Projectors who can experience a theme of being afraid they will run out of energy and/or appear weak, so they overdo it (and don't know when enough is enough!). The challenge here is for you to courageously stand up for the appropriate management of your energy.

Courage and the Spleen Center

The Spleen is the center for survival instincts and well-being. The fears of the Spleen may seem paralyzing but can be pushed through. The challenge here is simply to face your fears and strengthen your courage to move through them. (See the Resources Page for a link to access my series of articles on the Fears of the Spleen.)

The Courage Spectrum

Low expressions:

> Fear and anxiety, analysis paralysis, confusion, false bravado, not facing your fears.

High expressions:

> You move through challenges gracefully. You have the courage to trust your Strategy and Authority, and to make decisions and follow through with them. You have the courage to trust that your G Center is guiding you to what you need—in other words, you trust your process.

Sample Assessment Questions

- How is fear keeping you from doing what you want to do? Where is it holding you back?
- Are you getting stuck because of specific fear themes? Look at which of your Spleen Gates are defined in your chart and their associated fears: fear of being inadequate (48), fear of the future (57) or of the past (44), fear of letting others down (50), fear of failing (32), fear that it is all futile (28), fear that you will never get it right (18).

Self-Rating on Courage

How healthy is your expression and experience of Courage? How much does fear hold you back?

Rate yourself on a scale of 1-10

10 = I am courageous in facing my fears and taking appropriate action.

1 = I am fearful and holding back.

Resiliency Key: Vitality

Vitality is a balancing act between energy outflows and restorative inflows. It is about leveraging and using energy wisely and effectively and being a good steward of the energy available. The centers related to this Key are the Sacral Center, Throat Center, Will Center (also called Heart or Ego Center), and Root Center. Each of these centers has its own challenges related to Vitality.

Vitality and the Sacral Center

The Sacral is the center for lifeforce and workforce energy. Managing and leveraging energy to support vitality is a crucial issue for us as Projectors who do not have reliable access to the Sacral's motor energy. We take it in from others but do not have our own consistent flow of it. Plus, we can be afraid that we will run out of energy and/or appear weak, so we overdo things. The challenge is to use amplified Sacral energy wisely, learn how to tell when enough is enough, and embrace the concept of enoughness to manage vitality sustainably.

Vitality and the Throat Center

The Throat Center governs our communication and our ability to manifest effective action. This center manages energy, but it is not a motor—it has no energy of its own. When we as Projectors do not wait to be recognized and invited and do not use our Authority to know what to step into, we waste precious effort and can negatively affect our thyroid gland (which manages metabolism). Energy deficits and a compromised thyroid can degrade our overall well-being and drain our vitality.

Vitality and the Will Center

The Will Center is our source of willpower and the seat of our self-worth. This center needs cycles of work and rest when it is defined, and lack of rest can seriously undermine vitality. Exerting willpower to overcome a lack of rest can result in burnout. The undefined Will Center can struggle with self-worth and reach burnout by exerting amplified willpower to prove itself. The challenge here is to manage this powerful Will Center energy wisely to sustain a healthy quality of Vitality.

Vitality and the Root Center

The Root is the center for adrenal energy (adrenaline). I call it turbo-boost energy. When it is open, you will feel under constant pressure to get things done. When it is defined, there is an energy pulse that is either on or off. The challenge there is to navigate the pulse, so you work with the energy when it is on and do not push yourself when it is off. If this center is open, you need to manage your self-imposed pressures and learn to rest even when your to-do list is incomplete (which it always is).

The Vitality Spectrum

Low expressions:

> Burnout, exhaustion, reactivity, despair, overwhelm, confusion, apathy.

High expressions:

> You manage your Vitality well and have plenty of energy reserves. You set and maintain healthy boundaries. You balance energy wisely between work and rest, knowing that you work in spurts and then need time to recover. You trust your resilience and bounce back well after challenges to your energy.

Sample Assessment Questions

- Are you burned out? A little or a lot? What led you to where you are now?
- Do you overcommit and overdeliver? How is not knowing when enough is enough showing up in your life?

Self-Rating on Vitality

How healthy is your vitality and your ability to leverage your energy?

Rate yourself on a scale of 1-10

10 = I am high in vitality, managing my energy very well.

1 = I am seriously burned out or not managing my energy well at all.

Resiliency Key: Lovability

Lovability—feeling lovable and worthy of love—is focused in the G Center, also known as the Identity Center. This is where our sense of self and direction in life reside. It is also the location of our vibrational attractive power (called the Magnetic Monopole in traditional Human Design) that draws to us the people and experiences we need to fulfill our purpose. Its effect on us depends on whether our G Center is defined or open, but we all have a theme of learning to love and accept ourselves.

Lovability with a Defined G Center

You have a rather fixed identity and sense of self. You *are* who you *are* and are not easily influenced by others. You wonder and worry whether you can be loved for who you are, because you are not likely to change much.

Lovability with an Undefined G Center

You are designed to have a fluid and adaptable identity and direction in life. Who you are in the moment depends on where you are and whom you are with. You fundamentally question your lovability because of your chameleon nature. "How can someone love me when I am always changing?"

The Lovability Spectrum

Low expressions:

Depression, fear of rejection, fear of authentic self-expression, feeling unworthy of love, feeling unloved, feeling unlovable.

High expressions:

You feel inherently and unconditionally lovable. You fully love and accept yourself just as you are. You fearlessly express who you are, knowing that you are inherently worthy of love.

Sample Assessment Questions

- How easily do you receive and express love? What gets in the way?
- What parts of you do you hide because you feel unlovable?

Self-Rating on Lovability

How healthy is your expression of yourself and your lovability?

Rate yourself on a scale of 1-10

10 = I am inherently lovable.

1 = I don't feel lovable at all.

Resiliency Key: Self-Worth

Self-Worth allows us to move through life with confidence and to feel worthy of receiving and giving support. It is focused in the Will Center, which is also known as the Ego Center or Heart Center. The Will Center has energy for willpower, ego, and the power to influence others. This energy also relates to material resources, money, business, and, importantly, how we value ourselves and each other. Its effect depends on whether your Will Center is defined or open. As Projectors, we often associate our value with accomplishments and *doing* which can lead us to an unhealthy (and unsustainable) basis for our Self-Worth.

Self-Worth with a Defined Will Center

You have the willpower to influence others and manage your own behavior, although you may have a fear of being seen as selfish or "being in your ego." You need cycles of rest to balance your cycles of work, because you can push yourself into burnout if you undervalue yourself and/or disregard your need for rest.

Self-Worth with an Undefined Will Center

You question your Self-Worth and have a deep need to prove yourself. You probably undervalue yourself and your contribution to the world, often undercharging for your skills and services or giving them away for free. You have a pattern of feeling undervalued by others, which leads to bitterness. Pushing yourself with borrowed willpower leads to burnout.

The Self-Worth Spectrum

Low expressions:

Feeling unworthy, undervalued, having low self-esteem, needing to prove your worth/value, ignoring rest and self-care, and pushing yourself to the point of exhaustion or burnout, self-effacement, not valuing others.

High expressions:

You feel inherently and unconditionally valuable and worthy. You nourish and restore yourself as needed. You have core-deep self-confidence, set clear boundaries, and maintain excellent self-care.

Sample Assessment Questions

- How much do you base your value on your efforts and accomplishments? What are you trying to prove?
- How well are you taking care of yourself?

Self-Rating on Lovability

How healthy is your sense of Self-Worth?

Rate yourself on a scale of 1-10

10 = I am inherently worthy.

1 = I don't feel worthy at all.

Resiliency Key: Self-Trust

Self-Trust is rooted in trusting the connection to your inner guidance through awareness of your body's reactions. It is expressed as trusting yourself, keeping agreements with yourself, and developing your trustworthiness. There is also a component of trusting the Universe/God/Source which provides a deep sense of the broader context in which we all exist, and of not being alone. The centers related to this Key are the Head Center, Ajna Center, and Spleen Center. Each of these centers has its own challenges related to Self-Trust.

Self-Trust and the Head Center

The Head is the center for ideas and inspiration. The challenge here is navigating this center's lower expression themes which include confusion, doubt, and the struggle to know the unknowable. These can easily result in self-doubt and can hijack your Self-Trust.

Self-Trust and the Ajna Center

The Ajna Center governs mental energy which likes to understand things but feels anxiety when confused or when not knowing the answers. This uncertainty will undermine your Self-Trust at every turn. The challenge is to learn to trust your knowing at every level: logic, sensing, and pure knowingness.

Self-Trust and the Spleen Center

The Spleen is the center for intuition, survival, and in-the-moment awareness. It gives us gentle but brief nudges (intuitive hits) from our inner knowing that are easy to ignore or downplay. The challenge is to develop the habit of listening for (or feeling for) those intuitive hits and to learn to trust them. This takes practice, but the nudges themselves are instantaneous.

The Self-Trust Spectrum

Low expressions:

> Fear, anxiety, nervousness, paralysis (not moving forward), self-doubt, suspicion, hyper-vigilance, trusting others more than yourself.

High expressions:

> You are sure of yourself and of your intuition and inner knowing. You are unflappable no matter what is going on around you. You feel capable, dependable, and completely trustworthy. You trust your connection to Source and feel secure about your place in the universe.

Sample Assessment Questions

- How much do you trust your capabilities? Your body? Your intuition?
- How connected do you feel to Spirit/Source/God/Your Higher Self?

Self-Rating on Self-Trust

How healthy is your Self-Trust?

Rate yourself on a scale of 1-10

10 = I am tapped into my intuition and my connection to Spirit/Source/God, and I feel confident and trustworthy.

1 = I feel disconnected and/or untrustworthy.

Resiliency Key: Decisiveness

The Key of Decisiveness is based on your capacity to make good choices that are aligned with your unique energy and purpose. This includes knowing how to make decisions correctly for you, trusting that process, connecting with what you truly want, making the decision, following through, and staying flexible. The challenges here include doubting your ability to make good decisions because you have made poor ones in the past; lack of clarity about what you want; lack of energy to follow through; and trying to avoid the stigma of "making mistakes" especially if you have a 3 or 6 in your Profile.

Your Authority determines your personal decision-making process, although it can be affected by the following centers regardless of your Authority: Head Center, Ajna Center, G Center, Sacral Center, and Emotional Solar Plexus Center. Each presents its own specific challenges to Decisiveness.

Decisiveness and the Head Center

The Head is the center for ideas and inspiration. With an open Head Center, you take in inspirations and ideas from others and then feel pressure to implement them. With a defined Head Center, you think you should follow your own inspirations. Either way, there is no energy here for action. The challenge, whether your Head Center is open or defined, is to use your Strategy and Authority to make your decisions, and not get distracted, confused, or misled by your Head.

Decisiveness and the Ajna Center

The Ajna Center tries to figure things out using mental energy. With an open Ajna, you are a flexible thinker, but you struggle to be certain about your ideas and decisions. With a defined Ajna, your thinking is fixed, and your certainty can be unshakable—even when it is wrong. The challenge here is to trust your inner knowing and your decision-making process regardless of your mental certainty or lack of certainty.

Decisiveness and the G Center (aka Identity Center)

The G is the center for love, self-identity, and direction in life. With an open G Center, you will struggle to find your direction and to trust your decisions and your decision process. Your doubts about your lovability can also hijack your choices. With a defined G Center, you will have a more consistent sense of self and direction but can still question your lovability and wrestle with trusting that your decisions reflect your True Self.

Decisiveness and the Sacral Center

The Sacral Center supplies lifeforce and workforce energy. It is only defined for Generator and Manifesting Generator Types, where it provides the basis for their decision-making process—guidance through their Sacral sounds. As Projectors, our Sacral Center is always undefined, so Sacral sounds are not part of our process. But, because we take in and amplify Sacral energy, we can be affected by that energy and by the responses of defined Sacrals around us. The challenge is to distinguish that influence from your own energy and use your Strategy and Authority to reach clarity about your choices.

Decisiveness and the Emotional Solar Plexus Center

The Emotional Solar Plexus Center is the seat of emotional energy and passion. With an open Solar Plexus Center, you avoid conflict and try to keep others happy which can easily derail your decision process. With a defined Solar Plexus, your emotional waves deeply affect how decisions feel to you and you must take your time to feel your way to your correct choices.

The Decisiveness Spectrum

Low expressions:

> Confusion, hesitation, paralysis (not moving forward), feeling lost, pressured, or stressed, trauma from past decisions, blame, regret.

High expressions:

> You make good decisions for yourself that are aligned with your inner truth. You trust your decisions and your decision-making process, taking the leap of faith to follow your Authority as you learn to trust it. You follow through with your decisions as appropriate.

Sample Assessment Questions

- How do you feel about making decisions? Do you trust your Authority?
- How confident are you in your ability to make good, strong decisions that are right for you?

Self-Rating on Decisiveness

How healthy is your Decisiveness?

> *Rate yourself on a scale of 1-10*
>
> 10 = I am totally confident in my ability to make good decisions and follow through.
>
> 1 = I don't trust myself to make good decisions; I avoid making decisions.

Resiliency Key: Empowerment

Empowerment is the state of feeling connected to your personal power in a healthy way. With it, you feel capable and competent, you take responsibility when appropriate, and you take action correctly to "create your reality" and maximize the quality of your life. However, your sense of self-empowerment can be distorted by a negative mindset and the many issues related to Projector pain we explored previously. The centers related to this Key are the Will Center, Sacral Center, and Emotional Solar Plexus Center. All three are motor centers, with energy for creating resources, taking action, and expressing creativity, respectively. Each has its own challenges related to Empowerment.

Feeling powerful is a basic human need and we are at our most powerful when aligned with spirit and with our natural energy. Following our Strategy and Authority gives us direct access to our legitimate personal power. Sadly, there are many ways we disconnect from our power and give our power away. Feeling powerless is a prescription for burnout and bitterness and all their negative consequences. Feeling infinitely powerful emerges from a confident connection and alignment with God/Spirit/Source, and it supports our personal power.

Empowerment and the Will Center

The Will is the center for willpower, ego, and creating and managing resources. When this center is defined, you have consistent access to willpower energy and are likely to feel empowered and to empower others. When this center is open, you are likely to struggle with empowerment due to your inconsistent access to this energy. Exerting amplified willpower that does not belong to you can cause burnout as you push yourself (and, perhaps, others) so you can feel empowered. The challenge is to learn that you do not need to prove yourself. You can choose to access your power and feel empowered simply by choice.

Empowerment and the Sacral Center

The Sacral is the center for lifeforce and workforce energy. With an open Sacral Center, we Projectors struggle with the variability of our access to energy and are vulnerable to burnout when we push ourselves too hard. Our lack of consistent energy can leave us feeling disadvantaged and even powerless in comparison to the defined Sacral Types. The challenge is to embrace a new definition of sustainability and find ways of feeling powerful that don't rely on Sacral energy—or on any energy at all.

Empowerment and the Emotional Solar Plexus Center

The Emotional Solar Plexus Center is the seat of emotional energy and passion, and it plays a big role in empowerment through its impact on decision making. With a defined Solar Plexus Center, you might leap into inappropriate choices or feel stuck and powerless if not making decisions correctly by waiting through your emotional wave. With an open Solar Plexus Center, you may make decisions based on the responses of others and on not wanting to upset them, so you compromise your own needs and feel disempowered.

The Empowerment Spectrum

Low expressions:

Anger, depression, lack of forgiveness, confusion, hopelessness, despair, burnout, bitterness, feeling victimized, feeling powerless, blame.

High expressions:

You feel infinitely powerful and aligned. You express power in healthy ways. You empower others because you know life is not a competition and we all benefit when we all feel empowered.

Sample Assessment Questions

- In which areas of your life do you feel especially powerful, and where... not so much?
- How do you feel about activating your personal power? Your infinite power?

Self-Rating on Empowerment

How healthy is your sense of personal power and full Empowerment?

Rate yourself on a scale of 1-10

10 = I proudly claim my personal and my infinite power, and I empower others.

1 = I don't feel powerful; I don't want to feel powerful.

Resiliency Key: Authenticity

There are two aspects to the Key of Authenticity. The internal aspect is knowing Who You Are at your core—your True Self—and having inner alignment with that truth. This is who you know yourself to *be*. The external aspect is *expressing* your truth and taking aligned action. This is who you are showing to the world—your public face. When you confidently know and express who you are, you are not swayed or confused by the opinions of others. You have no pretense and are not afraid to be vulnerable. You accept and love yourself, and Who You Are internally is aligned with who you are showing to others.

When you are not being true to yourself and expressing yourself authentically, you send mixed and confusing messages to others making it much harder to be recognized and invited correctly. You will feel more dissatisfied leading to bitterness and burnout. You may receive harsher lessons in life, offering you opportunities to re-evaluate and realign with your True Self. Plus, it takes tremendous energy to maintain an inauthentic façade if you are pretending to be other than Who You Are. The centers related to this Key are the G Center and Throat Center.

Authenticity and the G Center (aka Identity Center)

The G is the center for love, sense of self, and direction in life. It is the seat of our vibrational attraction power which puts us in the right place and draws to us what we need to experience and learn. With a defined G Center, you know who you are, but you may feel that it is not safe to express, or even to be, who you are. With an open G Center, who you are changes so it is easy to feel confused about who to be and who to express. In both cases, identify and focus on your core qualities that remain consistent. Note that Authenticity and Lovability are intertwined here in the G Center.

Authenticity and the Throat Center

The Throat Center governs our communication and thus our expression of ourselves in the world. This is our primary interface with others. Whether your Throat Center is open, defined, or motorized, the biggest challenge is timing—waiting for and feeling for the correct time to express yourself. If your timing is off and you feel unheard or rejected (which is especially common for open Throats but also for unmotorized defined Throats), you are likely to shut down the authentic expression of yourself.

If you have a defined channel between the G and Throat Centers, you are extra sensitive to criticism. It is helpful to know this about yourself and intentionally try to be less sensitive to any real (or perceived) criticisms or judgments from others and not take them to heart.

The Authenticity Spectrum

Low expressions:

> Fear, insecurity, not being known or seen for Who You Are, not feeling loved for Who You Are, hiding out, regretting your choices, feeling empty.

High expressions:

> You are fully self-expressed in healthy ways. You know Who You Are and are

true to yourself. You have healthy relationships and interactions with others who recognize you and call out your talents. You create a life you love.

Sample Assessment Questions

- How safe do you feel to express the truth of Who You Are? Why or why not?
- Are there gaps between your True Self and the self you express in theworld? Where is this misalignment showing up?

Self-Rating on Authenticity

How healthy is your Authenticity?

Rate yourself on a scale of 1-10

10 = I am living in complete alignment with my True Self.

1 = I am hiding my True Self from others, and even from myself.

A Few More Thoughts on Healing

Life can be challenging, and in many ways that is a good thing. It forces us to grow, to step out of our comfort zone, to learn, adapt, forgive, and accept. It is through our challenges that we expand our possibilities and also identify weak spots. When we accept that, at some level, *we* put these challenges in our own path to learn from and grow—then we can stop feeling like a victim, start accepting responsibility, and begin embracing those learning opportunities with gratitude and awe. This not only helps us heal past and present wounds, but it also allows us to avoid much pain, trauma, and suffering in the future.

This brings us back to mindset. How you view yourself, others, and what happens to you in this life determines your experience of this life. Deliberately managing your mindset gives you the power to intentionally heal and guide your life. And now you also have the Resiliency Keys to help you be healthy, healed, sustainable, and resilient. May you make wise use of all of these tools.

I highly recommend that you rate yourself often on these Keys. Choose one or two Keys to focus on. Get a buddy for support. Be intentional and do your healing work. Build your resiliency. Be kind and loving to yourself. Have patience and lots of forgiveness—for yourself and others.

While you are healing, remember to put more emphasis on BEING HEALTHY, WHOLE, AND RESILIENT than on trying to heal. This way, you will not need to change your focus as you progress, and that emphasis will serve you for the rest of your life.

Chapter 16

Deconditioning and Open Center Hijacking

We previously established how important it is to make correct decisions for yourself and your life. There is a significant role our open centers can play in derailing correct decision making. It is appropriate to address that here in the context of healing our Projector pain, as bad decisions are huge contributors to experiencing pain and struggle in life. Consistently making correct decisions puts us on the path to healing and flourishing.

Let's take a moment to review how open centers work and why they matter for decision making: Whether you call them open or undefined, the white centers on your chart take in the energy of their defined versions from other people and they amplify that energy. This amplification of energy coming from outside of us can be deeply confusing, distracting, painful, and overwhelming. It can also hijack our decisions.

Conditioning and Deconditioning

Conditioning—the influence of energy from outside of us—happens through openness, especially through our open centers. Most people have one or more centers open, and therefore easily take in the energy of others. Only rarely does someone have all nine centers defined.

Conditioning, generally speaking, is not bad. It is part of the human experience. Through our openness, we interact with and explore the world around us. Only when it confuses us about Who We Are and distracts us from our correct decision-making process does it become problematic.

There are predictable behavior patterns that develop from each open center. These behaviors are our best effort under the circumstances (of not knowing about openness or conditioning, before we encounter Human Design) to make sense of and cope with these energies bombarding our energy field. These behavior patterns, however, are not healthy nor empowered behaviors. They are coping mechanisms at best. These coping mechanisms have a way of hijacking our decision process.

It is as if each open center has its own agenda and wants to get its own way in every decision we make. When we allow this hijacking, we are fully distracted from our correct decision-making process and end up with choices that rarely serve us well. At worst, these choices lead us directly into the pain and struggle we wrestle with so often as Projectors. These choices cause us to abandon our path and our growth and move deeper into our not-self behaviors.

Initially, conditioning by the outside world happens during our first seven years of life. By the age of eight, most of us no longer remember who we truly are because we have been deeply influenced by our parents, others we interact with, and society at large. Our not-self has developed during this time as a "conditioned programming" from these influences, and it hides and/or distorts our True Self.

Deconditioning is the process of becoming aware of our openness and of the influences we take in. As we gradually discern what is "us" and what is from other people, we begin to reconnect with the truth of Who We Are. As described earlier, it takes seven years to decondition our open centers and be able to fully operate from our defined energies—our consistent strengths—as well as to tap into the wisdom contained in our openness. We cannot completely remove past conditioning or prevent it from happening to us in the future (nor would we want to), but we can minimize and neutralize its negative effects and reduce its power over us.

Part of our deconditioning process is becoming aware of each of our open centers, their specific agendas, and their hijacking methods so we can avoid these distractions. With awareness and intention, we can stop the automatic unhealthy behaviors and make deliberate choices to follow our correct decision-making process. This steers us away from our not-self themes and patterns and moves us toward the empowered and thriving version of ourselves and the wisdom and gifts of our open centers.

Hijacking happens when our open center agendas override our Strategy and Authority as we are making a decision. Each open center itself is a potentially powerful derailer of our decision process. When we have more than one open center, they can weave together in the background to create a formidable hijacking force.

The Behavior Pattern and Hijacking Potential of Each Center

For each center, we will look at its predictable behavior pattern and how it can derail our decisions. There are a few examples to help you see how each one works, then you will see specific ways to avoid that hijacking so you can make consistently good decisions—which I promise will change your life. Check your personal Human Design chart to see which of your centers are open (white). If you do not have a chart, see the Resources Page for a link to get a free chart.

The Open Head Center

Predictable behavior pattern:

> Feeling pressure to live out other people's ideas, questions, and inspirations, instead of your own.

How it can hijack your decisions:

> Leaping into ideas and wrong choices through inspiration, confusion, or to release the pressure.

Examples:

- You are invited to do something and your Authority says no, but your Open Head says that it is such a great idea you just can't pass up doing it.
- You are invited to do something and your Authority says no, but you are feeling so much pressure to figure out how to guide the implementation of the idea (or worse, pressure to do the work itself) that you say yes.

How to avoid the hijacking:

- Ask yourself: Am I under pressure to answer other people's questions and live out their ideas and inspirations?
- Use your Authority to be selective about which ideas are yours to implement and which are simply for you to observe or share.

The Open Ajna Center

Predictable behavior pattern:

> Struggling for certainty; changing your mind; struggling to remember details

How it can hijack your decisions:

Leaping into wrong choices through pressure to decide and pressure to feel certain, and from the conditioning influence of others

Examples:

- You are invited to do something and your Authority says no, but your Open Ajna says it feels certain this is perfect for you.
- You are invited to do something and your Authority says no, but the inviter is pressuring you to decide, and you saw your parents cave in to pressure from others when you were growing up, so this is an easy pattern for you to follow.

How to avoid the hijacking:

- Ask yourself: Am I struggling to be certain? Am I trying to convince myself (and others) that I am certain?
- Use your Authority to be selective about which beliefs and choices feel correct for you and align you with your True Self; stay flexible; meditate or spend time alone to clear the influence of others; avoid over-reliance on your mind.

The Open Throat Center

Predictable behavior pattern:

Doing inappropriate things to get attention, recognition, or be heard; feeling that what you have to say is not valuable (low self-esteem).

How it can hijack your decisions:

Choosing to say or do things solely to be noticed, recognized, or appreciated; desperation to make things happen.

Examples:

- You are invited to do something and your Authority says no, but your Open Throat says that if you say yes, you will get the attention and appreciation you deserve.
- You are invited to take a job and your Authority says no, but you are so desperate to get something going in your life that you say yes so you finally get noticed and can make *something* happen

How to avoid the hijacking:

- Ask yourself: Am I doing inappropriate things to get attention and recognition?
- Don't push with Throat energy that hasn't been activated through recognition (because that will stress your vocal cords and thyroid gland); wait for correct timing; be quiet and let your aura do the talking; wait to be asked or invited before speaking.

The Open G Center

Predictable behavior pattern:

> Questioning your lovability; struggling for direction in life and a solid sense of self.

How it can hijack your decisions:

> Choosing what you believe will help you feel loved and valued; choosing from low self-esteem; desperation to know Who You Are and where you are going; being influenced by others.

Examples:

- You are invited to do something and your Authority says no, but your Open G says that saying yes will give you a new identity which you want because you don't know who you are, and you are desperate to figure it out (maybe this will be the right one!).
- You really don't need to buy another online course, this one isn't even something you need right now, and your Authority says no, but you get so caught up in the description of it in the sales video that you buy it because you've been convinced it will solve all your problems.

How to avoid the hijacking:

- Ask yourself: Do I question my lovability? Am I struggling to find direction? Do I love where I live, where I work, and who I am with?
- Follow your Authority to allow your G to take you where you need to be; relax, you don't need to figure it all out yourself! You do need to be out of the aura of others before you make decisions, because the Open G is so easily influenced by others.

The Open Will Center

Predictable behavior pattern:

Questioning your worth and value; trying to prove yourself.

How it can hijack your decisions:

Making a choice you believe will prove your value and worthiness; choosing from low self-value.

Examples:

- You are invited to do something and your Authority says no, but your Open Will says that saying yes will let you prove your value and show them they can't do it without you.
- You are invited to do something and your Authority says no, but your Open Will says that you are not worthy of getting a better offer, so you need to just take this one.

How to avoid the hijacking:

- Ask yourself: What am I trying to prove?
- Do not push yourself with willpower energy that you do not have (because an Open Will does not have consistent willpower). Use your Strategy and Authority instead, stand in your power, self-value, and inherent worthiness, and don't let your mind dictate what you should do.

The Open Emotional Solar Plexus Center

Predictable behavior pattern:

Trying to keep everyone happy; not speaking your truth; avoiding conflict.

How it can hijack your decisions:

Choosing from the fear that you might upset someone; not standing in your own power; feeling overwhelmed

Examples:

- You are invited to do something and your Authority says no, but your Open Solar Plexus says that the inviter will be so upset if you say no that you must say yes.

- You are invited to do something and your Authority says no, but your Open Solar Plexus is overwhelmed with the intense emotions around you, so you say yes to protect yourself from those emotions getting even more intense.

How to avoid the hijacking:

- Ask yourself: Am I avoiding truth and conflict, and trying to keep everyone happy? Is what I am feeling true for me, or are they someone else's emotions?
- Be aware of what is "yours" and what is not regarding emotional energy. Let go of what is not yours. Discharge emotional energy often. Step into your power. Don't wait when making your decisions (except to be in your own aura). Ultimately, you will be able to choose what you want to experience from the emotional energy flowing through you—like choosing to enjoy the flower-scented breeze as it flows through a screen door.

The Open Spleen Center

Predictable behavior pattern:

> Holding on for longer than you should to people, things, clutter, grudges, anger, addictions, illness, attitudes, etc., because you believe you will feel better by holding onto any of those.

How it can hijack your decisions:

> Choosing from fear (any of the Splenic Fears of your defined Spleen Gates); choosing from an unwillingness to let go of the past or to let go of what no longer serves you.

Examples:

- You are invited to do something and your Authority says yes, but your Open Spleen says no because you are still mad at that person over something that happened years ago.
- You are invited to do something and your Authority says yes, but your Open Spleen says no because you are afraid you might fail at it (or any of the other Splenic Fears).

How to avoid the hijacking:

- Ask yourself: Am I holding onto something for longer than I should? What could I let go of that no longer serves me?

- Trust your intuitive insights and awareness; push through any Splenic Fears that show up; pay attention to your health and safety and your body's immune system and its needs.

The Open Sacral Center

Predictable behavior pattern:

Not knowing when enough is enough; pushing with energy that is not yours.

How it can hijack your decisions:

Choosing from a place of pushing to make things happen or from a place of burnout. Assuming you have sustainable energy when you do not. Choosing from a fear of appearing weak or lazy.

Examples:

- You are invited to do something and your Authority says no, but your Open Sacral says that you must keep pushing yourself to be successful in life, so you say yes.
- You are invited to do something and your Authority says no, but your Open Sacral says that you can handle the extra work (and you don't want to be called lazy), so you say yes but end up exhausting yourself.

How to avoid the hijacking:

- Ask yourself: Do I know when enough is enough? Am I doing more than enough right now? Do I need to stop? Do I need to rest?
- Borrow the energy from Defined Sacrals around you but know when to stop so you do not burn out. Use your Strategy and Authority to create and maintain healthy boundaries. Respect that your energy flow is inconsistent so don't set expectations (from others or from yourself) of consistent energy from you.

The Open Root Center

Predictable behavior pattern:

Trying to get everything done so you can be free from the pressure you feel.

Often, that pressure is unconsciously self-imposed, but it simply comes from amplified Root energy from others that we experience as pressure.

How it can hijack your decisions:

Choosing from feeling pressured or stressed; choosing from panic or fear; having unrealistic expectations of what you can get done

Examples:

- You are invited to do something and your Authority says no, but your Open Root caves in to the pressure (real or imagined) to say yes.
- You are invited to do something and your Authority says no, but your Open Root says that you can add that to your workload, no problem, so you say yes and end up exhausting yourself.

How to avoid the hijacking:

- Ask yourself: Am I still trying to get things done so I can be free? Is this pressure self-imposed?
- Realize that it is just energy and you do not need to be a victim to it. Remember to be a screen, not a sponge, when you experience Root energy from others as pressure or stress. Prioritize what must get done and be realistic about which are the true priorities and what you reasonably can get done.

The Gift of Deconditioning

The seven-year deconditioning process is really an education process. Many advanced degrees in higher education take seven years to complete, such as medical school or Ph.D. programs, and mastering an instrument can take that long or longer. Deconditioning is like a higher-education degree in the endeavor of becoming yourself.

But it does not take seven years to see differences in your life. The moment you start to apply and experiment with your Strategy and Authority, you will begin functioning differently, deprogramming the old patterns, and reinforcing new healthier ones.

As you increase your awareness and discernment regarding your open centers, you begin to learn Who You Really Are, and you find yourself operating differently in the world. Old habits fade away, new perceptions emerge, the "shoulds" slowly disappear, and a new ease starts to take hold. When you stop pushing (yourself, others, projects, ideas, etc.), you can use that quiet space of no-pushing to listen for and feel for your truth through your decision-making Authority and through the definition in your chart which is consistent and reliable.

Surrendering to your internal guidance system (your Authority) is not meant in the negative sense of surrender—of giving up or giving in. It is an empowering choice that trusts what feels truly correct and aligned for you. It is also the path of least resistance for creating the life you want.

Here is a helpful hack to use as you are about to make a decision: stop, challenge, choose. Stop before you make your decision, to give yourself a moment to consider the motivation, consequences, and bigger picture. Challenge/test your choice to see if it is coming from your Authority (confirmed by how it feels in your body) or from your open centers (which are managed by your mind). Then make the choice from a deliberate and clear space, not from the influence of old patterns or the automatic hijacking of your open centers.

The last few chapters focused on ways to heal your wounds, restore your self-confidence, make better choices, and begin to step into your power. Now I would like to introduce you to a Projector who overcame deep wounds of abandonment in childhood and emerged as a powerful and deeply empowering world-wide influencer.

Meet a Projector - Dr. Wayne Dyer

Dr. Wayne Dyer was an internationally renowned author and speaker in the fields of self-development and spiritual growth, known to his fans as the "father of motivation." Over the four decades of his career, he wrote more than forty books, including twenty-one *New York Times* bestsellers. He created many audio and video programs, appeared on thousands of television and radio shows, and starred in ten National Public Television specials.

In addition, this one-motor Projector had three marriages, six children, and two stepchildren. He was a busy guy. His one defined motor was the Will Center which undoubtedly gave him the intensity and tenacity to accomplish so much, and it enabled him to empower millions worldwide through his books and programs.

He clearly embraced his role as a guide (to millions!). He did a lot of healing work himself and encouraged others to do theirs. Despite a childhood spent in orphanages and foster homes, he overcame many obstacles to make his dreams come true and spent much of his life showing others how to do the same. His main message was that every person has the potential to live an extraordinary life. And he articulated the possibility that every person could manifest their deepest desires—if they honor their inner divinity and consciously choose to live from their Highest Self.

Learn more about Dr. Wayne Dyer and details of his Human Design chart in my Celebrity Chart Review of him on my website. Find the link from the Resources Page.

Name:	Wayne Dyer
Birth Date:	10 May 1940, 03:13
Birth Place:	Detroit, MI, United States
Type:	Orchestrator (Projector)
Inner Authority:	Resource (Ego - Heart)
Profile:	1/3 - Resource / Explorer
Definition:	Split - Large
Strategy:	Wait for Recognition and Invitation
Themes:	Success / Bitterness
Incarnation Cross:	RAX Explanation 2
Channels:	2343 - Innovative Thinking (Structuring) 2551 - Higher Purpose (Initiation)

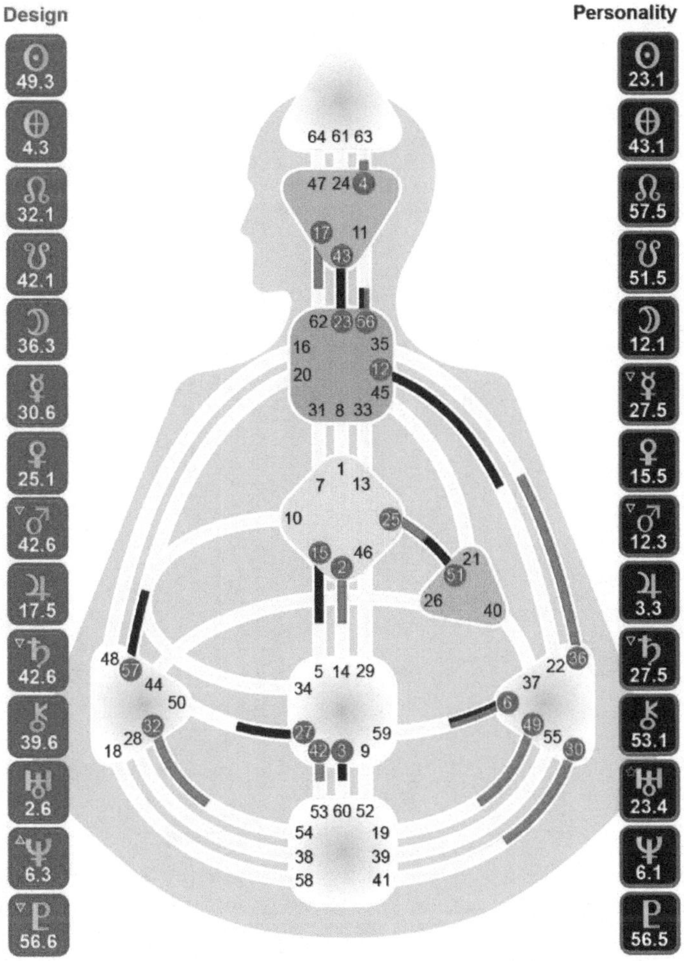

Design	Personality
49.3	23.1
4.3	43.1
32.1	57.5
42.1	51.5
36.3	12.1
30.6	27.5
25.1	15.5
42.6	12.3
17.5	3.3
42.6	27.5
39.6	53.1
2.6	23.4
6.3	6.1
56.6	56.5

PART FIVE

Becoming Empowered

Stepping into Your Brilliance

Resiliency gives you power and sustainability so
you can play full-out in every area of your life.
Here is how to put it all together.

If we fully occupy our own value, then we have nothing to prove. And our actions will reflect not only a deep alignment with the Cosmic Plan, but also a deep sense of the inherent value of not only ourselves, but others.

~ Karen Curry Parker

Your song is unique. Your aura sings for those who can hear.

~ Ella Aboutboul

PART FIVE

Becoming Empowered

Introduction to Becoming Empowered

To thrive and live life as an empowered Projector, you need to heal your wounds, clear your trauma, and restore your wholeness. There is nothing wrong with you; you are brilliant. To fully embrace your power, you may need some tender self-nurturing and deep inner work that will restore your resilience and confidence. Also, you might not fully know yourself and perhaps have not fallen in love with yourself yet.

Here is a simple set of steps to follow:

- know yourself
- accept yourself
- respect yourself, and
- begin to truly love yourself.

This is how to step into the fullness of Who You Are—imperfections and all. We are all imperfect. You, no more than anyone else. I promise you that.

Our imperfections and vulnerabilities make us unique and *uniquely qualified* for our special tasks and purpose. They are not even imperfections—they are part of the design we are here to express and learn from. They are how we grow.

When we choose to improve our lives, we take on a lifelong project that has clear benefits along the way. We release what no longer fits with our emerging sense of self and embrace what aligns with the truth of Who We Really Are. We finally start to relax, letting go of the anxiety that has gripped us most of our lives—the fear that there is something fundamentally wrong with us.

What I want you to do right now is make sure that your quest to become empowered as a Projector is motivated by wanting to enhance your life and your contribution, not by trying to fix your brokenness. YOU ARE NOT BROKEN. You may be wounded, you may be in need of healing, but you are not broken. There is nothing wrong with you. If you are still wrestling with this issue, I invite you to get a Human Design Reading, work with a Quantum Alignment System™ practitioner, and/or read this book again. You are amazing and vital to the evolution of humanity. Breathe. Allow yourself to BE just as you are.

The mind is always looking for meaning and purpose. But your body already knows how to LIVE your purpose. You just need to allow it. Do not let your not-self assign a purpose *to* you or endlessly search *out there* for your purpose. Your purpose is in your chart, and it is in your body. You are already living it.

A reading can give you greater clarity about your purpose and more confidence to step into it, but nearly all my clients discover (often to their surprise) that they were already drawn to and engaged in what is aligned and correct for them. That confirmation brings relief and helps them to trust themselves more and more.

To be truly empowered, you need to fall in love with yourself. Not in a weird or egotistical way. In a genuinely respectful way. In a way that honors YOU. In a way that says that you are worthy of your own highest expression of love. In that process, you become capable of truly honoring, respecting, and loving others. Unconditionally.

When you no longer take things personally and develop a deep trust in yourself, you will live beyond the judgments of others, feel good about yourself, and be in great shape for sharing your wisdom and making your unique contribution to the world. You will BE empowered.

The following was shared with me by a student, Juanita, who took my Success for Projectors course. Her words beautifully capture this powerful shift:

"This past year has brought huge revelations in loving and valuing myself. I turned all that wisdom that I had been giving out to others, towards myself. So, my view of the importance and value of others is now balanced with the importance of being myself as myself and for myself. I am now here for me first so that I can be there for others. I see that others have their path with the experiences they need in order for them to be guided into being their highest potential. Thus, I no longer see people as broken needing to be fixed. Their path is not my business until they reach a point where they reach out for assistance. I am now attracting and surrounding myself with supporting others who value me and respect my uniqueness. Love for self expands into love for all."

Chapter 17

Embracing Your Projector-ness

To step into our power, our brilliance, and our Projector-ness, we need to reach a state of acceptance, and hopefully even delight, in our unique gifts and characteristics and in our important role. What does that look like and how do we get there? The remaining chapters in this book will fully answer that question.

Here is a list of Projector-ness tips to get you started, synthesizing much that we have already covered. These tips will help you firmly step into the fullness of you as a magnificent being in the form of a Projector in this lifetime. In the coming chapters, you will see lists and tips specific to different areas of life.

- Be kind, loving, and gentle with yourself.
- Filter everything through YOUR truth.
- Set healthy boundaries.
- Value yourself.
- Know you are inherently lovable and worthy.
- Own your role in life and your value to the world; "own the throne!"
- Own your brilliance.
- Make peace with needing others to activate your energy.
- Be joyful and gracious.
- Trust, and re-frame.
- Breathe!
- Step into your wisdom.
- There is nothing to prove.
- You *and* the other must succeed.
- Manage your energy to FINISH STRONG.
- Leverage your impact.

- Hone your skills; develop your mastery.
- Allow flow to happen; don't resist.
- Don't push or prod; all flow, no force.
- Have happy and eager anticipation.
- Be of service.
- Wait for invitations with a positive mindset.
- Watch for politeness versus true invitation.
- Minimize what gets in your way.
- Don't compare yourself to others.
- Don't take things personally.
- When you feel stuck, go help someone else.
- Manage your thoughts and beliefs (your mindset).
- Do more BEING and less DOING.
- Let others help you; ask for help when you need it.
- Feel awe, wonder, and curiosity about life.
- Surrender to your Strategy and Authority.
- Learn enough Human Design to help you know Who You Are.
- Be fully alive every day… you will be ageless and happy!

To keep us laser-focused on our Projector-ness, let's circle back to the beginning of this book and our role as GUIDES. We have seen how we are designed to know others so we can guide them and their energy. We have also seen how we can get hijacked, burned out, bitter, and feel broken along the way.

To navigate these challenges and still fulfill our role, we need to take a clear-eyed look at how we can become more empowered and more empowering as guides. Since this is our role, let's become rock stars at guiding!

Here are some powerful questions to consider that will improve your guiding skills. Although some are worded as yes/no questions, dig deep for your thoughtful responses, not just for one-word answers. Consider specific examples that support your answers. Explore how you felt, how things played out, and what you might change in the future.

- When you have the impulse to guide someone, are you truly guiding or are you interfering? Did they ask for your guidance specifically? Did the impulse to guide come from you or from their invitation to you?

- When you guide others, do you have an agenda of your own? Are your not-self needs and open center demands getting in the way of your focus on the other person or are you selflessly there for the other's benefit?
- Are you attached to the outcome of your guidance? Are you trying to prove yourself? Get noticed? Be recognized? Please others? Why?
- Are you trying to fix others without being asked? Do you think you have all the answers? How does that feel for you? For them?
- What is the difference between guiding and managing someone? Is there a difference between guiding and advising someone? What is it? Is that an important distinction?
- How do you react when your guidance or advice is not well received or appreciated? Do you take it personally?
- How can you start using more questions and fewer "directions" when trying to help someone?
- Who are you without an invitation? Can you guide without one? Can you be successful without one? Can you express your talents and skills without one? Can you feel good about yourself without one? What would that look like?
- How do you use your time and energy? What is truly important to you, and do your actions and choices line up with what you say is important?

I hope you will use these questions to conduct a practical self-examination of your guiding style. Where are you doing well? Where do you need some work? Being an excellent guide of energy (and people) is a skill we are designed for. Embrace it fully, with new self-awareness, and intentionally hone that skill.

Although it may feel counter-intuitive, being quiet and waiting for the right timing is a far more powerful approach than trying hard to be noticed or heard or trying to force something to happen. Quiet confidence and good timing are the Projector's best overall approach to life, and these especially apply when you are guiding others.

Maybe you have had a lifetime of not being noticed or appreciated for your skills, talents, and contributions. Without proper recognition, it is hard for your gifts to be activated and you may have despaired of ever being truly seen and valued. As you step into your inherent power and value, you will feel a new sense of ease, confidence, clarity, commitment, and compassion (for yourself and others). You will fully own your space in this world, from which you can now make your full contribution to the world. The world needs YOU to be YOU, just as you are, and fully empowered!

Chapter 18

Money, Career, and Self-Promotion (Gasp!)

Money, career, and work are often major issues for Projectors. It can feel hard to hold a job, sustain a career, run a business, or attract abundance when we do not have the energy to do it in the same way that others do. It can be especially confusing to figure out how to market and sell services in a Projector-aligned way that actually works.

Let's start by talking about—and redefining—the concept of abundance. Our Western culture equates abundance and prosperity with money, material goods, and the numerical metrics we previously looked at. Further, our current culture views hard work as the prerequisite to abundance. The harder we work, the more we deserve. Right there, we see that these values are not aligned with open Sacral people like Projectors.

By contrast, look at indigenous cultures and their values. They do not house, clothe, feed, and value only those tribe members who work hard. The community (the tribe) takes care of everyone, and everyone has their place and their role, participating according to their capabilities. No one gets left behind or punished for not working as hard as others.

These cultures know that natural abundance, and being included and cared for, are birthrights of humans. We are designed to have everything we need and want and to be supported with adequate resources which are all around us on this lush and abundant planet.

To step into the new, evolving metrics of success, we must see abundance and prosperity from a holistic perspective. One cannot be truly abundant and prosperous if not also healthy, happy, and fulfilled. These aspects are unique to each of us. What helps me feel happy and abundant is probably quite different from what helps you feel that way.

So, how can we as Projectors sustain ourselves in today's work-oriented culture while enjoying the inherent abundance around us in ways that work for us and support us on all levels? The first step is to build a strong foundation.

Building a Strong Foundation

Use all the information in this book and all the tools at your disposal not only to know who you are at an intellectual level, but also to know yourself at a bone-deep and soul-deep level. This profound self-knowledge lets you fully step into and own your value as a human being, as a Projector, and as you. Trusting your inherent value—without having to prove yourself—is indispensable to your success as a Projector. This needs to be rock-solid.

You have deep intrinsic value to yourself, your loved ones, and to the world. From previous chapters you saw that the way to build self-worth and self-value is through mastery, especially mastery of systems, and then helping others through your extensive knowledge, skills, and wisdom. This attracts recognition and invitations which bring you energy and resources from others that help you to be successful in the world. But you are not dependent on recognition from others for your self-worth and value. Those are still internally sourced; they are enhanced by recognition from others but not dependent on it. Recognition can be used as helpful feedback or an indicator, like a gas gauge.

If you are not getting the recognition and invitations you want, especially around money, career, and business, be very deliberate in strengthening your self-worth. With practice, you will get better at it. Remember that we are all born worthy and loved by the universe. You were probably not taught that at a young age, or at any age! Most of us were not. There is nothing you must prove in order to be worthy.

Explore and experiment with the ideas of sufficiency and enoughness discussed in Chapter 14. Learn to recognize enoughness in yourself, in what you want and need, and in what you give to others. This is much easier when you are not trying to please everyone. Review the hijacking behaviors of your open centers in Chapter 16 so you notice those conditioned patterns when they show up, and you can make better choices.

Here are a few more tips for building your solid foundation around money and career issues:

- Redefine (and keep refining) your definition of success. Do not be seduced by materially-based measures of success. Trust your heart to know what feels like success for YOU.
- Allow the magic of life and the natural flow of energy to unfold without your interference, resistance, or attempts to control.
- Focus on the solution, not the problem, in each area where you struggle. But don't get too specific. "I want more money so I can pay my bills and get out of debt" is practical and feels okay but is not a vibration that will really attract an abundance of what you want. "I want more money so I can experience freedom and be generous and have the nice things in life that I want" has a very different feeling to it.
- Ask yourself: How could this be as *easy* as possible? Allow yourself to imagine the perfect unfolding. What would that look and feel like? Enjoy the envisioned ease and flow of it. It is not a cop-out to take the easy path. It is smart and correct energetically.
- Use "seed questions," not requests or demands or even affirmations. Asking questions, which we are all hardwired to do, releases them to super-consciousness and accesses the infinite field of possibility. Then the answers come back through the earth to us. Use expansive, curious questions, not specific (or sarcastic) ones. Here are some good examples:
    - What would it look like for everything to fall into place for me to be able to go on vacation this year?
    - What would it feel like if I could pay off all my debts and start saving for retirement?
    - Here is a wonderful question template from Karen Curry Parker: What needs to be healed and released for me to …? For example, to regain my health and vitality? To achieve the level of success in my business that I know I deserve? To get a job that uses my knowledge and pays me well?
    - These are excellent questions to ponder and release and then allow the answers to show up. Do not try to answer any of these questions yourself. Let the answers emerge in their own timing.
- Do not hold yourself back from wanting or achieving prosperity because you fear there will not be enough for everyone. When all Types are

playing their roles and operating correctly, there will be more than enough for all. People are always innovating, creating, and tapping new resources that are more sustainable. When you align yourself correctly and operate joyfully and abundantly, you make the best contribution possible to the whole. You help everyone get what they want and need by helping yourself get what you want and need.

Next, let's get specific about what gets in the way of accessing abundance and sustainability. Here again, there are two sets of factors: external and internal.

External Factors that Challenge Our Sustainable Abundance

We have already glimpsed these external factors: The work, money, and productivity paradigms of our culture today simply do not fit the natural energy and work style of Projectors. The Generator-driven get-ahead world we live in is not, and has never been, Projector-friendly. There is a collective belief that hard work and consistent hustle (exemplified by sustainable Sacral energy) is the only way to earn a good living and accumulate wealth. Having an open Sacral Center and no connection from a motor center to the Throat Center puts us at a disadvantage in this world. Because we cannot fake it for as long as some other Types, we must surrender to our design and let things work the way they are designed for us, while doing all we can to tip the balance in our favor as we move forward.

Here are some tips to help you shift these external factors to your advantage:

- Stack the deck in your favor with good visibility and positioning (but always do so with integrity).
- Be selective in where you put your attention; manage your energy and your mindset to support sustainable prosperity.
- Don't take things personally, especially in the world of work and money.
- Spend time around people who see you and value you.
- Spend time with people who share your values about abundance, prosperity, and sustainability.
- Do your inner work; a strong foundation of self-value is critical.

Internal Factors that Challenge Our Sustainable Abundance

There are two internal factors: the HOW factor and the WHAT factor.

Most of us do not know HOW to create abundance in our lives in ways that are correct, natural, energizing, and sustainable for us, and much of what we attempt does not work.

Trying to create wealth and abundance in ways that are not correct for *you* personally will never work. There are so many examples from the world of business coaches and lifestyle gurus. For example, you take a business building course that says to be successful as a coach you need to build a full coaching practice by attending ten to fifteen networking events per month and doing twenty coaching sessions per week. (One of my first business coaches told me exactly that when I was starting my business. Not correct for me.) That would put a lot of Projectors into full burnout (me included).

We must filter advice from others through what we know to be true for us. There are lifestyle gurus (mostly Manifesting Generators) who will tell you to take *massive action*. That is correct for some people. It might be correct for some Projectors, under the right circumstances (invited and it feels correct), but not if you are trying to force things to happen. Use your Strategy and follow your Authority. Forcing does not work and trying to follow the advice and pathways of others rarely works.

The next internal challenge is the WHAT: Often we are trying to create something that we don't really want. Again, courses and gurus as well as parents, friends, and loved ones will tell you what you *should* want. A business coach can promise to help you make a million dollars in your business but when you do the work and get there, you might discover you are not happy at all. It wasn't what YOU truly wanted. Or maybe you become an orthodontist because your parents want you to. Or you become a worker bee (not a guide) because you are smart, capable, hardworking, and you need the job, but it makes you miserable and you burn yourself out.

How can we avoid all of that, be smart, and go about creating what we truly want?

How to Get What You Want: Classic Three Steps to Manifesting

The classic steps to "manifesting what you want" will help you address those WHAT and HOW factors:

#1 Know what you want.

#2 Believe you can have it.

#3 Take aligned action.

Let's look at these more closely and adapt them for Projectors. Most people think of manifesting as "making things happen" and "creating something out of nothing." For Projectors, we could instead call these the three steps of "aligning with and allowing what you want." Not as catchy but far more accurate and much less stressful.

Step #1 - Know what you want. This can actually be hard.

The good news is that you do not have to be clear about this to get started. If you do know what you want, make sure it is really *your* desire. If you do not know what you really want, just enjoy yourself while waiting! It is challenging to know one's inner truth. What feels good and feels aligned is usually the best indicator.

ALIGNMENT GUIDELINE: If you are not sure if something feels good to you or not, then it doesn't! You will know it when something feels really good to you.

In your quest to discover what you want and what truly resonates with you:

- Keep your exploration open-ended.
- Engage with curiosity; focus on possibilities; don't jump to conclusions; don't give up.
- Follow the answers and directions that feel good to you.
- The biggest challenge is your conditioning and your not-self; what you think you want may not be what you really want; dig deep to connect with your true desires.
- Don't use your mind; use the wisdom and intuitive awareness of your body and your Strategy and Authority.
- You need to know and TRUST Who You Are and that can take time, so

be patient with yourself.

Step #2 - Believe you can have it. This is also quite challenging for many of us.

This is where your strong foundation and inner game of self-worth matter so much. When you feel good about yourself, you feel empowered, resilient, deserving, and worthy. Then, aligning with and allowing good things to come to you is so much easier.

The Nine Resiliency Keys we previously covered will help you see what is in your way and identify where you get stuck. Using EFT and other clearing techniques, and especially working with the Quantum Alignment System™, can clear those blocks, heal those wounds, and rebuild strength and internal resilience. All of this will support your belief that you deserve to have what you want and that it is okay for you to have it.

Step #3 - Take aligned action. In many ways, this is the easiest part.

This bears repeating: Follow your Strategy and Authority. When you live in alignment with the energy of your Type and make decisions correctly, you go with the flow, and you naturally align with your specific path and purpose—which makes everything you do easier.

Pay attention to your vibration—your baseline frequency. Be deliberate about what you put out to the world because you will attract whatever matches that.

As much as possible, do not force yourself to do things (especially in your business) that do not feel good to you. As you know, I am a pragmatist. Do what you have to do, but pay attention to how things feel. Don't just barrel through at any cost to you. Look for alternatives, options, easier ways, and help and support from others. If it feels like you are pushing a boulder up a hill every day to get something done, then maybe it is the wrong hill. Try this as a mantra: all flow, no force.

Emotional definition can influence your choice of actions, so give yourself time to find clarity if your Emotional Solar Plexus Center is defined. Also, an Open G Center can influence your actions. Make sure you are making choices from within your own aura, away from the influence of others.

Handling Projector Money Issues

There are three big predictable issues that Projectors struggle with regarding money and earning a living in today's world. The worldwide shifts to white collar jobs and working from home are helpful for us, but these issues are still challenging. Below are the three issues plus tips for handling each one. We covered many of these in previous chapters, but this section brings them together for easy reference and a good review.

Money Issue #1 – Sustainability in a job, career, or business.

- Become knowledgeable and proficient in systems and processes and develop your expertise so you can leverage your energy, time, knowledge, and resources.
- Be selective in what you say YES to; find the work that is right for YOU.
- Avoid burnout; listen to your body, not your mind or open centers.
- Create as much flexibility in your schedule as possible.
- Right opportunities for you will accommodate your variable energy levels.
- Reframe procrastination as sensing the right timing.
- Delegate work to others; focus on guiding the work.
- Plan ahead; take the long-term view; work smart, not hard.
- Ask for help, receive and allow help; pay it forward when you can.

Money Issue #2 – Waiting for invitations related to work and money.

- Stay in touch with contacts and cultivate new connections.
- Be findable and invitable.
- Help others as you can; creating good will and gratitude gives you positive standing and invites reciprocity.
- Follow your bliss; invitations will come more easily.
- Embrace the patience, wisdom, and leverage of waiting for the right invitations and right timing; keep a good attitude.
- Do what you need to do while waiting; hone your skills; make wise use of your time (which includes rest, sleep, and fun).
- Maintain your energy, health, and faith while you wait.

Money Issue #3 - Bitterness.

- Bitterness is understandable, but don't go there; it is not helpful.
- Avoid the "it's not fair" slippery slope; stand in your power.
- Don't look back or hold grudges or resentment.
- Do whatever it takes to heal wounds and repair relationships.
- Let go of what can't be repaired; bring closure to unfinished issues.
- Summon your courage; strengthen your self-worth.
- Stand in your value; ask for/charge what you are worth, but also be realistic about the value of your skills and experience.
- Focus on what *is* working and what you *do* want.
- Find healthy ways to soothe yourself and lift your energy and outlook.

When you take action regarding money, jobs, and business, do so from a positive energy flow as much as possible. Trust that things will work out for the best and choose to feel abundant and prosperous along the way. All of this raises your vibration and helps attract more of that to you. If you are in trouble financially, reach out for help from those who care about and can help you.

Handling Career and Job Choices

When it comes to Projectors making job or career choices or owning their own business, the same issues and same tips apply as we just saw with money issues. Plus, here are some specific tips for these challenges and choices:

- Career choices and job opportunities qualify for the "big decisions" category in decision making, so being invited into these is extremely beneficial and helps you enter them correctly.
- At the very least, you want an "energetic opening" for stepping into a career or job or starting a business, if not an actual invitation.
- It can be hard to get a job without applying for one, so go ahead and apply if you need to, but also work your network, stay in your bliss, and hone your skills.
- There is no magic formula for all Projectors; find the work and career that are right for you. Especially if your G Center is open, that can be fluid and change over time.

- Do what comes naturally for you and play to your strengths. For example, if you are not a details person, avoid jobs and professions that require attention to detail. If your brilliance is in interacting with people, do people-oriented work. Often, we don't give much value to what we are best at because doing it comes so easily. Do more of *that!* That is where your greatest leverage (and probably your deepest joy) will be. Get a Human Design reading so you are clear about your natural strengths and superpowers.
- Think outside the box in terms of roles and careers. The best fit for you may not exist yet because you bring a unique mix of knowledge and skills. When possible, help guide and craft the creation of new ways you can uniquely serve.
- Think in advance about a career path within your field that will work for you long term. You may love being a massage therapist when you are young and have lots of energy. Eventually you may want to teach or mentor or write books or blog about massage therapy instead of physically giving massages.
- Projectors are taking on more prominent roles; remember you are here to GUIDE so don't be afraid to take on a managing, directing, or leadership role if you have the energy for it and enter it correctly.
- Avoid being a worker bee if you can; leverage your knowledge and conserve your energy.
- Remember that you are holding the energy grid and "scrubbing" the karma of the planet, especially work and money karma, so always operate with integrity and model what is possible for humanity.
- Have faith, especially in the absence of evidence to support that faith. That is when faith matters the most.

How to Market and Promote Yourself Correctly

You have probably read or heard that Projectors are not supposed to market or promote themselves or actively sell their services or products. *Really?* Talk about trying to play basketball with both hands tied behind your back!

I am here to tell you something different.

I am here to tell you that you can and *must* market and promote yourself and actively sell your services and products. Do I hear a big collective gasp?

This is where it is important to distinguish between what really needs an invitation, and what does not. If you are in business for yourself or in the fields of sales or marketing, you need to know how to promote yourself (and your company) correctly so that your message is well-received *and* effective.

It can be completely correct for you to put up a website or Facebook page or Instagram account or whatever platform and style appeal to you, if those are consistent with expressing your True Self and are aligned with the people you want to reach. You do not need an invitation to do these things, although you may benefit from getting some experienced help with them. Make sure the person helping you knows Who You Are so the result truly reflects you. Being visible in these ways falls into the realm I call *stacking the deck in your favor*. Make it easy for people to find you and know who you are, what you do, and what you offer.

Your efforts will work best when your branding, style, and message are not only honest and consistent with your True Self, but also inviting to the visitor/reader. A soft approach usually works best, not loud or brash, and certainly not pushy (because pushy simply does not work for Projectors). Be sure to emphasize your natural strengths and what comes easily to you. The gems of truth about you contained in your Human Design chart are the best way to successfully shape how you present yourself to the world.

It will help you enormously to be invited to create your business or your course or your service offering. But that does not always happen. Do your best in the absence of invitations. Often the invitations will come as you get started and get a little traction. Before you spend a lot of time and effort to create a course, for example, test the waters first and see if there is genuine interest in such a course. You can even pre-sell it so you know there is demand for it and you are on the hook for getting it done. There are business coaches who teach this method, including Danny Iny, and I know it works because I've done it myself.

Do what you need to do to have a functional business that supports you. I would caution that it is not easy to create this. If your day job is your sole source of income, do not leave it until you can sustainably support yourself through your business. Here is where the biggest challenge happens for many Projectors: holding a full-time job while creating a business on the side. That can be exhausting, so pace yourself. Take baby steps and take care of yourself during this process. Heal your burnout first, and do not put yourself into burnout with this effort.

Try to make all of this as easy as possible on yourself. I cannot stress this enough. Get help. Trade services, if appropriate. Do not try to do it alone or implement all the pieces of your business by yourself. It is the rare individual who is good at doing everything. Daydream about how things could fall into place easily and beautifully. Put out seed questions for this to the universe. Allow the universe to bring you opportunities and conspire on your behalf to deliver the easy path. Easy is good.

Also, pay attention to your motivation and your "shoulds." If you are driven by money or what you "should" do, it will be much harder. If you are driven to serve others by doing what you love, you are more likely to attract the support, allies, and clients that will help you be successful.

Another factor that matters now and will matter even more with the 2027 shift is having integrity in your business and giving back to your community. A heart-based approach to business is central to the new business paradigm and the evolving metrics of success and fulfillment. When you truly care about the impact of your business on people and the planet, and when you explore your potential to make a difference in new and maybe unexpected ways, you will attract the clients, supporters, raving fans, and resources to fulfill your dream and your unique contribution.

Having a qualified business coach to skillfully work with you can help tremendously, especially one who knows Human Design and can coach correctly for *you*. There are more of these coaches every day, thanks to the spread of Human Design. You might join some online Projector groups and ask for recommendations. Don't be shy about getting some help.

Here are some additional tips to guide you as a Projector in business.

- Heal your burnout FIRST.
- Trust your instincts and passion, but also feel for the right timing and right invitations.
- Be of service to peers and colleagues but set healthy boundaries.
- Be cooperative, not competitive.
- Take a low-key, co-creative approach.

- Stack the deck in your favor.
- Have a website, give introductory talks or sessions, be active on social media, and/or ask for referrals BUT ONLY IF those feel correct for you.
- Get as much help as you can.
- Don't be afraid to specialize; the narrower your niche, the easier it is to market yourself.
- Don't try to do volume; do quality, not quantity.
- Capitalize on your guiding nature and the strengths shown in your Human Design chart.
- Leverage your time, energy, and knowledge; for example, create evergreen courses that do not require your direct energy to generate revenue.
- Have others facilitate things for you.
- Let your tribe find YOU, but you can help them do that.
- Be authentic on your website and social media.
- Get testimonials and "social proof."
- Don't do everything the gurus tell you; do what is aligned for you.
- Be introduced by someone when you speak to a group, lead a class, or teach a course.
- Empower and guide everyone who asks for your help to be their best self.
- Without an invitation, there is nothing you *must* do but plenty you *can* do.

Our greatest challenges are our greatest teachers and our biggest opportunities for growth. Money and its related challenges rank right up there with relationships as the biggest issues most people wrestle with, and this is especially true for Projectors. Let's explore Projector relationships next.

Chapter 19

Healthy Relationships

Relationships bring richness, personal growth, and companionship into our lives. Plus, there is nothing like a close relationship for bringing up our issues and wounds, and for challenging us to break through old patterns and emerge as more compassionate and mature.

Humans are fundamentally social creatures, and we are usually drawn to being with others. In order to fully thrive and be empowered and successful in life (based on your own definition of success, of course), you need to have healthy, supportive relationships. You don't need to have a lot of them, but you need at least a few.

The first thing to know is that our relationships are actually NOT personal. I know that seems weird at first. They usually feel *very* personal and very personally challenging, but when viewed through Human Design we see that our interactions are governed by the mechanics of the energy of each person's chart and how those energies interact. By knowing your own chart and the chart of the other person (lover, spouse, parent, child, friend, boss, co-worker, etc.), you can understand the easy energy flows and compatibilities, and the places of potential friction and misalignment of energy.

There are no "good" or "bad" relationships. Any relationship can work, with enough understanding and patience. There will be some people who are more compatible energetically with you, but that does not always translate into a great relationship. Plus, there are always non-chart factors, including your history and personal preferences, that come into play. But knowing the "lay of the land" of the relationship, by seeing the charts of two people and how their energies interact, can give us tremendous information and advantage. Entering into the relationship correctly, for each person (according to each one's Strategy and Authority), also has a significant impact on how the relationship plays out.

While relationships can be challenging for any person and for all Human Design Types, it will be helpful for us to identify the specific issues that Projectors encounter. But first, we need to start with the basics of how relationships work at the energetic level.

How Relationships Work Energetically

The openness in our charts is the medium through which we interact with each other. Any white area on your chart—centers, gates, whole channels—can be influenced by the corresponding defined areas on the charts of other people. The definition of others, and to a lesser degree the cosmic transits, condition our energy field specifically through our openness.

This is not a bad thing. It just IS. It is the way things work for us humans. We live in a constantly changing web of interactive energies that educate us about others and about ourselves, that can derail us from our truth, but that can also imbue us with wisdom and insight. This is how we learn and grow. Understanding these energy dynamics and applying them to our relationships can have a profound impact on the quality of those relationships.

Ra said the only thing more important than relationship dynamics is how we enter our relationships. Following Strategy and Authority will prevent us from entering the wrong relationships and help us enter the correct ones in the correct way. But the pull of passion, romance, and excitement from the Emotional Solar Plexus Center currently dominates the planet and can distract us from that relationship clarity.

The secret to all relationships is awareness and acceptance. In other words, let others be who they are. With patience, you can support others in being who they are designed to be and accept who they are right now. Ideally, this allows you to have honest and effective communication that nurtures the relationship long-term. Relationships are not about changing yourself or the other person.

A local client of mine was struggling with her relationship with her boyfriend (they were both in their sixties). In her reading, we talked a little about his chart but mostly, of course, about her chart. I saw her a few weeks later and asked how things were going. She said their relationship had improved tremendously. When I asked what changed, she said that she stopped expecting him to be someone that he is not.

Then she added that she also stopped expecting herself to be someone that she is not. Quite a profound shift.

The Energy Dynamics and Attractions within Relationships

In each relationship we have with another person, a temporary composite of the two sets of energies is formed—even if you are just walking past someone on the street. The influence from that passerby is just fleeting, but it is through our ongoing relationships that we are deeply conditioned by the people in our lives.

The energy dynamics of a relationship are all about chemistry and mechanics—it is not personal. When we remember this, and take the emotional reactions out of the dynamic, we can have a calmer and happier relationship experience without losing the passion or spontaneity that may exist there naturally.

With the magic of Human Design software programs, we can merge two people's charts into one **composite chart** that readily shows how each chart influences the other and how together they form a temporary energetic integration (a new quantum field).

There are two powerful attraction mechanisms that exist in the realm of composite charts and that influence our relationships. The first is the **electromagnetic** configuration.

When one person has one gate defined in a channel, and the other person has the opposite gate defined in that same channel, there is an electromagnetic attraction. Any defined half of a channel is always energetically seeking to complete the energy flow by connecting with the other defined half of the channel. When both defined halves of a channel connect within the composite of two charts, it creates a complete energy flow in the relationship.

This can draw two people together and help maintain their connection and relationship over time. It is usually the source of the spark first felt when attracted to someone. This, of course, also exists in non-romantic relationships where we can more easily see that this dynamic is an energetic attraction, not a physical or sexual one. Most romantic relationships have one or more electromagnetic connections, but some have none.

The second powerful attraction mechanism in the realm of composite charts is the **bridging of a split.**

A "split" is a separation between the groupings of defined centers on a personal chart. The centers within a grouping are connected by defined channels. Some charts have only one group of centers, in which all their defined centers are connected to each other, which is called Single Definition. Some charts have two groups that are not connected to each other, called Split Definition. There are also charts with three groupings (Triple Split) or four groupings (Quadruple Split).

We can feel incomplete due to our splits, and we are energetically drawn to people who supply the "missing" gates or channels that bridge (connect) our split or splits. We feel more whole, like we are firing on all cylinders, when we are around someone who bridges our split(s).

A Relationship Composite Reading will look at the two individuals' charts and their composite chart to explain the relationship dynamics between them, including the areas of flow and compatibility and the areas of potential struggle and what to do about them.

Relationship Challenges for Projectors

Now let us look at the specifics of how the natural talents and characteristics of Projectors affect our behaviors—and drive the dynamics—in our relationships.

There is profound wisdom and practical understanding available in exploring the issues of Projectors as children and Projectors as parents, but those are beyond the scope of this book. Those issues are addressed in my Success by Type course for Projectors and my Success for Projectors course.

What follows is an exploration of the general aspects of being a Projector that affect our relationships.

We as Projectors are here to **guide** the energy of others, so we naturally want to help others and give advice. Whether we are actually helpful, and whether our help is well received, depends on how we approach this.

When you are in a relationship with someone, it is usually not correct for you to try to manage, guide, or direct that other person unless they have specifically asked for guidance, and they specifically want *your* guidance. You will want to check your tendency to give **unsolicited advice** (even when it is for their own good!). And remember to use the phrasing technique you learned in The Little Decisions in Life section of Chapter 5.

Waiting for big invitations can definitely impact your relationships. The other person may be on hold in some way while you are waiting, and your attitude and mindset while waiting can deeply affect them.

Little invitations matter too. If the other person has asked for (invited) your guidance or advice, then they have opened an energetic space that you can speak into, and they will hear you. If you are just blurting out advice and suggestions without their invitation, they are not going to hear or value your advice. They will misinterpret what you say, feel irritated with you, think you are pushy, bossy, or nosy, or simply ignore you. Energetically, your advice will not feel good to them, even though you intended to be helpful.

Remember that it is just energy. Please do not take any of this personally. As Projectors, it is our **energetic configuration** that can put others on the defensive, even when we don't say a word! When you learn to work in alignment with your energy, you can become extremely effective and helpful in ways that are correct for you and feel good to others.

Watch out for **bitterness** or resentment showing up within your relationships. It is not healthy to allow any level of bitterness to linger there. Review Chapter 13 for tips on avoiding and dealing with bitterness. Ideally, when you are using your energy correctly, others will ask for your advice and guidance and will respect you, and bitterness will not show up.

Our drive for developing **expertise** in systems and areas of study can cause us to be very focused and even forget to have fun sometimes. Many non-Projectors simply do not understand the Projector's quest for knowledge, awareness, and proficiency, and we Projectors can easily feel isolated and left out. It helps to have people around who understand and support us, and who invite us into their activities and also allow us to pursue our own activities.

Sexuality can be an issue in any romantic relationship, and sexual energy for an open Sacral being (which is all Projectors) is quite different than for a defined Sacral being (all Generators and Manifesting Generators). The open Sacral Center gives Projectors an unlimited capacity to experience and express sexual energy, so you will need to experiment a little to find what works for you and you may not want to make a long-term commitment to your first sexual partner.

With **variable levels of energy**, we have a vital need to manage our energy and set healthy boundaries in relationships, which at times can cause upset and unfulfilled expectations. It is important to communicate your needs clearly, patiently, and with compassion—for yourself and for others—so others know what is going on with you. You may want to explain your energy dynamics, especially that you can work very hard sometimes but need to rest and restore after that. That pattern does not make sense to most Generators and Manifesting Generators, so you need to help them understand you. If you are in burnout, explain your situation and ask for the time and support you need so you can heal.

Variable work energy can also be a sticking point in relationships. The Sacral beings in your life will not understand that you cannot work the same way they can—unless you explain it to them. They still may not understand or like it. It can feel very uneven in a relationship if the other person does most of the work and the income earning. See if you both can associate value with what you do to contribute to the partnership, so an equitable balance is established. It can help for the Sacral person to understand they are designed to work (and to love their work) and you are designed for a different function.

Alone time is vital for Projectors to discharge energy picked up during the day and restore integrity to their energy field. Inform others of your needs for alone time, and maybe invite them to do something with you after you have rested. It can also tremendously help Projectors to sleep alone some or all of the time, so negotiate that with your partner with love and compassion.

By design, Projectors need more **attention and energy** from others than most people. This can seem needy to others. We also function best when we are invited, even for small things like cooking dinner together. Help others understand that receiving **recognition and invitations** from them keeps you healthy, balanced, and happy. When the other person gives you that recognition and attention, it can be a beautiful exchange of energy and work very well.

Not knowing when enough is enough can be a big issue in relationships. If you also have an open Spleen Center, you will hold onto things (clutter, anger, grudges, opinions, relationships) for longer than you should in addition to not knowing when enough is enough. All of this can, understandably, be hard for and frustrating to the other person. These are both open center issues (Sacral and Spleen) so focusing on your deconditioning of those centers and avoiding those predictable behavior patterns can help you move into the wisdom and away from the conditioned behaviors of those open centers.

A final point here is the impact on our relationships of our Projector gift and the challenge of **knowing others better than we know ourselves**. This can be baffling to others who often see us more clearly than we see ourselves. This personal challenge of ours also leads us to **talk through our decisions** with others (remember your personal Authority from Chapter 6). Our need for a sounding board listener can drive our friends and loved ones crazy, especially those who want to give us advice and not just listen. Being clear and honest in communicating your needs, and being compassionate and grateful to your listeners, can really help.

Advice for Projectors

Here are some how-to tips to help you have healthier and happier relationships. A few of them may not be easy to implement, but I encourage you to take these seriously. They *will* make a difference in your life and relationships.

We have mostly covered these in earlier chapters, and this list brings them together in one convenient place.

- Ask or offer before giving guidance or advice or wait quietly until they ask for it. Don't just tell people what they should do, or you'll come across as bossy, pushy, a know-it-all, etc., even with your best intentions to be helpful.
- Do not judge or criticize. This is harder to avoid if you have Gates 17 or 18 defined in your chart. Use your amazing gifts and talents wisely, in service to others, not in judgment of them.
- Be clear about your areas of knowledge and expertise. Do not assume expertise where you do not actually have it. Always be open to learning more, even where you do have high-level proficiency and deep knowledge.
- Wait patiently, wisely, and with a positive mindset to receive recognition,

invitations, and openings to speak into.

- Intentionally have a baseline energy frequency (your vibe) that is open to invitations and recognition, and welcome those. Stack the deck in your favor so you are easy to find as well as approachable.
- Stay out of the bitterness, resentment, and "it's not fair" spectrum. It repels and confuses people and makes you more miserable than you realize. It also keeps you stuck.
- Do not get caught up in another person's energy, especially if you have many open centers. Remember to be a screen, not a sponge, so you are not carrying around energy from others. Distinguish what is you and yours, and what is not. Let go of everything that is not yours.
- Set healthy boundaries, especially regarding energy, expectations, and responsibilities. Use your decision-making Strategy and Authority.
- Manage your energy wisely; sleep alone as needed.
- Cultivate your self-value—it resides within you and is independent of recognition from others.
- Be the lighthouse: Let your aura communicate your powerful beacon/message and draw the right people to you. Stand grounded in who you are and why you are here (even if you do not know the specifics yet). Stand firm in knowing that the right people and opportunities will find you (that is how this attraction-based universe operates), if we just allow everything to work as designed, including ourselves!
- Believe in and stand in your power and your importance to the world.
- Do not try to keep up with other Types, or even with other Projectors.
- Do not compare yourself to *anyone.*
- It usually works best to give your attention to one person at a time. Be aware that others around you may be jealous of your attention to that one person.
- Ideally, only step into groups when you have been invited, and only hold positions as leader, guide, or adviser—not as worker bee! But also, follow your bliss. For example, if you want to do some volunteer work, follow your heart and do that, but it may go better if you know someone there or someone introduces you or facilitates your entry there. But don't hold

back if none of that happens. Just do everything with your new awareness of what is truly correct and ideal for you, and what is not.

- You are here to know others, so be sure to look outward at them not inward at yourself. Too much self-reflection and self-exploration can tangle you up and choke off your progress. Recognize others for who they are and who they are designed to be (their potential). Also, be aware of their impact on you and your impact on them.
- You cannot change others, nor can they change you. Make peace with What Is even if you do not like it. Focus on what you do like (in yourself and others), which will bring forth more of that. When you focus on what you don't like, you bring forth more of that.

Advice for Others in Relationship with a Projector

Now we look at how to have a relationship *with* a Projector, whether you are a Projector yourself or one of the other Types. Here is a list of helpful tips.

- Invite the Projector and include them in activities. Help them feel seen, recognized, and valued. They may have a history of feeling invisible or like an outcast.
- Ask for their advice. They can be an impressive resource for you, and they usually have valuable input. Give them some attention and energy and invite them to share their ideas with you.
- Recognize them for who they are and their strengths; do not judge or criticize them. For example, do not call them lazy or weak.
- Allow them to be who they are; do not try to change them or improve them.
- Facilitate invitations for them. Help things be easy for them so they can contribute their brilliance and wisdom without exhaustion.
- Be a sounding board for them, without giving unsolicited advice.
- Respect their need to manage their energy and to have some alone time, including the need to sleep alone.
- If they overstep their bounds, be patient and understanding; they genuinely want to help but may not go about it effectively sometimes. Do not take it personally. When you are the recipient of a Projector's

incorrect use of their energy and wisdom, it is easy to feel irritated, turned off, and even repelled. This is normal. Even Projectors can feel this way toward other Projectors. However, you then miss the wisdom and advice that may very well benefit you. If you feel you just want to get away from them, get out of their aura for a while and then ask for their opinion or guidance the next time you see them—*before* they offer it. This corrects the energy flow between you.

- Do not push them into things that YOU think would be good for them. Let them make their own choices in their own time using their Strategy and Authority, but also be a sounding board and support them when they need that. Love them as they are.

Relationships with Each of the Types

Patterns that emerge in a relationship between two people often are rooted specifically in their Types. Next, we will look at the issues facing a Projector with a partner of each Type. While the main focus here is on intimate relationships, much of the information also applies to family, friendships, and work relationships.

Projector-Projector Relationship

I know of several long-term relationships between two Projectors, including my own of more than twenty-six years. It can work and it can work long term, although it does have its challenges. When the energy and nuances of each person are understood, it makes a huge difference.

Strategy is key when you have two Projectors in a relationship. Let them invite each other. Let them recognize and value each other and ask for opinions and guidance from each other. When couples do this, it can work beautifully.

A relationship between two Projectors is usually a nice, calm type of relationship that is very appealing to many Projectors. Because they are both here to guide others and the world, they can provide guidance together in very powerful ways and support each other in doing that.

There are potential challenges. If they do not understand their energy dynamics, they can both be critical of each other which can be toxic in a relationship. They can be bitter and never feel recognized for their wisdom, particularly if they are not being asked for their advice. There is also the issue of sustainable energy. Who is going to work and earn income? Who is going to do the yardwork and the housework? These issues can be very challenging for two Projectors.

If together they define the Sacral Center through an electromagnetic, that will give them Sacral energy within the relationship. They are still open Sacral beings on their own, but when together, they get Sacral energy from the combination of their two charts. This can be helpful for having energy and getting things done, but it can also disturb their sleep and they may sleep best alone.

Also, sexuality can be an issue for two open Sacral Centers. They can be very wise about sexuality and have an unlimited capacity to express sexual energy, but a Projector couple can also lack the spark for sexual energy if they keep the Sacral open in their composite.

Projector-Reflector Relationship

This is an interesting combination. The Projector can support the Reflector in taking the time the Reflector needs to make decisions and adjustments, and the Reflector will gratefully feel understood and loved. The Projector will need recognition, appreciation, and invitations from the Reflector. When they both understand what each one needs, it can be a very beautiful relationship.

The same potential exists here for defining the Sacral Center through an electromagnetic as it does in a Projector-Projector relationship, with the same benefits and challenges. And the same work, money, and sexuality issues can exist as well.

The Reflector can be very anchored and even be the CEO of a large corporation or have other major responsibilities. They can also be a gypsy and just want to float freely and not be tied down. The Reflector and Projector would need to negotiate the relationship so that it works for both. The Reflector will need a lot of consistent support and energy from the Projector.

Projector-Manifestor Relationship

Again, we have two open Sacral beings, but this combination is a bit different because the Manifestor has a motorized Throat Center and can more easily make action happen in the world than other open Sacral Types. This can help to solve the issues of work and money in the relationship, although both people will still need to manage their energy.

For a healthy relationship, the Manifestor needs to recognize the wisdom of the Projector, and the Projector needs to wait for the Manifestor to ask for help or guidance.

The Projector can be the Manifestor's greatest resource, but Manifestors are here to initiate action and make things happen. They are not here to be told what to do and, more than any of the other Types, they do not like to be told what to do. If the Projector is using their Projector energy incorrectly giving unsolicited advice, that clash could be significant. Neither will feel respected or honored.

It is important for the Manifestor to understand that the Projector is not deliberately criticizing, although it may feel like criticism. For the Manifestor to access the wisdom of the Projector, the Manifestor must recognize and invite the Projector to share that wisdom and then actually listen to that wisdom.

As we saw with the first two relationship combinations, the two people in this combination can also potentially create definition in the Sacral Center together and experience the benefits and challenges of that extra energy within the relationship.

Projector-Generator and Projector-Manifesting Generator Relationship

The key here, again, for a healthy and strong relationship is for each party to follow their Strategy and respect and honor the Strategy of the other. The Projector can take the lead in guiding the relationship if recognized and invited. If not, their partner will perceive the Projector as bossy or controlling.

The Manifesting Generator in particular does not want to be managed by the Projector unless they have asked for help. To either Type, the Projector could say something like, "May I help you with this?" or "I have some suggestions that may help. Would you like to hear them?" This is a healthy way to approach it, allowing the other to answer with their Sacral response.

It helps for the Generator or Manifesting Generator to know that Projectors want and need recognition and attention. Without this awareness, the Projector can seem emotionally needy. When recognition is given, there can be a beautiful flow of energy, and the Projector can be a brilliant resource for the Generator or the Manifesting Generator in that relationship.

The defined Sacral person is often the one who gets things done in this relationship, especially when the Projector does not have the energy to do those things. This can be an excellent combination where the Projector guides and directs, and the Generator or Manifesting Generator accomplishes tasks using the wisdom of the Projector—as long as there is understanding, agreement, and no resentment about it.

I have had Generator clients say, "The Projector is always bossing me around. I don't like being their worker bee." Generators and Manifesting Generators are actually here to be worker bees, but the specifics need to be negotiated in the relationship so both parties feel honored and valued for the energy (Sacral) and guidance (Projector) they each bring.

It is very useful for the Projector to almost exclusively use yes/no questions with the Generator or Manifesting Generator so that the Projector activates the lifeforce energy response of their partner. This helps their partner access their own internal guidance, which is a wise exchange of energy between them and a great way to keep the relationship strong.

Often Overlooked Relationships

To close this chapter, let's address several relationships we all have in life that are often overlooked when understanding and working on our usual and more obvious relationships.

We have talked a lot about self-value and self-love, but not specifically in the context of one of our most important relationships in this life—our **relationship with ourselves!** I invite you to now use this context. Treat yourself as if you are a Projector whom you deeply love and respect—your best friend ever. How would you want her to treat herself? How could you support and nurture him? Try this and see what insights and new awareness show up. Remember to know yourself, accept yourself, respect yourself, and love yourself. My deepest hope for you is to wake up each morning *loving* being you and *loving* being alive. If your circumstances are lousy, you can still love yourself and love that each day you have an opportunity to make the best of things and improve your circumstances if you can. Even if your circumstances are already good (or even perfect), things can always get even better. No matter what goes on around you, you can still love yourself unconditionally. That is one of the single most powerful things you can do to begin turning your circumstances around.

Many of us have a **relationship with God/Source/Higher Power** that gives our life added meaning and deeper connections. It often gives us community and shared values and practices. It teaches us faith and gives us a bigger picture perspective. If it supports you and your growing consciousness, cultivate this relationship and nurture your faith in your faith.

Ra Uru Hu referred to the neutrino stream that is the basis for the flow of energy to and through this planet as "the Program." It is this energy that activates and carries the planetary influences that imprint us at birth and condition us throughout our lives. Although we may be unaware of it, we all have a **relationship with the Program**. We are constantly under its influence and cannot escape it. We have two choices. We can accept and enjoy the Program and go with the flow, or we can resist and struggle, force and push, deny and reject it. Surrendering to the Program is not about giving up or being a victim. It is about making peace with What Is and making the best of it, with the least amount of stress and strife. Which are you choosing?

Finally, we have an inherent **relationship with the planet** on which we live and with all of life around us. How we treat ourselves and each other is often reflected in how we treat nature and all living things. It is worth looking at life holistically and viewing our role, our potential, and our contribution to the global level's greatest good through that perspective. If you believe that every thought, word, and deed matters, it gives you a different relationship with our Mother Earth and all her inhabitants than you had before.

I have saved for the next chapter what is probably the most important issue for Projectors in our journey to becoming truly empowered: How we take care of ourselves and our energy so we can truly thrive.

Chapter 20

Energy, Self-Care, and Thriving

This is perhaps the most important chapter in this book, which is why I have put it near the end. This is where we put all the puzzle pieces together so we have a complete picture of what it looks like to be empowered as a Projector, and how we can become and sustain that in our lives.

The first thing I want to state unequivocally is that vibrant health and a thriving, empowered life is absolutely possible for a Projector! A vital component of this state of being is resiliency.

As we have seen, resiliency is the ability to recover quickly and spring back into shape when pushed, challenged, or stressed. It requires doing what you need to do to keep yourself in great shape physically, mentally, emotionally, and spiritually, and to have accumulated reserves you can draw from when needed. It means having more than enough of what you need in good times so you can easily get through the tough times. It means long-term sustainability—Projector style.

Remember that balance is a dynamic state of being. It is not static or rigid. It bends and flows, adapting and changing over time. When you are flexible and operating from the high expression of each of the Nine Resiliency Keys, you ARE resilient. When you combine that with the information in this book about becoming a successful Projector, you ARE empowered. When you apply all of this to your life over time, you WILL THRIVE in ways you cannot even imagine right now.

So, let's get busy putting it all together.

"How Do I Get my Life to Work?"

I hear this question often from Projectors who are struggling. No matter what they try, it doesn't seem to work, and I've seen their life circumstances go from bad to worse to much worse. How do they reverse that trend and start moving upward? Is there a way that unlocks the good stuff into their lives?

Not only are we each unique in our energy configurations, but we also have unique genetics, conditioning, experiences, desires, and preferences. There is not one key or trick or solution that will work for every Projector.

That said, there is one approach that allows for and works with each person's uniqueness—**alignment**. This means aligning your thoughts, words, actions, and beliefs with *your* truth, your inner knowing, your heart, and your soul. It means facing and learning the lessons that are right there in front of you, the ones that are keeping you stuck. It means having integrity with yourself. It means doing the work, healing the pain and, step by step, discovering your right path.

In order to align, you first need to make peace with What Is. We cannot change anything if we do not acknowledge where we are starting from. Only then can we have better clarity about how to get where we want to go.

You don't have to like where you are starting from, but you have to acknowledge it. You need to be clear-eyed about your current circumstances, issues, and patterns. Because people rarely see themselves clearly, and this is especially true for Projectors, you may need professional counseling or trusted friends to give you honest feedback about what they see is going on with you.

It is vital to avoid judging or blaming yourself. You have done the best you could with what you had, from where you were, and with what you knew. That was then, and this is now. You are now light-years ahead of where you were last week, or yesterday, or even three hours ago. When ready, allow the feedback from others and your own new clarity about yourself to seep in and start to shift your energy and mindset. Then start taking baby steps in the direction that feels right. Mindset and self-value are the best places to start.

You are breaking new ground, so be patient with yourself. Ask for help. Accept, acknowledge, appreciate, and be grateful for the help you receive. Give back as much as you reasonably can right now. Pay it forward as you are able. Sometimes complete surrender is necessary before you can hear and feel the true calling and direction of your heart and soul. If you are exhausted or in serious burnout, you need to heal that first.

Characteristics that Impact Our Energy and Empowerment

Below is a list of the major Projector characteristics and tendencies that impact health and well-being and therefore affect our ability to thrive and be empowered. These are also possible sources of burnout so this list will help remind you of the patterns to avoid. The experience and expression of these characteristics will be different for each Projector, but the themes are quite consistent. If the low expressions of these issues do not resonate with you, I am giving you a high five and saying to keep doing what you are doing!

If they *do* resonate, this review will help you make peace with them and make healthier, more aware choices related to them. We have seen these characteristics in previous chapters, but now we are looking at them specifically through the lens of health, resiliency, and self-empowerment.

Not knowing when enough is enough. This alone can be a serious recipe for burnout because you end up pushing yourself, running on fumes, and eventually frying your energy circuits. Focus on enoughness and sufficiency, and use amplified Sacral energy from others wisely but not to your detriment.

Inconsistent energy. It is especially hard to work consistently to earn a living in this Generator-modeled world. While we are not designed to work in that way, most of us must work so do your best and take extra good care of yourself while looking for as much flexibility as possible in your work schedule. On top of that, you might be in the wrong career for you, or the right career but the wrong job, all of which will drain your energy and leave you feeling disempowered.

Working all the time. We are converting the Sacral energy around us and flowing it through us. We are cleaning the collective aura of the lifeforce energy on the planet. We are keeping the energy grid of the planet intact, while others work and play. No wonder we are tired; even when it looks like we are "doing nothing" we are working hard!

But please don't use this as an excuse to remain in burnout or feel like a victim. This big picture view can help you make more sense of your experience and make peace with it so you can leverage your energy appropriately and release your true wisdom and brilliance.

Comparing ourselves with other Types, or even with other Projectors. This sets up a self-judgment or even a competitive atmosphere that can quite predictably lead to low self-esteem and/or burnout.

Needing recognition and invitations to activate our energy and take on big projects. We are not here to initiate without an invitation; we are here to wait for the right recognition and invitation. It is easy to exhaust ourselves by trying to initiate things and make things happen when we are *not* waiting, *not* positioning ourselves wisely, and *not* operating correctly as a Projector. It is easy to blame ourselves (or others) when we are not receiving recognition and invitations.

Needing to wait. It can be exhausting to wait if you are not trusting that this IS your best approach and that it is worth the patience. Waiting can also elicit negative reactions from others, which can lead to self-criticism and a negative self-image—all of which can lead to a lack of resiliency and eventually to burnout.

Here to guide the energy of others. We try to guide and to create order from chaos, but often it does not work very well. It can feel like such an uphill struggle, yet we try so hard to do it right and be of service. It is even more painful when we get criticized and feel rejected, bitter, and isolated. All of this is deeply damaging to our well-being.

Here to achieve mastery and immerse ourselves in a knowledge base (or two!). This can be a joyful, exciting, and fulfilling experience if done correctly, or exhausting and discouraging if not done correctly.

Being deeply conditioned by others. This conditioning can hijack you from your True Self. You may feel you have to create a mask or false persona to present to the world, and that takes tremendous energy to maintain. Trying to be who you are not, but who you *think* you should be, can completely wipe you out.

Not here to know ourselves. Not easily knowing yourself can be confusing and frustrating and cause you to make choices that are not in alignment with your Truth. Misaligned decisions are setbacks on the path to empowerment and vitality.

Needing to talk through our decisions. Most Projectors benefit from this process (review Chapter 6 on decision-making Authority), but it can frustrate those around you who may complain that "you talk too much" and who may be baffled and ask, "how can you not know yourself?" If you do not have reliable sounding board friends for this process, your decision making can suffer, and you can end up making less than ideal choices for yourself.

Struggling with sleep. Many Projectors struggle with sleep, probably from the open Sacral Center carrying Sacral energy picked up during the day, but also perhaps from the energy grid work done at night. Sleep is the number one thing that affects our health on an everyday basis and is even more important than exercise or food. Whether you are burned out, recovering, or avoiding burnout, be sure to GET ENOUGH SLEEP. In fact, get more than enough for a while to re-build your energy reserves.

Not having trust/faith; living in fear or anxiety. Living in fear or anxiety causes chronic stress which is terrible for your health and resiliency, and which leads to burnout. Living without faith in yourself, in the universe, or in the process of how things work, can lead to self-doubt, suspicion of others, feeling alone, or feeling helpless and powerless—all of which will wreck your well-being and resiliency. What fears are Projectors prone to? Primarily, the fear of not being valued or recognized, not being seen, not measuring up, and not fulfilling potential. Also, look at the defined gates on your Spleen Center and the Splenic Fears associated with those gates. (See my free blogpost series on the Fears of the Spleen from the link on the Resources Page.)

Guidelines for Self-Care and Stepping into Your Power

These guidelines will help you **become** resilient, **stay** empowered, and **recover** quickly from burnout so you can regain your well-being and resiliency as fast as possible. We have seen most of these earlier in the book. They are brought together here as a good reference list of the most important items to keep in mind.

Of course, add your own items to this list as you discover what works best for *you.* These are not the last words on resiliency and empowerment. They are a beginning point—the basics.

Manage YOUR energy. Spend, conserve, replenish, and enjoy your energy in ways that work for you. Leverage energy every chance you get, to produce big results with small effort. Treat your energy as the precious resource it is. It is renewable but finite so it must be deliberately managed. One way is to set reasonable expectations of yourself by not comparing yourself to others and by having a realistic sense of what you can do. Also, manage and set the expectations of others so you no longer let yourself be derailed by their expectations. Value yourself and your energy so much that you set and keep healthy boundaries. Remember to give to others from your saucer, not from your cup!

Actively cultivate self-value. Feel and believe within yourself that you are a success, on your own terms, especially given what you have had to work with. Give yourself a lot of credit for getting to where you are now! Acknowledge your efforts and celebrate your successes, no matter how small. Re-build your self-confidence. Use the Nine Resiliency Keys (of which Self-Worth is just one) to keep yourself at the top of your game in every area of life.

Ask for help; receive help gratefully. We've covered this several times, but it is important enough to be included on this list.

Learn how to rest and take care of yourself. Seriously. We are notoriously bad at truly resting, mostly because we are trying to prove ourselves and we feel anxious that we might not measure up. Find activities (including naps!) that replenish the soul and restore energy. Allow yourself to BE, just as you are. Even just for a few minutes each day—have nothing to DO. You are more than enough without doing anything. To replenish yourself, spend time in nature, move your body (dance, yoga, walking, play with kids and/or dogs, garden), volunteer to help others, cook, do crafts, learn something new. The possibilities are nearly endless.

Wake up each day feeling good about YOU. Experience and express joy every day. Relax some of your high standards for yourself and for others. Have more fun!

Guide with wisdom, but only when asked. Your most powerful tools are questions that illuminate the issues and allow the other person to gain new clarity. When you are guiding, do so from a place of service, not from your own agenda.

Use your Strategy and Authority. Learn to wait with a positive mindset. Discern the correct recognitions and invitations and say no to the wrong ones. Be very selective about whose energy you connect into. Be authentic in all your interactions. Practice with and learn to trust your Authority so you are making aligned decisions that support your highest good and serve the fulfillment of your important role.

Let go of the wounding and the blame of the past (and the present). Let go of what happened and how unfair it was. Let go of whose fault it was—yours, theirs, God's. Let go of your identity as a wounded self or as a burned-out self. To heal from pain and burnout, you must become and BE someone who is building health, strength, and resiliency. Avoid being someone in recovery. Identify with the end result you want, and do this day by day, breath by breath, and thought by thought.

It is possible to have unwanted physical issues and still be happy, healthy, resilient, and empowered. Having an unwanted condition or challenge does not mean you have failed or that it is impossible for you to thrive. Quite the opposite. Maybe there is a very valuable lesson for you to take from the experience. Maybe there is a life-changing message you can give to others about it. Be as happy and resilient as you can possibly be every day, and work to expand those possibilities at every opportunity.

Re-craft your story so it empowers you. Shifting and transforming the stories and repeated phrases you say about yourself and your life is a powerful tool. See the next chapter for specific ways to do this. Don't underestimate the impact that replacing your old painful, disempowered stories can have. If you believe that people commit to their life circumstances before birth for the purpose of evolving their consciousness, then embrace that you chose this Projector experiment this time around. Feeling doomed, hopeless, helpless, or flawed does not serve you one tiny bit. Those feelings do tremendous harm. Call yourself out on these feelings and intentionally replace them.

Every day, move in the direction of unconditional self-love. Remember that this progress is rarely linear—there will be hops, leaps, and backsliding. But you will be on the right path, with clarity about where you are headed. Every bit of forward progress counts, every shift matters, and even the setbacks are part of the process.

Allow synchronicities, magic, and wonderful surprises to show up in your life. This is a direct relative of being invitable and findable so you can be well positioned for recognition and invitations. Cultivate a quality of wonder, awe, and openness that not only allows but actually attracts wonderful things to you. Let yourself be surprised and delighted. They say that when you look for things to be happy and grateful about, you will find them. It is true.

Words to live by. Occasionally we come across a paradigm shifting idea or phrase that changes our life forever from the first moment we hear it. I came across one of those a few decades ago when listening to an Abraham-Hicks CD. Abraham said:

"Speak to everyone about what you like. Speak to no one, not even yourself, about what you don't like."

It might take a while to fully grapple with and implement this in your life. (I'm still working on it!) It provides a grounded and practical way to leverage the Law of Attraction. Applying this can completely shift what you talk about and what you think is important to share with others. Do you really want to keep repeating the story of how someone cut you off in traffic this morning, or complaining about something unfair that happened to you years ago? Or can you let those go completely and focus on what you *do* like and want more of? If you have complainer-friends, this shift will alter those relationships. But it will be for your benefit, and ultimately for the greater good of the planet. Remember the big role Projectors are here to play!

Before we wrap things up with a chapter on retelling your personal story, let's meet one more famous Projector. She was dangerously burned out before she got serious about taking better care of herself. Then she shared her story and her message with the world about how to create a balanced life and thrive on one's own terms.

Meet a Projector - Arianna Huffington

Arianna Huffington is a no-motors Projector with only the Head, Ajna, and Throat Centers defined. This co-founder and original CEO of the *Huffington Post* online news outlet (which later became the *HuffPost*) hit a serious burnout point before she learned to slow down and take better care of herself. She is a great example of burnout, recovery, self-empowerment, and a new version of success.

In 2007 she had been working nearly around the clock when she passed out sitting at her desk. She woke up with blood around her from her head having hit the desk. This caused her to redefine success for herself and ponder the question "What is a good life?" She used her access to media to create a national conversation about what makes life fulfilling and meaningful. She continued to work very productively, part of the time as editor-in-chief during major transitions of the company being bought by bigger enterprises, although she made crucial changes in her daily work-life balance and really "walked her talk."

She was a nationally syndicated columnist and author of thirteen books prior to writing her book, *Thrive*, which is about living a more mindful and meaningful life and defining success on our own terms. She then gave lectures and workshops on the topic. Her chart shows her propensity for stories, details, depth, family, spirituality, and her love of humanity. In 2013 she was added to the *Forbes* Most Powerful Women List, and she has won numerous other awards and recognitions.

Learn more about Arianna Huffington and details of her Human Design chart in my Celebrity Chart Review of her on my website. Find the link from the Resources Page.

Name:	Arianna Huffington
Birth Date:	15 July 1950, 15:00
Birth Place:	Athens, Attiki, Greece
Type:	Orchestrator (Projector)
Inner Authority:	No Inner Authority (No Inner Authority)
Profile:	2/4 - Responder / Stabilizer
Definition:	Single
Strategy:	Wait for Recognition and Invitation
Themes:	Success / Bitterness
Incarnation Cross:	RAX Maya 2
Channels:	1762 - Formulation (Acceptance) 2461 - Cosmic Perspective (Awareness)

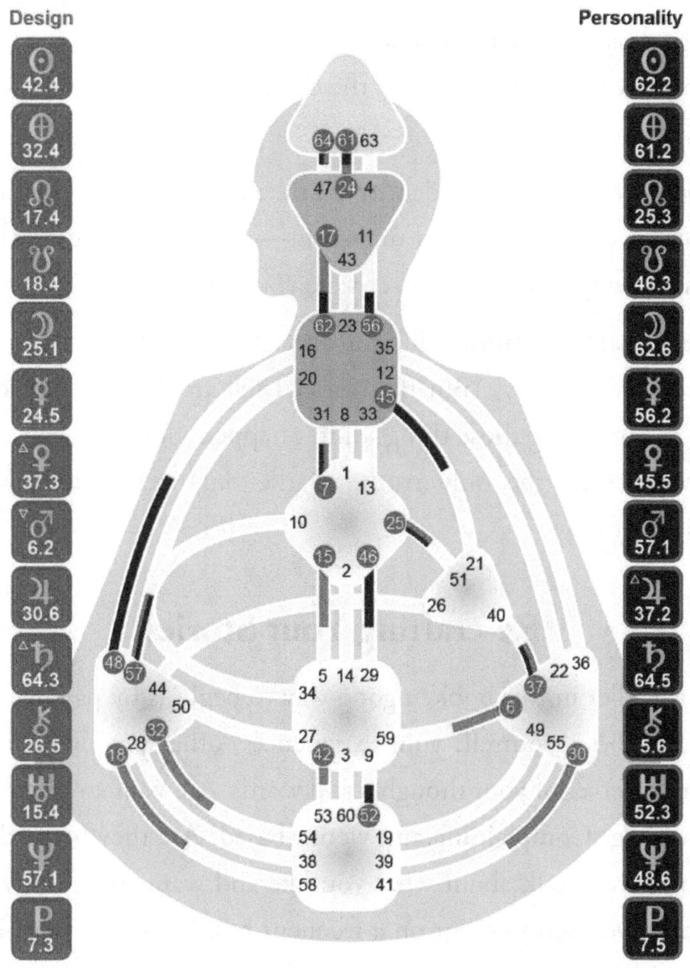

Quantum Human Design © Karen Curry Parker. All Rights Reserved.

Chapter 21

Telling a New Story

To become truly empowered, you need beliefs, behaviors, a mindset, and habits that support complete self-empowerment every day and that help you flourish and thrive for the rest of your days.

To change those beliefs, behaviors, mindset, and habits, you need to start telling new, more empowering stories. But for the changes to be permanent, you must also change your identity.

The good news is that your identity is still all about the stories. The stories we tell—about ourselves, our lives, and the world—create our sense of who we are. To transform your identity and your life, change your stories!

Some people argue against telling a different story about their life and their experiences because they say, "But the stories I tell are TRUE. Those things really happened." I'm not saying those things didn't happen, but what you *say* about what happened may not be the only truth, or the only perspective. Maybe a new perspective is possible.

Re-crafting Your Stories

As we saw earlier in this book, a good way to begin is by paying close attention to what you say about yourself, your experiences, other people, and the world in general. Be the observer of your thoughts and words. Are your stories mostly negative and disempowering? Complaining and victim-based? Are they focused on what you don't want, or do you talk about what you like and want more of? What vibe and what message are you sending out on a frequent basis? Are you putting out a lot of mixed messages?

Once you see your patterns with new clarity, begin to identify the big and/or recurring stories that irritate, deflate, or anger you the most. Those are the ones ripe for re-crafting.

To start with, pick a slightly easier one so you can practice, then move to the tougher stories. Choose a different perspective and a somewhat more empowering telling of that experience. Pretend you are an outsider hearing it for the first time. What different assumptions or conclusions might an outsider make, not knowing your issues and history with it? See if you can be more general and less personal in describing it. You might try a few different versions of retelling the same event. (What if you could choose to not tell that story at all anymore?!)

Here's an example. Let's say someone cut you off in traffic recently, zooming recklessly in front of you, nearly causing an accident, and it makes you hopping mad every time you think about it. You tell the story often, getting mad every time, because it was such an injustice, so unfair, and so dangerous. Perhaps it actually frightened you, but you cover that with anger and with feeling like a victim. What if that person was racing to the hospital because a loved one was dying? What if they were angry about something and taking it out on the world? What if they were just being stupid and reckless? Is it worth your getting mad repeatedly about it? It probably had nothing to do with you personally. Instead, maybe you could say this about it, "Someone cut me off in traffic and I'm grateful they didn't cause and involve me in an accident. It was close." That is still the truth, but there is less anger and sting in your words. What if you never brought it up or even thought about it again?

Here is another example. Let's say you are mad at your sister because three years ago she broke a promise to you that really broke your heart (and made you mad) and you have not spoken with her since. Your story about it is that she broke a promise to you, and you cannot forgive her for it. Have you ever broken a promise? (Really, never?) When you did, maybe you did not know how important it was to the other person, or that it really upset them. Maybe you had extenuating circumstances that prevented you from keeping that promise. Maybe you tried to communicate ahead of time, but your communication did not get through. Maybe you did not know that it never went through. Maybe you wanted to tell your side of the story, but the other person never gave you the chance because they no longer talk to you. Maybe you never even had the chance to say you were sorry. Or, maybe you had just forgotten about the promise and never meant to hurt that person. There are so many possible scenarios.

Now, imagine that your sister is YOU from that story. What could you say now that would be a little softer about your sister? "My sister really hurt my feelings a few years ago but there must have been something going on with her, she usually doesn't do things like that." Or if she does often break promises to you, you could say, "It's part of a pattern of hers and maybe I need to not take it so personally; she probably didn't mean to hurt me deliberately." Even if it was deliberate, your holding on to anger, resentment, and lack of forgiveness is hurting you more than her. You get the picture. Practice changing the words you use in talking about it. Your softer words will ease your feelings, and your softer feelings will ease your actions. Maybe you'll become willing to hear her side of it, or maybe you can just forgive her and get on with your happy, abundant, empowered life. A truly empowered life has no room for resentments, grudges, and withheld forgiveness.

A Positive Reinforcement Story

A simple, positive, and empowering way to shift your story and your identity is to start noticing any movement or improvement in your desired direction and reinforce it. An easy way to do this is to say, "I'm the kind of person who ___" and add to that sentence the action you did that you are reinforcing. My colleague Robin Gallob learned this from Wendy Hart, who calls it *prizing.* It is a statement of what is true, so you are not lying to yourself. By recognizing the action that proves this quality is true for you, you strengthen that quality.

For example, when you notice something positive in your life, say, "I'm the kind of person who notices what is going well for me." When you take your time to make a decision, waiting through your emotional wave (if you have Emotional Authority), say, "I'm the kind of person who trusts my Emotional Authority and waits through my wave to make wise decisions that align me with my True Self." When you say no to an invitation that does not feel good, then say to yourself, "I'm the kind of person who values themself enough to say no when the invitation isn't right for me, and that feels good."

You could also use this phrase to inspire yourself to become who and how you want to be. "I'm the kind of person who has money and resources that come easily."

That may not be true right now, but it might help to say it out loud and feel into what it would be like to have it *be* true. This is a form of seeding that is essentially an affirmation. This approach doesn't work for everyone but could be worth trying. "I'm the kind of person who senses when to speak and when to wait, and who waits patiently and joyfully."

For the Fantasy Lovers

Here is a fun (and optional) way to craft and reinforce a new and empowering version of you. Create a new story about you and your progress in life as a fairytale/fantasy told in the third person. To do this we will use a "story spine" which is a framework for the structure of a compelling story. This was created by Kenn Adams for use by improv actors (those who work without a script, making up a scene/story on the spot). It gives us an excellent framework for creating our own empowering new story.

1. Once upon a time…
2. And every day…
3. Until one day… (this is the Pivot Point)
4. And because of that…
5. And because of that…
6. And because of that…
7. Until finally…
8. And ever since…

To get you started, here is an example that creates a little more of the story but still lets you fill in the details.

****

Once upon a time there was a beautiful woman who was smart and kind and who wanted to help others and fulfill her unique purpose on the planet. But she was ____________ and ____________.

And every day she struggled with ____________.

Until one day, she learned that ____________ and she began to practice doing ____________.

And because of that, she started to ____________ differently.

And because of that, she was able to ____________ better and be more effective with ____________.

And because of that she was able to fundamentally shift her ____________.

Until finally one day, she realized she was ____________ and that she had always ____________ and was now fulfilling her purpose with grace, ease, and pure delight.

And ever since, she has been ____________ and ____________.

****

Now, write your own story. Let your imagination run wild but keep the essence of *you* in the story. Have fun with it. You may surprise yourself with what you come up with.

Fall in Love with Your Projector Self!

We have come through this empowerment journey together, and now it is time for you to spread your wings and take flight. You are extraordinary and the world is lucky to have you. You are a gift and a blessing. Just as you are.

What I want *for you* is to feel calm, peaceful, valuable, and strong deep in the core of your being. I want you to fall in love with your amazing self. Breathe. Relax. Be grateful for All That You Are, in all your brilliance, your uniqueness, your humanness, and your Projector-ness. Step into your power fully and thrive joyfully. I want you to feel you are coming back home… to your True Self.

What I want *for all Projectors* is for us to step up and stand strong and empowered in our vital role of guiding the evolution of consciousness and compassion on the planet. We are here right now for a reason. This is our time to shine. This is our role to play. This is our contribution to make. We can do it on our own terms. Let's lead by our example and inspire through our guidance.

What I want *for humanity* is for everyone to have access to resources and support so they can thrive, for everyone to be honored for their unique contribution and accepted for who they are, and for the development and timely implementation of creative, sustainable, and equitable solutions to the challenges facing our society and planet.

If I may, I humbly offer a new affirmation for Projectors everywhere:

I am fully aligned with my unique and brilliant True Self,
and I love being an empowered Projector!

What's Next

You now have new knowledge, deep awareness, and powerful tools to support your growth into a truly empowered Projector. You may be wondering about the best next steps for you. You know enough to be ready to move forward, and there are many possible options. Which should you choose?

That is a very personal choice and one that I encourage you to use your personal Authority to help you decide! If you are in a hurry to consider your options, go directly to **EmpoweredProjector.com/resources** for a list of free and paid resources and next steps you can explore right away.

If you are still here, there are three basic directions you can pursue.

#1 There are **free materials** on my website HumanDesignforSuccess.com, including nearly 200 blogposts, to expand your understanding of Human Design and of yourself. But that is the slowest way, and it lacks a personalized and integrated perspective about you and your chart. (Also, please be discerning about other free information you find on the internet—not all of it is of high quality or accuracy.)

#2 There are **online courses and live programs** from my website and other qualified teachers. I offer courses about Types and centers, and specific courses for Projectors. These provide more detailed and organized information to deepen the study of yourself and Human Design. But this choice still lacks the personalized application and integration of the information for YOU.

#3 The quickest and most effective way to learn more about YOU and apply that information directly to your life is through **interactive private readings**. These give you a personalized explanation and synthesis of your chart details so you can have a fully integrated interpretation and immediately apply those insights and wisdom to your daily life, your relationships, and your important decisions. Find a practitioner you trust. Visit the link above for information about available readings with me. If you don't know which reading to choose, learn more about them on my website, and contact me from there if you want help deciding.

Be sure to pick up your list of the Top Ten Awesome Things About Being a Projector from the Resources Page. Enjoy it and add your own items to the list!

Resources Page

To supplement what you learn in this book, here are some resources that will broaden and deepen your knowledge about yourself and others, through Human Design. You will find all the resources below on the online Resources Page at this link: **EmpoweredProjector.com/resources**

Links to:

- get a Human Design chart for yourself or others
- join my Empowered Projector Facebook group
- see Celebrity Chart Reviews of famous Projectors highlighted in this book
- read the Fears of the Spleen series of blogposts
- read about Relationship Composite charts and readings

Free downloads you can request to supplement the book's content:

- Top Ten Reasons to Wait for an Invitation handout
- Top Ten Awesome Things about Being a Projector handout
- 3 Mistakes Projectors Make webinar replay
- 4 Crucial Stages of Self Growth handout

Courses and Programs information:

- Success for Projectors online course
- Success by Type–Projector Module online course
- Success by Centers online course
- Healing the Projector live program

Human Design Readings information:

- Initial and Full Readings
- Life Path and Soul Mission Reading
- Readings packages and other Specialty Readings

Links to recommended books for purchase about Human Design

Quantum Alignment System™ information

Notes

1. The Quantum Human Design term for the Type. Used with permission.
2. Lynda Bunnell and Ra Uru Hu, *The Definitive Book of Human Design* (Carlsbad: HDC Publishing, 2011), 129.
3. https://en.wikipedia.org/wiki/Axial_precession
4. Karen Curry Parker, *Introduction to Quantum Human Design* (Colorado Springs: GracePoint Publishing, 2020), 28.
5. https://brenebrown.com/articles/2013/01/15/shame-v-guilt/
6. http://positivepsychologynews.com/news/steve-safigan/2012051622128
7. https://quotepark.com/quotes/1294595-fulton-j-sheen-patience-is-power-patience-is-not-an-absence-of-a/
8. https://www.psychologytoday.com/us/blog/evil-deeds/200906/anger-disorder-part-two-can-bitternessbecome-mental-disorder
9. https://mackeyadvisors.com/what-is-enoughness/

Acknowledgments

My eternal gratitude goes to Karen Curry Parker for her generous and tireless work to expand the potential of Human Design and uplift people everywhere. Without her, I would not have found this work, engaged with this loving community, or discovered my own true calling. And this book would never have emerged.

My amazing book editors at GracePoint Publishing have earned and deserve my highest praise. Shauna Hardy's unwavering support and guidance of my work helped to shape this book and gave me the courage to keep going even when it felt hard. The skillful edits of Laurie Knight and Deborah Levering have elevated and polished my work to high standards. My heartfelt thanks to you three and to the entire team at GracePoint.

The contributions and support from my fellow Projector, colleague, and friend Robin Gallob have immeasurably improved this book. Her knowledge, care, attention to detail, and skill with words are impressive and a powerful combination, and she shares my commitment to helping Projectors thrive. I am deeply grateful to you, Robin.

I appreciate and applaud my Human Design colleagues everywhere who study and practice and then help others through this extraordinary body of work. I am especially indebted to my Projector clients and students who have shared part of their journey with me and allowed me to contribute to their lives and learn from their experiences.

I am also eternally grateful to my amazing life partner Charlie Vance, who contributes to and supports my work (and me) in so very many ways, and who has patiently put up with my long hours writing and editing this book. You make me laugh, you light up my life, and I love you.

About the Author

Evelyn experienced such a profound shift in accepting and loving herself and others when she learned about Human Design in 2008 that she has studied the system intensively ever since and shares it with people all over the world through readings, courses, and hundreds of blogposts on her website.

Her international M.B.A. and Master of Public Administration degrees led her to successful careers in business and the federal (U.S.) government. Now, she integrates those experiences with her fascination for Human Design, her deep interest in personal growth, and her love of helping people.

Through the natural energies she carries in her chart, she has a keen ability to translate the complexity of Human Design into simple, practical, logical, and effective self-knowledge and wisdom that transform the lives of her clients and students.

Her greatest joy is helping clients and students accelerate their journey of personal growth and success by understanding their inborn energetic structure, their correct decision-making strategy, and their life path and soul purpose. She is especially dedicated to helping her fellow Projector Types embrace their full power, vital role, and unique brilliance.

She enjoys a happy combination of Human Design readings, teaching, writing, speaking, and creating transformational programs from her home in central Florida. Visit **HumanDesignforSuccess.com** for a free Human Design Chart and Decision Maker's Kit, and to learn more about Evelyn. You will find her Human Design chart on the Meet Evelyn page.

About the Author

For more great Human Design books visit
Books.GracepointPublishing.com

If you enjoyed reading *Becoming an Empowered Projector* and purchased it through an online retailer, please return to the site and write a review to help others find this book.

Made in the USA
Coppell, TX
29 December 2023